A Psychoanalytic Approach to Treating Psychosis

A Psychoanalytic Approach to Treating Psychosis shows how, by understanding the antecedents and dynamics of psychosis, a psychoanalytic approach can offer a long-term alternative to the only psychotropic therapy and an explanation of the infantile origin of the illness.

This ground-breaking examination begins by clearly explaining complex terms and theories from the most significant thinkers in psychoanalysis. Split into three parts, it then explores the problems faced when following one specific technique for understanding the psychotic process. Practical as well as theoretical, Part 2 illustrates how to prepare an appropriate setting for the patient, including the importance of listening and the analyst's approach, as well as highlighting key features of the condition, such as delusions, hallucinations, infantile withdrawal and psychotic dreams. Acknowledging that psychosis is a psychic transformation which the mind works as a sensorial organ, the author asserts that the seeds are sown in childhood through emotional trauma, leading to withdrawal into a fantasy world.

Brimming with real-life vignettes throughout, Part 3 is dedicated to a unique and lengthy case study to illustrate the challenges of working with such patients. It also looks positively towards future research on psychosis informed by insights from neuroscience.

Innovative and accessible, this book will be essential reading for anyone working in psychosis, including psychoanalysts, psychiatrists, psychologists and physicians.

Franco de Masi is a former president of the Centro Milanese di Psicoanalisi and Secretary of the Training Institute of Milan. He has published papers in international psychoanalytical journals and books translated into English, French, German, Spanish and Polish.

A Psychoanalytic Approach to Treating Psychosis

Genesis, Psychopathology and Case Study

Franco de Masi

LONDON AND NEW YORK

First published 2020
by Routledge
2 Park Square, Milton Park, Abingdon, Oxon OX14 4RN

and by Routledge
52 Vanderbilt Avenue, New York, NY 10017

Routledge is an imprint of the Taylor & Francis Group, an informa business

© 2020 Franco de Masi

The right of Franco de Masi to be identified as author of this work has been asserted by him in accordance with sections 77 and 78 of the Copyright, Designs and Patents Act 1988.

All rights reserved. No part of this book may be reprinted or reproduced or utilised in any form or by any electronic, mechanical, or other means, now known or hereafter invented, including photocopying and recording, or in any information storage or retrieval system, without permission in writing from the publishers.

Trademark notice: Product or corporate names may be trademarks or registered trademarks, and are used only for identification and explanation without intent to infringe.

British Library Cataloguing-in-Publication Data
A catalogue record for this book is available from the British Library

Library of Congress Cataloging-in-Publication Data
Names: de Masi, Franco, author.
Title: A psychoanalytic approach to treating psychosis : genesis, psychopathology and case study / Franco de Masi.
Description: 1 Edition. | New York : Routledge, 2020. | Includes bibliographical references and index.
Identifiers: LCCN 2019046799 | ISBN 9780367430429 (hardback) | ISBN 9780367416416 (paperback) | ISBN 9781003000884 (ebook)
Subjects: LCSH: Psychoanalysis. | Psychoses.
Classification: LCC BF173 .D394 2020 | DDC 150.19/5—dc23
LC record available at https://lccn.loc.gov/2019046799

ISBN: 978-0-367-43042-9 (hbk)
ISBN: 978-0-367-41641-6 (pbk)
ISBN: 978-1-003-00088-4 (ebk)

Typeset in Times New Roman
by Apex CoVantage, LLC

Contents

Foreword		vii
HOWARD B. LEVINE		
Introduction		1
PART 1		7
1	Psychosis: The problem of a specific technique	9
2	Non systematic models	15
3	Kleinian contributions	30
PART 2		47
4	The setting and transference in psychosis	49
5	The psychic withdrawal and the psychotic part of the personality	54
6	Dreams and delusions in psychosis	62
7	Hallucinations	81
8	Trauma and the Super-ego in psychosis	90
PART 3		97
9	A psychoanalytic therapy	99

vi *Contents*

10 Clinical considerations   130

11 Future perspectives   138

References   144
Index   149

Foreword

How do we understand psychosis?
The enigma unveiled?

Howard B. Levine, MD

Broadly speaking, there are two fundamentally different theoretical discourses in psychoanalysis regarding psychosis, each of which has its roots in the writings of Freud. In the one, psychosis is a malignant variation of early psychic development and the forces that produce neurosis, but its metapsychological formulation remains continuous with neurosis and with early, normative primitive mechanisms and mind states that have not been sufficiently transformed and are believed to have failed to develop.

In the second discourse, one that is persuasively advanced by Franco de Masi in this book and in his other writings, psychosis is of a different order than neurosis, structurally and metapsychologically. It is a particular form of seductive psychic retreat, an altered mind state and alternative (false) reality that often begins very early in life, has the power to seduce, colonise and conquer the more reality adapted functions of the mind and reflects 'a mysterious world that no discipline has so far been able to explain convincingly' (de Masi 2009, p. xxiii).

Support for the first position may be found in Freud's (1911) understanding of Schreber's psychosis as a particularly severe variation of Oedipal conflicts; in Freud's (1924b) assertion of 'the unity and intimate connection of all the disorders that present themselves as neurotic and psychotic' (p. 204); and in his description of dreams as 'a psychosis . . . [that] can be undone and give place to normal functioning' (Freud 1940, p. 172). (Note the implied link here between psychosis and the primary process of neurotic dream work, a link that readers of this book will realise is far from substantiated in the clinical setting.)

Similar to this line of thinking in Freud, Klein considered psychosis as analogous to and continuous with normative infantile mental states, the former being an exacerbation of the latter. As de Masi carefully explains (Chapter 3), Klein believed that 'the disposition to psychosis depended on primitive impulses and anxieties that were normally transformed in the course of infantile development' (de Masi 2009, p. 3). The determinative factors for Klein, and for a number of her viii *Foreword*

followers such as Segal, Rosenfeld, Meltzer and to some extent Bion, involved the vicissitudes of the death instinct and the presence of pathological envy and destructive phantasies towards the primary object (mother figure).

In contrast, Freud (1894) had earlier argued that psychosis (paranoia) was a defensive flight from an unacceptable, unbearable reality,[1] that the primary problem in psychosis was a withdrawal of cathexes from representations of reality and that psychotic symptoms – delusions, paranoia, hallucinations – were miscarried attempts at restitution and reconnection with that reality (Freud 1911). It was not until later that Freud (1915, 1924a) began to more systematically consider that the response in psychosis of withdrawal of cathexes from representations of reality might involve a mechanism (*Verwerfung*: foreclosure, or *Verleugnung*: disavowal) that was different from that of the 'ordinary' repression (*Verdrangung*) found in neurosis or might produce or reflect a very different metapsychological situation.[2]

Bion (e.g. 1970) offers a potential insight into this second metapsychological view of psychosis when he notes that intolerance of pain can drive a patient 'to destroy the thought function and therefore to deprive himself of the only means whereby he could confront or modify the situation of frustration' (de Masi 2009, p. 19). Winnicott (1971) describes a more passively endured but similarly destructive process in terms of de-cathexis. (Think, too, of Robertson's (1970) descriptions of children who begin to fall into a miasmic decline following too long a separation from their maternal objects.)

Bion (1970) also followed this later trend in Freud, when he noted that while neurotic patients banish painful realities to the repressed unconscious where the ideational perception of those realities remain more or less intact, 'psychotics destroyed the instrument [i.e. the psychic thought function, and the capacity for perception] that would have enabled the unconscious to understand the psychic experience' (de Masi 2009, p. 19) that was the source of their agony. Whether or when this disabling of vital psychic functions has motivational intention (unconscious but intentional attacks on linking) or is passively (traumatically) undergone is a moot point. Either condition may obtain, and speaking metapsychologically, the consequences are similar (see Bergstein 2015 for further discussion).

Based on extensive clinical experience treating psychotic patients, an experience that is richly illustrated in this text, it is de Masi's contention – and a very important contribution that should be paid careful attention to by analysts and analytic therapists at all levels of experience – that *psychotic disorders take root in the seductive, dissociated world that is begun to be built up and resorted to in childhood to replace a potentially traumatic and/or disruptive actual reality*. These movements begin long before overt, psychiatric clinical manifestations of psychosis appear. What is crucial is that 'There is no thought in the withdrawal, only dissociated sensory content that wipes out psychic reality' (Chapter 5).

The origins of and stimulus for this withdrawal may include the infant's reaction to primary objects that are unable to accommodate the infant's or child's emotional communications or who invade the infant's or child's mind with disturbing emotional projections. Thus, while not yet qualified as a 'defence' in the neurotic sense of the term, the withdrawal may serve as a protection against aversive contact with primary objects and the relational world.

The price for withdrawing, however, is considerable: 'Constantly creating an imaginary sensorial reality saps energy from emotional and affective development, hamstringing experience the individual needs for growth, and compromising . . . the development of personal identity' (Chapter 5). What is sacrificed is the psychic and emotional truth that Bion described as being as essential for psychic development as alimentation is for physical growth and somatic well-being.

Interestingly, de Masi has found that:

> When emotional input is lacking on the part of the caregiver, the child uses his own body for the purposes of arousal; sensation, devoid of a relational quality that develops only within good affective caretaking, deviates. To combat a sense of disintegration, the deprived child clings to a series of sensations (a light, a voice, a smell etc.) that can serve to hold together the scattered parts of the personality, or he uses the body in masturbatory terms.
>
> (Chapter 5)

Other authors, such as Aulagnier (2001), Fain (2019), Tustin (1986) and Miller (2014) have described a similar turn from the object relational world to autosensorial self-stimulation as a 'survival' mechanism and developmental derailment in infants and young children who find themselves helplessly ensnared in situations of overwhelming deprivation or impingement. The turn away from the relational world of objects and external reality to sensorial self-stimulation has been implicated in the aetiology of various conditions that lie at the limits of analyzability, such as perversions, addictions, impulse disorders, somatic discharge or the creation of autistic nuclei and defences.

De Masi concludes that it is not so much destructiveness that spurs the child who is destined to become psychotic, but a particular seductive pleasure and/ or need to escape from frustration and pain that drives him to leave the relational world in favour of building 'another world' that he himself creates and can omnipotently govern. The latter, to which the patient may repeatedly retreat in the face of subsequent frustration, helplessness and deprivation, is then perceived as superior to psychic reality precisely because of the sensations it can generate as the patient alters his sense organs and destroys the psychic organs of knowledge. This is a malignant process through which the psyche loses its capacity to function as an organ of thought and instead becomes an organ whose primary purpose seems to be that of generating sensations. Eventually, this initially euphoric world turns persecutory and malignant.[3]

Prior to doing so, however, this dissociated world can be resorted to by the child as a defence against a real world made uninhabitable by prolonged maternal depression, lack of parental emotional involvement, intrusive impingement or other sources of early or severe agonies and frustrations that drive the organism x *Foreword*

'beyond' existential pain. As in drug or alcohol addiction, the patient is initially seduced by the pleasurable state of the psychic retreat[4] and does not understand or consider the dangerous consequences that can follow from this kind of operation. While often unconscious – or perhaps better described as 'reflexive' – there is a repeated 'choice' that is made between facing pain or frustration and effacing and withdrawing from reality. The clarification and interpretation of this 'choice point' – along with the strengthening of the non-psychotic functions of the psyche – become important features of the treatment process.

Once this dissociated world is constructed and takes hold, it opposes the acceptance of and contact with ordinary reality and its frustrations. It attempts to colonise the more normal parts of the mind, further subverting frustration tolerance and promoting omnipotence of thought. Increasingly, the patient is detached from relationships, psychic truth and the capacity to think with discernment about external and emotional reality. Vitality and emotional growth are sacrificed for the illusory power of sensory pleasure. Eventually, the patient's mind no longer works as a thought organ but becomes a perceptive organ that continuously produces sensorial phantasies, which are felt as real. All of this and more is richly illustrated by de Masi in the detailed clinical examples of psychotic presentation, analytic process and working through.

At the heart of de Masi's argument is the assertion that psychosis is an organisation distinct from neurosis. It is not about psychic conflict and symbolic meaning and does not concern the repressed unconscious. It is a particular experience of withdrawal and dissociation into a world of sensorial fantasy, an alternate reality or psychic retreat, a solipsistic and grandiose world that is anti-thought, closed off from the perception, understanding and processing of external, relational reality. Psychosis, then, 'is not an unconscious process, but a morbid state that transforms consciousness' (Intro). Instead of developing thought and nourishing psychic reality, the mind is used as a 'sensory organ' (Chapter 5).

The ability to create a sensory world separated from reality originates in the dissociated reality created in psychic withdrawal and gives rise to delusions and hallucinations. Hallucinatory and delusional states are testimony to an extreme development in which the newly created internal reality is projected onto the external world with a compression or complete loss of separateness between external and internal space. The confusion is not only between the external and internal world, but first and foremost between the sensorial and the psychic world. In the delusional state, the patient does not think: he 'sees' and 'hears'. He 'sees' via the mind's eyes and 'hears' via the mind's ears. The mind behaves as if it were a sensorial organ.

Central to de Masi's formulation and understanding of psychosis are the ideas that delusions, hallucinations and psychotic dreams evade symbolic meaning and associative linkage and so cannot be meaningfully associated to in the same way as neurotic dreams and fantasies (Chapters 6 and 7). Unlike the night dreams of neurotics, which normally use emotional narration to create their plot, delusions do not arise from the dynamic or repressed unconscious. It is not possible to 'wake up' from a delusional experience because the delusion is a concrete perception and not a symbolic narration. Nor are hallucinations or delusions psychic elements from which 'hidden meanings' may be discerned or extracted via free association. Construction and creation of meaning may be possible *de novo* and *apres coup*, perhaps, but hallucinations and delusions cannot be explored and 'unpacked' the way that the night-time dreams and daydreams of neurotics may be.

It is for this reason that delusions are tenacious and often irreversible. What the dreams of psychotic states can inform us about, however, are impending psychotic regressions or the dysfunctional present state of the psychotic's mind (Chapter 6).

Given the problem of how to understand and treat psychosis, I find myself in agreement with de Masi that

> the analogy between the [infant's] primitive [mind] state and psychosis is unsustainable. . . . Whereas psychosis is a subversion of thought that leads to the disintegration of the mind, the magic world of the infant is open to the unknown and [with the appropriate help of a good enough object] makes for the construction of a personal meaning to be assigned to that world.
>
> (de Masi 2009, p. 30)

If the psychotic patient does not robustly associate, cannot work with symbolic associations or the hidden symbolism of dreams – the latter when produced are not seen as 'rebus puzzles' offering a royal road to unconscious meanings, wishes, fears and conflicts, but are equivalent to sensorial experiences – then how is treatment to proceed?

What de Masi has concluded after years of extensive clinical experience – and here the reader of this book will have a chance to study and share some of that experience, because de Masi includes the detailed, almost week-by-week, report on the analytic treatment of a psychotic patient that ended positively – is that the answer is twofold. The analyst must:

1   Clarify and describe the psychotic's mental state in order to help him distinguish between his healthy and delusional parts while identifying the pains, threats, seductions and frustrations that trigger each choice point that leads to a withdrawal from reality.
2   Work to help strengthen the patient's 'emotional unconscious' – i.e. his nonpsychotic psychic functioning and emotional capacities so that frustration tolerance and affect tolerance and the capacity to think in the face of anxiety and pain will develop and be maintained.

'The analyst's task is to creatively understand how to strengthen the patient's healthy part in order to contain and reduce as far as possible the omnipotent part, which exercises great power over the patient' (Chapter 3).

Treatment may initially require hospitalisation, adjunctive resort to psychotropic medications or may begin with less frequent sessions and eschewing the use of the couch. However, full and intensive analytic engagement, including the

xii *Foreword*

reconstruction of the history of the psychosis, will usually prove necessary, if one is to achieve a definitive reworking and strengthening of the patient's non-psychotic mental functions.

The latter will almost inevitably require the repeated exploration and description of the way in which the pathogenic resort to psychotic withdrawal detaches the patient from his relationships, including that with his analyst, and functions as a 'drugging structure that tends to drain away the person's vitality and sacrifices his emotional growth for the power of sensory pleasure' (Chapter 5).

Psychotic patients must ultimately be taught the difference between what may feel pleasant but is destructive to the mind and that which is good and constructive, albeit often frightening and painful, and that psychosis is the price to pay for avoiding suffering at the cost of perverting reality. This is by no means an easy or quickly accomplished task. In the words of the author:

> Psychosis may be seen as a destructive way of dealing with mental pain, a psychic strategy directed at self-annihilation (de Masi 1996), which leads imperceptibly to the crossing of the threshold of tolerance and to the final destruction of personal identity. This self-destruction, whose origin lies in the subject's earliest object relations, becomes the tragedy enacted in the psychotic state, when the patient no longer possesses the unity and potential space of existence whereby he can feel alive, whole and separate from others. The psychotic patient must face his own psychic death, the unbearable pain of the destruction that has taken place, confusion with the rest of the world, which rushes in on him through hallucinations and delusions, and the anguished search for his own self in others.
>
> (de Masi 2009, pp. 62–63)

Notes

1 Although it should be noted that his assumption was that the unbearable reality was the actual memory of a childhood sexual experience and that the underlying defensive mechanism in paranoid psychosis was repression – i.e. identical to that of hysterical and obsessional neurosis.
2 See also Freud's (Freud and Abraham (1965, p. 206) 1914 letter to Abraham, where he noted that, in contrast to neurosis, where repression dissociated thing presentation from word presentation, in the narcissistic neuroses (i.e. psychosis), libido is withdrawn 'from the unconscious thing presentations, which is of course a far deeper disturbance' than neurosis.
3 A very powerful illustration of this process is conveyed in the Ingmar Bergman (1968) film *Hour of the Wolf*, in which a psychotic artist begins to draw the malign characters of his delusions in his sketch pad as if they were real figures encountered in his life. Bergman then mirrors that experience for the audience by blurring the distinction between reality and fantasy in the very action of the film that is shown on the screen. We do not know if the ghastly and perverse scenes of the party to which the artist and his wife are invited are real or are psychotic delusions being depicted on the screen. Eventually, the artist kills himself.
4 See also Abensour (2013), *The Psychotic Temptation*.

References

Abensour, L. (2013). *The Psychotic Temptation*. Hove and New York: Routledge.

Aulagnier, P. (2001). *The Violence of Interpretation*. Hove and New York: Routledge.

Bergman, I. (1968). *Hour of the Wolf*. A Film (Swedish Film Institute) written and directed by Ingmar Bergman.

Bergstein, A. (2015). Attacks on linking or drive to communicate? *Psychoanalytic Quart*, 84: 921–942.

Bion, W.R. (1970). *Attention and Interpretation*. New York: Basic Books.

de Masi, F. (2009). *Vulnerability to Psychosis*. London: Karnac Books.

Fain, M. (2019). Mentalization and passivity. *The International Journal of Psychoanalysis*, 99: 479–484.

Freud, S. (1894). Neuropsychoses of defense. *S.E.*, 3: 43–61. London: Hogarth, 1962.

Freud, S. (1900). The interpretation of dreams. *S.E.*, 4–5. London: Hogarth.

Freud, S. (1911). Psycho-analytic notes on an autobiographical account of a case of paranoia (dementia paranoides). *S.E.*, 12: 213–226. London: Hogarth.

Freud, S. (1915). The unconscious. *S.E.*, 14: 159–204. London: Hogarth.

Freud, S. (1924a). The loss of reality in neurosis and psychosis. *S.E.*, 19: 183–190. London: Hogarth.

Freud, S. (1924b). A short account of psycho-analysis. *S.E.*, 19: 191–212. London: Hogarth.

Freud, S. (1940). An outline of psycho-analysis. *S.E.*, 23: 141–208.

Freud, S., & Abraham, K. (1965). *A Psycho-Analytic Dialogue: The Letters of Sigmund Freud and Karl Abraham 1907–1926* (H.C. Abraham & E.L. Freud, Eds. and B. March & H.C. Abraham, Trans.). London: Karnac Books, 2002.

Miller, P. (2014). *Driving Soma*. London: Karnac Books.

Robertson, J. (1970). *Young Children in Hospital*, 2nd edition, with a Postscript. London: Tavistock; New York: Barnes & Noble.

Tustin, F. (1986). *Autistic Barriers in Neurotic Patients*. New Haven and London: Yale University Press.

Winnicott, D.W. (1971). *Playing and Reality*. New York: Basic Books.

Introduction

I should like to begin by saying that I do not believe psychoanalytic thought has as yet managed to formulate hypotheses that can explain the origins and development of the psychotic process. Freud, despite having reflected on the nature of this morbid process, was to leave us a complex theoretical and clinical system that is particularly useful for neuroses but not for psychoses, the psychotic patient operating very differently from the neurotic patient.

Pioneers of psychoanalysis tried to address therapy for psychotic patients using the technique that was effective for neurosis, which was also the method they had been trained in and were well acquainted with. I, too, after many years of analytic practice, when I began to take into my care patients who had come out of a psychotic break, would listen to them as I did neurotic patients. Although there were at times improvements, relapses were also a frequent occurrence. One psychotic patient in particular, in my care for seven years, who had shown considerable progress to the point of making me believe he had overcome his illness once and for all, had an irreversible relapse after an analytic break during the summer holidays. From that moment on, I reflected at length on the reasons behind his relapse and on what I had neglected during the analysis.

Clinical psychoanalytic technique is based on the analyst's ability to understand the patient's mental state and describe the patient's psychic experiences to him so that he may be helped to understand his own mind. For Freud this goal could be reached by studying unconscious processes, thereby overcoming resistance to censorship and repression. He believed that in every individual anxiety and suffering were produced by a part of his thoughts and beliefs that had become unconscious: hence the patient's inability to understand what lay behind his malaise.

The unconscious is not, however, confined to this dynamic functioning that Freud described; alongside it are processes outside awareness that concern emotions and thought, which are implicit and not directly known to the subject experiencing them. Processes that become altered in psychosis principally concern the unconscious that operates to produce awareness of ourselves and our relationship with the world and, to a lesser extent, the Freudian dynamic unconscious, which is of secondary importance here. Everyone has reflexive consciousness based on symbolic abilities, language and a type of autobiographical memory that allows us to live in the present, reflect on the past and anticipate the future; these functions are, however, severely impaired in psychosis.

2 Introduction

Analysts who work with psychotic patients need to understand how they can restore mental functioning within the analytic relationship in order to repair damage done by the psychotic invasion; frequently, this is a new and complex situation in that what has been learnt during personal analysis or during the treatment of other patients cannot be relied on. Given that the psychotic patient does not associate, we cannot work with associations, nor can we use dreams, which, when actually produced, are not symbolic but equivalent to concrete sensorial experiences. In addition, it is not easy to identify with a patient who lives in a psychotic state, since we have never experienced anything similar. This is all the more reason why we need to examine from a new angle how delusional activity becomes established in the mind. Furthermore, with regard to the first break, it cannot be viewed as a single and limited episode; the process of the disorder needs to be understood, and we must expect new psychotic manifestations to occur in the course of therapy.

The approach to use with the delusional psychotic patient is to describe his mental state in order to help him distinguish between his healthy and his delusional psychotic parts. The latter is not recognised by the patient as a sick part, but one that is good and healthy.

The omnipotent psychotic mental state appeals to the patient's vanity and narcissism, making him believe he is superior and endowed with special powers. The analyst therefore needs to have experience in working with these mental states and describe to the patient the continuous transformations that the psychotic part operates on him, in particular the propaganda it exercises on his mind when it offers a pleasant world, one that is, however, dissociated and far from reality. I am of the opinion that the psychotic patient has lived most of his life in a fantasy withdrawal, which is why the delusional experience constitutes nothing other than the development of an old inclination that is no longer containable.

I should now like to briefly mention my reasons for writing this book. Part of my reflections on the psychotic illness and my way of analytically dealing with it can be found in my book entitled *Vulnerability to Psychosis* (2006). In this second volume, written more than ten years after the first, are further reflections that centre more on the patient's therapy and on providing additional contributions to the genesis and psychopathology of the psychotic process.

Over the years, I have not ceased to wonder at the fact that such a sparse audience has been found for psychoanalytic input on psychosis among psychiatrists, psychologists and psychoanalysts alike. Intuitions of great past analysts on this illness thus risk being left aside and rendered obsolete, their clinical and therapeutic significance fading well into the background. And yet, if psychoanalysis were to consult with other disciplines, first and foremost psychiatry and neuroscience, methodological wealth and depth that other disciplines inevitably cannot acquire would emerge. Contemporary psychiatry, in particular, which seems to have altogether abandoned the psychodynamic and phenomenological orientation of the past, has undertaken to identify, as the latest edition of DSM shows (DSM-5 2013), a series of symtomatologies for which suitable pharmacological solutions can readily be found. Naturally, I do not wish to underestimate the benefit and effectiveness of psychotropic drugs, but despite being a necessary part of treatment for psychosis, when effective, they are not resolving, confined solely to limiting visible symptoms; moreover, they tend to be taken for extremely long periods, if not for the remainder of the patient's life.

A variety of experiences has fashioned my conception of the psychotic illness and its treatment. For fifteen years, I worked as a psychiatrist in a public hospital with prevention, diagnostic and treatment services, where many psychotic patients were under my care. Still today, more than thirty years on, I can perfectly remember a number of them and reflect on their more-or-less unfortunate state of affairs. After leaving the hospital, I kept up my interest in psychosis through psychoanalytic literature but only began to take some psychotic patients into my care once I felt that my analytic identity had been consolidated.

In the beginning, I tried to listen to the psychotic patient in the same way I did the neurotic patient, and in spite of my surprise at the patient's unpredictable course, I employed the usual set of tools for neurosis to deal with his anxieties and defences. I expected associations and tried to understand dreams, but over time this way of working proved inadequate: that is, of little help in preventing regression and relapses into psychosis. Indeed, treating the psychotic patient in the same way as the neurotic patient carries the risk of not highlighting in time how the psychotic part functions, all the while it stealthily colonises the mind towards an acute break. After much reflection on the reasons behind this lack of success, I gradually sharpened my listening until I had built up a specific vision of the origin of and analytic treatment for the illness.

My clinical work was further developed in my role as supervisor. For twenty years now, I have discussed clinical cases of individual colleagues with adult psychotic patients in their care and held monthly supervision sessions with them as a group. Yet another equally important experience is my supervisory work of therapies with severe children, which I discuss either individually or in a group context with child analysts and psychotherapists. I have understood how psychosis begins in childhood and that it often goes undetected by the environment. Parents tend to underestimate what has already become a psychotic withdrawal, seeing it as some kind of game or childhood fantasy. The child's isolation and sensorial withdrawal are frequently considered normal and not the expression of his capture by the psychotic construction.

The psychoanalyst's field of observation is rich in heuristic potential in a way that no other clinician's is; we work in direct contact with the patient's inner self and so can see how he constructs his psychosis from *within*. Moreover, we can go back to re-examine his childhood, when the first seeds of psychosis were sown, and draw attention to the emotional traumas that hindered development, driving him to repudiate psychic reality.

Among the pathologies in which adequate knowledge on their origin and development escapes us today, psychosis certainly features prominently. This pathological process develops outside words and beyond the sufferer's awareness; as mentioned earlier, it is not an unconscious process as in neurosis, but a morbid state that *transforms consciousness*, the nature and danger of which the patient ignores. In the psychotic state, awareness of one's individuality is lost, and perception of external reality as existing outside them is absorbed into the Ego,

4   *Introduction*

whose boundaries disappear. No longer can a distinction be made between what is dreamt, created or just imagined; everything that is constructed in the imagination presents itself to the patient beyond a shadow of a doubt as *the* only true reality.

Both past and present efforts to treat psychosis can provide useful information on the nature of the illness; recapitulating these efforts, I aim to show how, despite the phenomenological complexity of the symptomatology, the key nuclei of psychotic transformation and the reasons underlying it can be understood in order to frame an effective therapy.

Firstly, I have considered past psychoanalysts who have left a written record of their work; at that time, no adequate theoretical frame for them to work within existed, nor could use be made of others' clinical experience, and so their work was carried forward on completely unknown terrain. Only later, particularly thanks to analysts who referred to Melanie Klein's thought, was a wider and more structured theoretical body of knowledge built up. This theoretical enrichment gave momentum to the first systematic efforts to provide analytic treatment, which were not, however, accompanied by corresponding and documented results on a therapeutic level; I believe this could explain why, after a period of interest in psychosis therapy, psychoanalytic contributions steadily fell away. Psychoanalysts as a whole most likely acknowledged this illness's mysterious origin and difficult therapeutic course silently, however, without clear scientific debate where light could have been shed on such difficulties.

In the book, I particularly seek to highlight the beginnings of the psychotic process in childhood. Some children, as many authors who have dealt with this subject have pointed out, are already carriers of specific signs of mental malaise (the psychic withdrawal), which can spill over into a clear psychotic manifestation in adulthood.

I hope to put across the complexity of psychosis starting from the *clinical level*. It is my belief that clinical work, not to be separated from theory, of course, can bring to light the underlying psychopathological structures through a better understanding of the difficulties, which include resistance to change. Nowadays, many are the complex approaches used by psychotherapists, psychiatrists and psychologists alongside psychoanalysts to treat psychotic patients. I do not make a radical difference between psychotherapeutic and psychoanalytic treatments, the number of sessions or couch versus face-to-face, but I do believe the main focus of attention in clinical work should be the specific features of the psychotic state and analysing with the patient his readiness to be conquered by the illness.

The psychotherapy of psychotic patients, despite being complex, produces results for the patient, who would tend to regress and increasingly isolate himself if left alone. Given that the psychotic patient develops a bond of absolute dependence with his family and social group, thus shrinking his world more and more to avoid anxieties he cannot brave, the purposes of therapy are to reinforce his jaded vitality, support the healthy part of his personality, and contain the action of the psychotic part. Although he can neither acknowledge nor express it, the patient is aware that he needs help: hence his development of a strong tie with the therapist; one need only consider the deterioration and relapses that frequently

Introduction 5

occur when therapy is temporarily suspended, during the analyst's holiday time, for instance. This is because the therapist operates as the patient's healthy Ego, and when absent, the psychotic part has more opportunity to conquer, seduce or overpower the patient's healthy part.

Below are a few basic points that may be helpful to all therapists:

- Psychosis usually begins during childhood, with the child withdrawing into a world of sensorial fantasy. The psychotic breakdown proper, which sees the development of a delusion and hallucinations, is nothing other than the manifestation of the pathology that in many cases originated in childhood. This path is more frequent when the illness is processual, but less so when there is one single episode that will possibly see a late outbreak connected to trauma.
- Once established, the delusional experience is difficult to transform; it is a new sensory-built reality that develops gradually, which differs greatly from the dream or the daydream.
- The patient's resistance to speaking about and working through the psychotic break concerns his fear that by evoking it he can be recaptured by it. Recovery without specific psychological treatment tends to be poor.

The book is in three parts. In the first part, I have summarised the great efforts made by pioneering analysts who treated psychosis, taking into consideration only those who undertook psychoanalytic therapy in its usual setting and therefore not including the numerous colleagues who worked within an institutional or group context.

For the sake of practicality, I have arranged analysts who worked in a traditional setting in two groups. In the first are the *non systematic* analysts: that is, those not working within a structured theory, but on the basis of their clinical intuition. In the interests of brevity, I have chosen to consider only a few: Fromm-Reichmann, Searles, Sechehaye, Rosen, Federn, Benedetti and separately Lacan. And in the other group are analysts who drew their inspiration from Melanie Klein's thought, working with a structured and coherent theoretical apparatus that permitted the psychotic patient to be systematically taken into one's care.

In the second part of the book, I look at specific features of psychosis, such as delusions and hallucinations, whose dynamic meaning and resistance to change must be contextualised. Psychosis does not involve some functions of the mind only, but the entire psychic system, which is invaded by sensory elements.

In the third part is a detailed description of the therapy of a psychotic patient who began his analysis with me a number of years ago. When he started his therapy, he had already suffered a psychotic break and was being treated with psychotropic drugs. Over the course of his therapy, the delusion situation frequently recurred obstinately and dangerously. The delusion was changeable in that the characters or figures changed, but the structure of the core delusion stayed the same. I chose this case because my work with this patient enabled me to understand the different ways the patient obstinately clung to the delusion, and moreover, it gave me the opportunity to show the various and difficult passages towards stable improvement.

Part 1

1 Psychosis

The problem of a specific technique

Psychosis

I use the term *psychosis* to indicate that form of severe mental disorder that manifests chiefly in young adults but which is not rare in childhood, adolescence or middle age either. In the past, the consequences of the illness were so severe that psychiatrists treating the condition named it *dementia praecox* (Kraepelin 1883) and *schizophrenia* (Bleuler 1911). Besides its alarming symptoms, psychosis was dreaded because of its course, as it saw a gradual deterioration of the patient's mental and relational abilities, his fate inevitably being an asylum, at times for the rest of his life. Instances of spontaneous recovery from psychosis were also reported, Kraepelin himself having related cases that developed in this manner, and in 1838 the English nobleman John Perceval wrote in one of his books about his fall into psychosis, his confinement in an asylum and his subsequent recovery.[1]

Today the clinical picture of psychosis has greatly changed on account of the availability of medication. The disorder no longer necessarily takes an inevitable chronic course but consists of recurring critical episodes. Although this does not mean recovery, a balance can be reached whereby the individual may lead a life that is not particularly satisfying but is at least not institutionalised. Mental health professionals will intervene at the first sign of the illness nowadays, and when hospitalisation cannot be avoided, it is short term only; in addition, psychotropic drugs can be used to stop the disease process at least temporarily. Thanks to a trained medical team, the condition can be prevented from worsening and developing into chronic forms of mental deterioration. As just mentioned, the current course of psychosis is that of an intermittent illness, critical episodes alternating with periods of well-being in which social contact and relational skills are limited. The more severe and lifelong clinical manifestations described in past psychiatric treatises, which clearly manifested during extremely long periods of hospitalisation, are rare today, practically having disappeared altogether.

In the past, the patient's regression was certainly due in part to prolonged institutionalisation: lengthy periods of isolation from the healthy population, coupled with unsuccessful therapeutic care, meant that the destructive device which is specific to psychosis was given free rein to unfold. At times regression was aided by transferring patients on a regular basis to hospitals with less effective care: whereas

10   *Part 1*

first admissions were to an environment that could provide intensive psychiatric care, in the case of relapses, the patient would be transferred to less specialised hospitals where prolonged isolation favoured the patient's regression.

Today, not only does a psychotic patient receive care early on, but his care plan goes beyond the clinical manifestations: one specialised team takes care of the symptomatology together with environmental and family factors that may contribute to the illness. In Italy, especially over the past few decades since the closure of psychiatric hospitals, huge individual and group efforts have been made to stop the illness from progressing and to reintegrate the patient into the community.

Psychotherapeutic treatment is indispensable in the course of the illness. From the first episode, the patient's fate will be shaped by the orientation of the psychiatrist and care team. If the psychiatrist's orientation is biological, psychotropic drugs will be the cornerstone of treatment. Psychotropic drugs are certainly extremely helpful to alleviate or suppress the more evident symptoms – that is, hallucinations and delusions – but they are confined to treating the symptoms and not the causes of the illness. At times, on the strength of persecutory anxieties, the patient categorically refuses to take medication, and when he does agree to take it, he tends to experience passivity; as with any medical therapy, the patient expects to 'be cured' without necessarily understanding how.

Should the patient be under the care of a team whose orientation is psychodynamic, initial care goes beyond prescribing psychotropic drugs: the doctor, who in this case is more open to dialogue, whenever possible, will suggest a psychotherapeutic course and refer the patient to a colleague trained for this task through personal analysis and therapeutic work that enables him to understand and communicate with the psychotic patient.

A specific technique

Freud formulated a theory and a technique for treating neurosis but did not believe that the same technique, based on the analysis of transference, could be applied to therapy for the psychotic patient. According to his line of thought, a complex – that is, an idea or a wish in conflict with other needs of the psyche, usually of a moral nature – is at work in the neurotic patient and ends up being repressed in the unconscious, manifesting as symptoms of suffering. Over the course of treatment, the patient relives this conflict in the transference with the analyst and discovers the childhood origins of his complex; this results in greater awareness of his unconscious functioning, the neurosis thus being got rid of.

Freud's idea was that psychotic patients could not be analysed as they were unable to develop transference; despite returning to the problem of psychosis many times, without, however, studying it systematically, during the last part of his life, Freud described several defence mechanisms, such as denial and splitting, that paved the way for subsequent developments in understanding psychotic and perverse mechanisms. At the same time, he encouraged and supported pupils of his who worked with psychotic patients, such as Abraham and Ferenczi, in the hope that a theory to effectively deepen understanding and treatment of psychosis could be developed.

The first analysts to undertake analytic therapy for psychosis could not but refer to Freud's model for neurosis, even though it would have been preferable to move beyond this framework of reference: no easy feat, though, considering that not even today do we have a thorough understanding of the origins of the illness (biological, environmental, psychological) or its development.

If we examine psychoanalytic literature, we can see that the outcomes of analytic therapies for psychotic patients regarding recovery are not so clear. For example, we do not know whether these so-called recoveries are effectively that or simply temporary remissions. It seems, however, that cases of full recovery are but a few (Mariotti 2000).

As previously mentioned, psychoanalytic technique, the foundations of clinical work, consists in the analyst's ability to understand the patient's mental state so as to describe his experiences and thus activate his understanding of psychic processes. Freud, in order to reach this objective, worked to reduce defences, in particular censorship and repression, and he tried to make the patient more aware of that nucleus of hidden truth at the root of his suffering.

Our mental functioning is based on our ability to make many of our emotional perceptions unconscious; for example, dream work allows us to carry out complex operations in order to understand and assign meaning to what we have experienced outside awareness. Analogously, in analytic work, repression is resolved, enabling us to trace back the experienced emotional reality via associations.

Unfortunately, this work cannot be done with the psychotic patient, as his emotions and conflicts are not dealt with using repression, his very instruments of perception and knowledge having been distorted and wiped out. This is why a technique and an orientation are needed that differ from those applied in the treatment of neurotic patients.

Analytic theory of the psychotic state has both continuous and discontinuous explanatory models of the disorder. The *continuous* hypotheses present psychotic development as the result of mechanisms at work in normal development and neuroses, whereas in the *discontinuous* hypotheses, psychosis represents a radical break with normal thought functions and emotionality, which are replaced by completely different mental processes, about which we still know relatively little (London 1988).

The continuous or *unitary* hypotheses seek to keep analytic theory of psychosis and neurosis linked and tend to interpret psychotic behaviour as originating unconsciously in intrapsychic conflicts similar in nature to those of neurotic patients. Discontinuous theories instead are *specific*, resting on the assumption that psychosis is a distinct disorder that does not concern the repressed unconscious, this being my orientation.

For the continuous models, the delusional experience derives from a psychic conflict, occurring therefore at a level of unconscious functioning that governs the mental life of the normal person and the neurotic patient. Caper (1998), for example, claims that the unconscious delusional fantasy can be gradually transformed into a normal unconscious fantasy.[2]

Conversely, by postulating a clear divide between neurosis and psychosis, discontinuous theories sustain that withdrawal is a dissociated experience that is

12   *Part 1*

neither integrable nor transformable in the psychic world. Even when a degree of awareness seems present in the patient, it makes no contact with the delusional belief.

A clear example of judgement dissociation to save the delusion can be found in the memoirs of President Schreber (1903). Although Schreber was capable of understanding the mental state of other patients, he was not with regard to himself. He expressed this as follows: 'I am fully aware that other people may be tempted to think that I am pathologically conceited; I know very well that this very tendency to relate everything to oneself, to bring everything that happens into connection with one's person, is a common phenomenon among mental patients'.

This explained, he added: 'But in my case the very reverse obtains. Since God entered into nerve-contact with me exclusively, I became in a way for God the only human being, or simply the human being around whom everything turns, to whom everything that happens must be related' (p. 276).

As stated previously, in psychosis the patient is largely unaware of the dangerous mental state related to this pathological process; once set in motion, the process produces changes that are difficult to reverse and which paralyse or destroy the recognition of psychic truth. The complexity of the problem of analytic technique regards the fact that psychosis does not concern the dynamic unconscious but a more basic form of mental functioning that leads to the patient distorting his thought function outside awareness. The psychotic patient destroys the very tools that would allow his unconscious to understand psychic experience; he is unable to unconsciously repress and process experiential content (he cannot 'dream') and is therefore unable to benefit from work done by the unconscious.

Consequently, the analyst cannot use with the psychotic patient the same approach that he does with the neurotic patient; he must 'forget' what he has learnt from his personal analysis, from clinical practice with other patients and from discussions with colleagues.

The analyst must be aware of the fact that these patients do not have symbolic thought; they are unable to understand psychic reality via the use of emotions, be they conscious or unconscious and their minds are saturated with sensory elements that will then underpin the development of delusions and hallucinations. These concrete sensorial elements cancel out the inner psychic world by invading and dominating mental processes and sensorially 'permeating' the mind. Psychotic dreams fall outside symbolic processing, acquiring instead a quality of concrete sensory facts.

I would like to state here several reasons why I believe psychoanalysis has encountered great difficulty in treating psychosis:

- Psychoanalytic therapy was built around problems related to neuroses, and for a long time, psychoanalysts tried to treat psychosis using the same methods employed for neurosis.
- Psychotics are not very rewarding patients: they have frequent relapses and tend to discourage the therapist, who expects improvements to be stable, as in the case of neurotic disorders.

- Frequently, it is not possible to treat psychotic patients in therapy with a dual setting only. Collaborating with a psychiatrist is needed for the prescription of medication, should this be necessary, and with support figures such as family members for the patient's extra-analytic life.
- Analytic technique for psychotic patients is very particular. On this subject, Rosenfeld (1987) maintained that analysts should learn from scratch how to treat psychotic patients, since what was learnt for the therapy of 'normal' patients cannot be applied with psychotic patients. Analysts should even consider acquiring new therapeutic skills through specific training.
- The analyst should have a certain familiarity with psychotic patients before taking them into therapy; naturally, this knowledge is more easily acquired after having had this kind of patient in one's charge in a healthcare institution.

Borderline states and psychosis

I shall not discuss the clinical differences between the two syndromes but just mention several psychopathological structures common to borderline states and psychosis that are due to a deterioration in unconscious functions, in particular those of emotional awareness.

Whereas neurosis is the result of discordant functioning of the dynamic unconscious, borderline structures stem from an alteration to the emotional-receptive unconscious: that is, the mental apparatus that symbolizes affects and understanding and modulates emotions. A similar distortion but with a different outcome is observed in psychosis, in which the communicative function of the unconscious is continually weakened or completely wiped out by the invasiveness of a solipsistic and grandiose world that closes itself off from the perception of external reality.

All manifestations of borderline symptomatology, such as constantly oscillating between moments of extreme dependence and flight from relations, brings to mind a total lack during childhood and adolescence of those processes that favour the development of symbolisation and the containment of affective states. Patients are dominated by violent emotions that they are incapable of describing or understanding, let alone processing: in other words, the unconscious based on repression did not get structured. Frequently, it may be ascertained that the disorder developed following continual childhood traumas, whereas in psychotic conditions, it is not always possible to trace evidence of such. In psychosis, for various reasons, a process of detachment and isolation from one's emotional-relational world is performed, and a psychic structure (the psychotic part of the personality) that replaces contact with the real world is created.

In the course of the analytic process of borderline and psychotic patients, the problem is not so much to make the unconscious conscious, but to develop the patients' originally wanting intuitive abilities. This is difficult work, as these patients are unable to use associative thought that would permit psychic facts to be understood intuitively.

The unconscious emotional-receptive function is similar to implicit knowledge: it functions as does procedural memory, which is indispensable for relational and

14   *Part 1*

emotional experiences. In the case of patients destined to develop a borderline state, this ability is damaged from the beginning, whereas in psychotic patients, it undergoes gradual deterioration by psychopathological structures such as delusions, which develop during the course of the illness; another difference is that the distinction between ill and healthy parts in psychosis is sharper, and the course of the illness depends on the power the psychotic part has to invade and colonise the healthy part. In the borderline patient, impulsiveness, self-destructive acting out and alternating emotional and dazed states predominate. Delusion development is highly probable in the psychotic patient, but rare in the borderline patient.

The patient who is destined to become psychotic has lived since childhood in a withdrawal dissociated from reality, a secret place where he builds a world of concrete fantasies and images, wiping out emotional functions that would enable him to understand psychic reality. Mental operations performed in the psychic withdrawal do not observe the rules of normal psychic processing; for example, they cannot be repressed or 'dreamt' so as to be transformed into thoughts. One problem in therapy is that the patient does not usually communicate the operations that occur in the withdrawal because he idealises them and is unaware of their pathogenic power; he therefore cannot foresee their consequences, among which is the likelihood of delusion development.

In the beginning, these psychotic procedures produce pleasant and exciting mental states, but then, when the process gets out of control, they create distorted and distressing perceptions, such as hostile hallucinations that the patient feels he is the target of.

This kind of experience in which sensorial excitement replaces thought is also present in borderline patients, but to a lesser degree; while the latter oscillate in and out of various mental states, psychotic patients go down a road that is often irreversible.

Borderline patients are unable to control their emotions, which they cannot even understand and must expel in order to reduce their anxiety; psychotic patients, on the other hand, tend to isolate themselves, use their bodies as a source of stimuli and treat the world of grandiose fantasies as a real world.

As previously mentioned, one objective of analytic treatment is to develop the patient's functions of self-awareness and his emotions. It is therefore important to prepare a specific setting that allows for the development of these experiences that the patient has never lived; in other words, the analysand must be helped to build a real identity through the relation with a new object, the analyst.

Notes

1 This book was republished by Gregory Bateson in 1961.
2 Incidentally, this also seems to be Winnicott's point of view (1971).

2 Non systematic models

Models

Analytic therapy for psychosis was first used systematically at the *Burghölzli* Psychiatric Clinic in Zurich on the initiative of its then director Eugen Bleuler. This saw the arrival at the *Burghölzli* of many psychiatrists. Some of them went on to become future analysts, eager to treat patients with the analytic method; among them were Carl Gustav Jung, Karl Abraham, Arden Brill, Max Eitingon and Ludwig Binswanger. Jung was the most ardent exponent of the free association method, which he believed could beneficially be applied to psychotic patients in order to discover their emotionally charged pathogenic complexes; it was his conviction that the psychotic patient's thoughts were not absurd but contained a message that needed deciphering. And in fact, through the use of psychoanalytic tools, modifying one's listening and opening up new therapeutic paths, the symptomatology of people who were otherwise destined to an irreversible regression could be understood.

After this, various therapeutic institutions that offered psychotherapeutic treatment for schizophrenic and psychotic patients were created. One of these was the *Bellevue Sanatorium* in Kreuzlingen, Switzerland, under the direction of Ludwig Binswanger. Meticulous psychological care was provided there; also, during psychotic breakdowns and while in hospital, patients could carry out work and study activities and attend lessons and workshops to aid their mental recovery.

In the United States too the dissemination of psychoanalysis had raised hopes of recovery with the founding/the foundation of clinics such as the *Chestnut Lodge Sanitarium*, where patients were treated with analytic therapies proper. Several important analysts worked here, their documented work being an integral part of the history of psychosis therapy. Among these were Frieda Fromm-Reichmann and Harold Searles. Both were influenced by the great American psychiatrist Harry Stack Sullivan, who had created a psychotherapeutic unit at the *Sheppard and Enoch Pratt Hospital* in Baltimore. Here, a group of doctors, nurses and assistants helped patients find their feet again in interpersonal relations. Sullivan had observed that even severely regressed schizophrenic patients responded positively to the therapeutic group work. In fact, most patients seemed to improve, if not fully recover, with this method centred around the interpersonal relation.

16　*Part 1*

Sullivan believed in the psychogenesis of schizophrenia as well as in working with transference with these patients, who, in his opinion, preserved the ability to enter a relationship, even in cases of severe pathological splitting.

Many are the analytic contributions on psychosis therapy. Of these, I have listed here the most representative: Freud (1894, 1910, 1915b, 1922, 1924a, 1924b, 1932), Abraham (1924), Federn (1952), Arieti (1955), Rosen (1962), Fromm-Reichmann (1959), Arlow and Brenner (1969), Hartmann (1953), Pao (1979), Fairbairn (1952), Winnicott (1954, 1971), Bion (1957, 1958, 1965, 1967), Rey (1994), Lacan (1955–56), Aulagnier (1985), Searles (1965), Segal (1956, 1991), Rosenfeld (1965, 1969, 1978), Katan (1954), Meltzer (1983a), Meltzer et al. (1975), Ogden (1982, 1989), Resnik (1972) Benedetti (1980), Rosenfeld (1992), Volkan (1997), Racamier (2000), Freeman (2001), Symington (2002), Jackson (2001), Williams (2004), Lombardi (2005), De Masi (2000, 2006), Lucas (2009).

I have sought to divide the various analytic models of psychosis into two groups: *intuitive-non systematic*, or *eclectic*, and *theoretical-systematic post-Kleinian*. This division may not seem ideal, considering the complexity and wealth of analytic work on psychosis, but I feel it is useful in order to establish an initial distinction between the various positions.

Whereas the *non systematic* or *eclectic models* mainly make reference to intuitions and experiences derived from clinical work, the *post-Kleinian systematic models* refer to complex, well-organised theories that often preceded the study of psychosis (as in the case of Melanie Klein).

The non systematic models highlight the patient's alienated condition and his imprisonment in a state of regression; the therapist must therefore enter into contact with him and lead him towards the world of relations. According to the non systematic authors, interpretations are not about what is communicated but are a possible means to take the patient towards recovering the self and symbolic thought. Madame Sechehaye (1951), with her patient Renée, is an extraordinary example of this course.

For the sake of brevity, from the many interesting non systematic authors I have chosen just a few: Fromm-Reichmann, Searles, Sechehaye, Rosen, Federn, Benedetti and separately Lacan.

Non systematic or eclectic models

In that same period when clinics were being prepared for psychotic patients, individual therapies were also beginning to take root. Taken into consideration was how the patient was to be seen and communicated with, which analysts solved by letting themselves be guided by their own intuition and spontaneity; the style of therapy therefore largely depended on each analyst's personality. At that time, of course, there were no pharmacological therapies to contain the psychotic process.

Several analysts were convinced that patients they had treated had made a recovery, even though it is difficult to establish whether recovery was permanent or only a temporary remission of psychotic manifestations. In any case, their work is testimony to effectively communicating with the psychotic patient as well as receiving responses from him.

Frieda Fromm-Reichmann

Frieda Fromm-Reichmann was born in Karlsruhe, Germany, in 1889 and died in Rockville in the United States in 1957. She was forced to flee to Palestine, France and then to the United States because of Nazism. For twenty-two years she worked as a psychiatrist at Chestnut Lodge alongside other psychiatrists and psychotherapists, such as Harold Searles, with whom she developed a good working relationship.

She was a psychoanalyst who had little love for convention, not only generally speaking, but in her work too; despite believing in the fundamental concepts of psychoanalysis, such as the defences, transference, the unconscious and the importance of childhood for personality development, she above all focused her attention on the analyst-patient relation.

Frieda Fromm-Reichmann believed that the analyst's participation in the therapy of the psychotic patient needed to be very active and not confined to impersonal interpretations of his communications; she herself did not define her way of working as psychoanalytic but viewed treatment as *intensive psychotherapy*. In the case of psychosis, she thought that the classical attitude of neutrality, the analyst as a blank screen or mirror, was unsuitable; instead, she was convinced that the therapist needed to transmit interest in the patient in order to reawaken his spontaneity. She did not ask the patient to lie on the couch, nor did she intend to get closer to the patient by breaking down his defences with transference interpretations.

In the beginning, Frieda Fromm-Reichmann had adopted a rather optimistic vision of the illness, giving much value to the analyst's reparative potential. She believed that psychotic patients had suffered significant childhood traumas during the stage in which they lived in a narcissistic and grandiose world. This kind of traumatic suffering, caused above all by a mother lacking in empathy, made them particularly sensitive to life's difficulties and driven towards illness, where they recreated the autistic and omnipotent world of early childhood.

She had observed that the psychotic patient became suspicious and disheartened when the therapist tried to enter his secret world, and for this reason, she recommended beginning therapy only after a sufficiently long period of interviews. In her opinion, the patient needed to explore the figure of the analyst for an adequately long period before accepting him. Each mistake or shortcoming by the therapist could provoke a serious disappointment that repeated the childhood trauma, whereas his strength and solidity recreated a good maternal-like relationship in which the patient could gradually develop better contact with reality.

Frieda Fromm-Reichmann thought that the analyst had to adopt an attitude of total acceptance with regard to the patient's behaviour, even when it was bizarre. This tendency, a little naive and excessively reparative, was gradually abandoned when she took into consideration the patient's aggressive aspects, too, such as hatred, violence and pathological splitting. To avoid adverse regressions, she then began to analyse more thoroughly the negative transference. Here, it was not about injuring the child present in the adult schizophrenic, but rather addressing

18   *Part 1*

the adult that existed before the psychotic illness. In this sense, she abandoned the idea of being an ideal mother and developed instead an interest in the internal dynamics and the conflict between the patient's regressed part and his adult part.

Only later did she speak about how important it was to identify and clarify the *distortions* the patient made regarding the figure of the therapist and to understand in what way the therapist's words were understood by the patient. She also underlined the fact that the psychotic patient was stirred by extremely ambivalent impulses; on the one hand, he wished for contact with the therapist, but on the other, he feared losing himself in him.

Something important that Frieda Fromm-Reichmann suggested was that the content of psychotic communications should not be interpreted as the objective is not to make the unconscious conscious, given that the psychotic patient is invaded by unconscious material that bursts into consciousness. In order to respond to hallucinatory and delusional manifestations, she adopted a respectful manner without interpreting by using this sort of sentence: 'I do not see and do not hear what you see and hear. Let us try to understand the difference between our experiences'.

In the last part of her work, Fromm-Reichmann underlined the importance of working with the non-psychotic part of the personality, and she was convinced that in order to reach the patient's regressed part, it was necessary to be in contact with the healthy or adult part, however modest it might be.

Over the years, she moved away from the hypothesis of trauma and abandoned the idea of needing to be a reparative maternal figure; great effort was made on her part to enter into contact with the intrapsychic pathology that underlay the psychotic disorder.

At a certain point she decided to write a book in collaboration with a patient who was considered to be recovered after three years of therapy. The agreement was that each of them would write one part of the book, but Frieda, elderly and extremely busy, was unable to complete her part; it was her patient Joanne Greenberg who published the book entitled *I Never Promised You a Rose Garden* (1964), which met with much success and on which a film was then based. The book is really very stimulating, also from a psychopathological point of view, in that it describes in detail the thoughts and actions of this ill young woman and her progressive submission to the psychotic organisation that dominated and terrorised her. The psychotic part conquered and intimidated her, as would an evil prompter that distorts reality. Since childhood, this young woman had created a psychic withdrawal where she believed she lived, an alternative world to the real one; she had distanced herself from her family reality, which in many ways had been traumatic, creating this ideal world, the Kingdom of Yr, which was a sort of paradise. This ideal world progressively transformed into a tyrannical structure that controlled her every action, threatening and intimidating her. For a long time, the gods of Yr had been agreeable companions who shared in her solitude. When camping, where she was hated, and at school, where her oddness increasingly distanced her from the others, the Kingdom of Yr and her isolation expanded hand in hand; her gods were cheerful, amusing characters whose only expectation was her wish to meet them. But then the Kingdom of Yr changed from a world of beauty and solidarity into one of fear and pain, which the patient became accustomed to subjecting herself to without rebelling; she thus plunged from the rank of queen in a comfortable, glittering world to being a cruelly treated prisoner.

I have summarised the plot of the book because it highlights a typical transformation in the psychotic process. Early on in the illness, the psychotic organisation does not present itself as a pathological entity but as a structure that takes care of the patient, removing him from depending on others and letting him experience a mental state of euphoria. Then, when the patient tries to break away from its power, it turns into a criminal gang that imprisons and threatens to kill him. During therapy, the pathological organisation intimidates him and turns him against both therapy and analyst. Among other things, the therapeutic task is to remove the patient from the domination of the psychopathological structure.

Fromm-Reichmann herself described the case of a patient who revealed her secret during a session, and then in the following session, the patient was terror stricken; in a state of distress, she explained to the therapist that a voice had threatened her to death because she had told her of 'their' secret.

Harold Searles

Searles started working at Chestnut Lodge in 1949, and he remained there for fifteen years. He had many resident patients and collaborated with Frieda Fromm-Reichmann, whom he expressed his debt of gratitude to on many occasions. Numerous are his publications on psychotic patients and their therapy. Searles underlined the psychotic patient's difficulty in forming a dependence relationship with the therapist or, rather, in his giving up his omnipotent fantasies. In his opinion, the patient defends himself by projecting his needs onto the analyst, which explains why the analyst becomes despised and belittled; therefore, one may say that the schizophrenic patient does not have the problem of *how to relate* with others, but *whether to relate* with others. In particular, Searles sustained that schizophrenics, whose sense of cohesion is weak, are ambivalently persecuted by distress and by their wish to become non-human objects such as machines, trees or animals.

He was particularly interested in the psychotic transference, which is often persecutory, as the patient believes that he is hostilely treated by the analyst when, in actual fact, it is he who projects his hostility onto the analyst. Searles believed that the psychotic patient develops a primitive transference similar to that of a nursling who lives in a world of partial objects; the therapist should therefore regress in the beginning and function as a part of the patient so as to then help him differentiate himself and reach a certain degree of separateness and integration similar to that of the neurotic patient.

With regard to chronic patients, Searles recommended creating a prolonged phase of therapeutic symbiosis, in which the patient can use the therapist as an object to constantly project parts of himself onto, like an auxiliary Ego. He also highlighted how important it was for the therapist to be aware of the symbiosis with the patient in order to experience and treat it with a balanced and serene

20   *Part 1*

state of mind. Therapy needed to centre on the description of the patient's mental state – at times partitioned, at others integrated – to favour the transformation of transference psychosis into transference neurosis and concrete thought into symbolic thought. It was important not to interpret the transference, since the patient would be unable to understand interpretations during this stage.

Searles often adopted bold and unconventional positions, arousing much controversy among colleagues. For example, in his paper 'Oedipal Love in the Countertransference' (1959), in which he described a state of mutual dependence in the symbiotic transference as something inevitable, the love countertransference being a signal of such, he then went on to describe his fantasies of falling in love with some neurotic and psychotic patients, male and female, to whom he even communicated his feelings. In his opinion, this technique brought benefit to them, as they felt important and of worth due to their being able to arouse feelings of love in the analyst.[1]

Searles truly idealised the patient, whom he experienced as a young child with a weak Ego that needed strengthening also through this kind of gratification. There is a degree of idealisation present even in one of his last papers 'The Patient as Therapist to His Analyst' (1975), where he again described the intimate relationship between analyst and patient and that despite perceptual and ideational difficulties, the patient has the intuitive ability to understand the therapist's mental processes. In my opinion, even if the patient is extremely sensitive to the analyst's understanding of him, this does not mean that he can understand the other's mind, an ability that, by definition, is compromised in psychosis.

I would like to end this brief summary of Searles' contribution to psychosis by referring to one of his papers on the relationship between the psychotic illness and the perception of one's own death. Here (1961), he claimed that terror at the thought of dying triggers psychosis: becoming psychotic is a choice in order not to face up to the thought that life is mortal. Among the various cases of psychotic patients who showed such distress, Searles described in particular one of a woman who, after three and a half years of psychotherapy, was able to acquire a more realistic image of the world and herself. This patient would spend most of her time in the hospital park gathering fallen leaves and dead birds and small animals, which she tried to bring back to life with bizarre magical practices. It was clear that she thought she was like God bringing the dead back to life. One autumn day, while she was sitting beside Searles, it came across that the patient was in a painful state of mind, and then, with tears in her eyes, looking at the leaves she had gathered, she said: 'I can't turn these leaves into sheep, for example'. Searles replied, 'Perhaps you are beginning to understand that human life is like that too; just like the leaves, human life ends in death, too'. 'Yes', replied the patient. Searles also said that this woman was convinced that her parents were alive, despite the fact she knew they were dead.

If I were to say something about this case, the patient's intention to reanimate dead things just to resist facing death anxiety is not evident in my opinion. Fascinating as it may be, Searles's hypothesis that fear of death underpins psychosis has not been proven; if this hypothesis were true, psychotic disorders ought to appear when death anxiety is more evident: that is, after middle age. As clinical experience shows, patients who are very distressed by death do not develop psychosis, and psychotics usually deny time and, consequently, the transitory nature of life.

Frieda Fromm-Reichmann and Harold Searles treated psychosis during the same period at the same institution. They underlined that patients were able to establish a significant relationship with the therapist when the latter was able to understand their communications. Both believed that the analyst was not to be neutral, as was prescribed at that time in the therapy of neurotic patients, but that he needed to be willing to identify with the patient. (We may recall the importance Searles gave to the countertransference, to fantasies and to the therapist's identifications.)

Their idea was that if the analyst moved towards the patient, then he too would move towards the therapist, leaving his retreat. Recovery was possible for Fromm-Reichmann when the patient could be provided with an object that was different from the traumatic childhood object; for Searles, an intimate relationship within a symbiotic transference needed to be reached with the patient. Both believed that psychosis began in early childhood when the infant is helpless in relation to emotional traumas; it is as if the psychotic patient returns to an early stage of development, and therapy should provide for his regressive needs. Searles underlined the need to experience regression to primitive mental states with the patient to promote individuation processes. Neither Searles nor Fromm-Reichmann ever stopped taking care of severe and chronic psychotic patients, and all credit goes to them for opening up psychoanalytic treatment to psychosis. Their position helped generate a more positive vision of psychotic patients, who until that point in time had been considered virtually incurable.

Marguerite Sechehaye

Marguerite Sechehaye was born in Switzerland in 1887 and died in Geneva in 1964. She was a very well-known Swiss psychoanalyst at that time in the field of analytic therapy for psychosis. After her psychoanalytic training with Raymond de Saussure, she began to frequent Melanie Klein, Donald Winnicott, Anna Freud and René Spitz. With the publication of her book *Autobiography of a Schizophrenic Girl* (1951), in which she described her *symbolic realisation* method, she revived hopes of being able to cure psychotic patients. During her work at that time, she aroused a great deal of interest within the psychoanalytic field and beyond. In the book, the patient, Renée, describes her illness and recovery alongside the analyst's account, which provides her viewpoint and therapeutic method. Inspired by the book, in Italy the subject of schizophrenia treatment became more widely known through a film (1968) directed by Nelo Risi with the help of Italian psychoanalyst Franco Fornari.

Renée was a severe psychotic patient who began to feel ill in childhood, with distressing mental states that made her see the world as a changed, incomprehensible and strange place. She had been a delicate baby with early trauma: at four months, she was found wasting away so much that gastritis was diagnosed; the cause was in actual fact insufficient maternal milk. A grandmother took care of her but passed away when she was eleven months old; her death triggered acute despair in the child, who manifested violence against herself. Renée continued to live with her family, who were totally incapable of understanding her mental state and, at times, would make fun of and mock her, despite her clear malaise.

During her adolescence, her refusal of food, extreme weight loss and a lung infection led to her being admitted to a sanatorium, where she stayed for two years. Subsequent to this, she manifested acute psychosis with psychomotor excitation, visual hallucinations and delusions of guilt. Her core delusion was that she lived in Tibet, a cold, desert-like region, lit up by blinding light, with no human presence at all; there were powerful, cruel, sarcastic characters there who dominated her and made death threats against her. In the course of her therapy with Madame Sechehaye, Renée was hospitalised on numerous occasions for her acute psychotic breaks featuring destructive and suicidal impulses.

After several years of therapy, the key episode that gave rise to the technique of *symbolic realisation* was the following. One evening, Renée, who was staying on a farm at the time, told Madame Sechehaye in a mixed-up and delusional fashion that she had been reproached by the farmer's wife, who had caught her while she was picking unripe apples from the trees. When Madame Sechehaye offered her all the apples she wanted, Renée answered that she wanted Mama's (that is how she referred to Madame Sechehaye) real apples and pointed to her breast; at this point, the therapist let Renée lean her head against her shoulder and offered her small pieces of apple, which she accepted. This moment of intimacy produced an almost miraculous effect: a newfound period of well-being for Renée.

From that moment on, Madame Sechehaye worked to find an indirect and symbolic way to enter into contact with the patient's unconscious desires. For example, she took care of a small soft toy, washing it, drying it and putting it to bed until Renée herself accepted being taken care of without feeling attacked by blaming inner voices. Madame Sechehaye tried to understand a little at a time what the patient's real needs were, which Renée defended herself so stubbornly against, and what instead were only compensatory wishes; to this end, she created symbolic situations mediated by objects, gifts or words with which she tried to enter into contact not only with Renée's repressed childhood wishes, but also with unexpressed hatred and grudges harboured against her parents. In this period, Renée's mental state was extremely dramatic, marked by recovered vitality as well as relapses into psychosis that required hospitalisation, at times even in a secure unit. According to Madame Sechehaye, many relapses were due to her own mistakes, when she confused 'compensatory wishes' with real 'symbolic needs', for instance.

Although this was a single case, it aroused considerable interest, thanks to the book and the film of the same title. Madame Sechehaye's hypothesis was that schizophrenic psychosis was a primitive regression caused by early trauma in an environment totally lacking in empathy, leading the patient to build an alternative inhuman world which he would then fall victim to. Her reparative therapy consisted in identifying essential unmet needs that were actively denied by the patient herself, which needed to be satisfied symbolically. We do not know whether Renée truly recovered from her illness or whether she benefitted from a fortunate remission. From Madame Sechehaye's account in her book, Renée completed her studies once her therapy ended and went to live with a female friend in a small town near Geneva.

Renée's positive development remains the sole experience brought about using this therapeutic technique. For long periods, the patient had been under the therapist's immediate care, being looked after by her even physically: Madame Sechehaye put her up in her own home and, when necessary, saw to her hospitalisation. Reading the book, one is taken by Renée's complex psychotic world and the author's clarity of thought. The patient's recovery, the fortunate release of a recluse from a psychotic prison, does seem almost miraculous. The technique of symbolic realisation did not have many followers, though; it faded with its creator, leaving the impression that this extraordinary outcome had been due to the two players' exceptional willingness to develop this relationship – a difficult course to repeat.

John Rosen

Today Rosen has practically been forgotten. In the 1960s and 1970s, however, he was well known for his psychotherapeutic method with psychotic patients: that is, *direct psychoanalysis*.

Rosen sustained that in order to be a good adoptive parent to the psychotic patient, it was not enough to be affectionately kind or warmly welcoming. At times, the therapist needed to be strict and authoritarian, not only to assure the patient that the situation was under control, but also to show him that he (the patient) was not at all able to kill with a wish or at a glance (1962, p. 14).

Rosen thought that a psychotic patient needed to be taken care of as does a newborn: care needed to be round the clock, and given that the analyst could not be there constantly, several assistants were needed to support the patient in the therapeutic unit: a small house with all the basic comforts. The patient could thus have the situation under control and feel that he was being treated like a human being. He was to be seen by the psychoanalyst every day without scheduled time limits, and during this time interpretations, *direct* and non-symbolic, were needed to dismantle his delusional experiences; collaborators could attend sessions to support the therapist in seeking to impose reality on the patient.

Rosen would often use a direct and aggressive style with patients. For example, if a patient spoke non-stop, the analyst could say: 'This fake nutrition will not actually help you to have your mother's breast. You use your mouth endlessly to have something to feed on, but this pretence will not help you at all' (p. 125, author's translation). Or a patient who would spin around quickly might be addressed as follows: 'Turning round and round will not make you escape death. If your mother were to say "drop dead", you would not do it. I am the only one here who can decide between life and death, and I want you to live' (p. 143, author's translation).

24   *Part 1*

I have cited these two examples of direct interpretations according to Rosen's technique (there are dozens in his book) to illustrate how an authoritarian concept of care comes through, aimed at 'awakening' the patient from his delusional beliefs.

Yet another exemplifying case is that of a paranoid patient who was convinced he was being pursued by the FBI for having burnt a relic in a church and, hospitalised, believed that he was in prison for a police interrogation. Rosen, together with his assistants, staged a scene. When the patient stopped accusing himself, Rosen said that he himself was the real arsonist and that the patient was a liar in search of publicity. Another psychiatrist also accused himself of the same crime. At this point, two false FBI agents – two assistants dressed up as officers – came onto the scene shouting that all three were under arrest, and then, after pretending to have checked a list of arson suspects, they left exclaiming that the three of them were only seeking publicity since none of them were on the list. Rosen then turned to the patient and reproached him for having made everyone look stupid. He sustained that after four days, the patient understood that he was in a psychiatric hospital and that his ideas were insane.

Clearly, Rosen's technique was often no more than the application of striking manoeuvres to manipulate the patient's mind in a bid to make him abandon his delusional ideas. It is no wonder that direct analysis disappeared from the therapeutic scene together with its creator's notoriety.

This technique, did, however, appear to offer new perspectives on the treatment of psychosis in the 1960s and 1970s. Even Frieda Fromm-Reichmann (1959) said that many of Rosen's interpretations, although arbitrary, were effective thanks to his convincing and constant intensive approach: what he was doing, however, was not so much treating psychotic patients as helping them come out of their acute psychotic states more speedily; much more is needed to treat the patient when the episode is behind him, and the psychotic process continues to produce distorted thought.

Paul Federn

The most original pioneer and, for a long time, the only European interested in developing a therapy for psychotic patients was Paul Federn, who had begun to treat a catatonic and restless female patient in hospital, whom he then decided to continue the therapy with at his home, where his wife looked after the patient during the day. The patient improved and was well for the rest of her life. This outcome convinced Federn of how important it was to give the psychotic patient in therapy female maternal care (Alanen 2009). Federn's most well-known assistant was Gertrud Schwing, who wrote a book on working with Federn and even went on to become a member of the *International Psychoanalytical Association*.

In his writings, Federn underlined that the psychotic patient's withdrawal from reality was never absolute, and in order to carry therapy forward, it was important to develop a positive transference (nowadays referred to as a positive relation), whereas the negative transference, when it emerged, needed to be interpreted and transformed. He was convinced that an analysis featuring transference psychosis in which the analyst had become the persecutor could not under any circumstances be carried forward, the only solution being a change of therapist.

Federn, like Frieda Fromm-Reichmann, was of the view that the customary analytic technique, such as using the couch and free associations, needed to be abandoned. He had patients who had become manifestly psychotic during their previous therapy with other colleagues, and so he learned to pay attention to signs that a psychotic break was imminent. In the case of a manifest psychotic state, however, the analyst initially had to share and accept the falsifications operated by the patient's delusion, and only once a relationship of trust had been built could he then begin to speak to the patient about the delusion distorting or wiping out reality.

The concept of the 'Ego' was of cardinal importance in Federn's writings: the sense of unity and the 'Ego feeling' concern the perceptual continuity of the self, which remains subjectively the same despite changes that occur over time; the 'Ego boundary' separates what belongs to the Ego from what is alien to it; naturally, this is not a real boundary of the person, but a psychological characteristic that can change during the various stages of existence. The Ego boundary would, in the final analysis, be a kind of sense organ that distinguishes between inner and outer and demarcates the Ego from external objects. Federn considered psychosis an 'Ego disease' that entails an inability to maintain the necessary boundaries and continuity of the Ego. When the inner Ego boundary is missing, so is the distinction between conscious and unconscious, and in this case, the patient experiences dreams as if they were delusions or hallucinations. Ego boundaries tend to be lost due to an excessive presence of falsified ideas that alter the perception of personal identity. Federn believed that patients did not abandon reality but developed a false conception of it.

Important reflections on analytic technique derived from this model. Federn suggested that therapeutic work with psychotic patients should not consist in interpreting symbolic meaning, including transference interpretations, as this would increase any confusion for an Ego that was already excessively dispersed. What was needed was therapeutic work to reinforce the patient's sense of identity, protecting him from extreme distress and improving his 'intentional thinking'. 'In psychosis', Federn wrote, 'the main damage consists of the loss of cathexis of the ego boundaries' (1952, p. 166). The Ego, due to its fractured frontiers, is exposed to the invasion of hallucinated reality. Whereas Freud postulated that the delusion was an attempt at reconstruction or, rather, at libidinal recathexis of the object, Federn held that it was the consequence of having falsified reality and lost the Ego boundaries.

A specific therapeutic practice stems from this conception, changing the rule of free associations: if the psychotic patient is beset by an excess of senses and meaning, his imagination should not be encouraged by the production of free associations but kept in check. One of Federn's most significant affirmations is that 'in neuroses we want to lift repression, in psychoses we want to create re-repression' (1952, p. 136). The aim is not to 'make the unconscious conscious',

26   *Part 1*

but to 'make the unconscious unconscious again' (p. 178). Through the positive transference, in the position of the Ego ideal the analyst must repair the patient's constitutive deficit and offer him a form of identification that can strengthen his Ego feeling.

Whereas in neuroses the transference is used to make repressed material manifest, in psychoses it is needed to establish a therapeutic relation that can provide support for the patient's identity deficit. Federn was convinced that the classical analytic method tended to aggravate the psychotic state; in this connection, he cited cases of patients referred to him by colleagues, who had become outright psychotic in the course of their treatment. The therapeutic method used by Federn to help the patient come out of the psychotic state involved the analyst also assuming an educational role: he needed to represent reality and be present in the patient's relational life when need be. Federn entrusted educational tasks to nurses in the hope that they too could be trained by psychoanalytic institutions; at the same time, he also shed light on the determining role of the family environment, which, if lacking, or worse still, if hostile, offered no hope for the patient's recovery.

What Federn deserves credit for are his highly significant intuitions on the nature of the psychotic process, such as the all-important need to boost the Ego's healthy part (even using psycho-educational measures) and that all symbolic interpretations need to be excluded from therapy, given that the patient may perceive them as disclosures of other realities and not as implicit and unconscious meanings held within his own psychic reality.

Gaetano Benedetti

Gaetano Benedetti specialised in psychiatry at the Burghölzli clinic in Zurich under the direction of Manfred Bleuler; he furthered his psychiatric and psychotherapeutic training while working alongside Ludwig Binswanger, Madame Sechehaye, Christian Müller and Carl Jung. Taking as his starting point Freudian psychoanalysis, several phenomenological currents and existentialism, Benedetti devoted himself to the theory and clinical work of psychoses, which comes through in his important book *La Psicoterapia Come Sfida Esistenziale* (1997) (*Psychotherapy as the Essential Challenge* – author's translation).

Benedetti thought that psychotic phenomena brought about a 'loss' of Self, in particular the mental and emotional symbol of the Self; this is why the patient withdraws into himself, creating a personal phantasmatic world, and tends to compensate for the loss of human relations by relating with all non-human objects that surround him, multiplying the possible meanings and assonance between words. Given the loss of Self-image and symbols, for Benedetti treatment was a course based on a 'progressive psychopathology', by means of which the analyst participates in the human meaning of the symptom, assigning to it symbolic value that is new and positive. Psychotic symptoms have communicative intentionality that activates when the therapist identifies with the patient through empathetic experiences. The encounter between the psychotherapist, with his experience and personal humanity, and the psychotic patient locked in psychosis is a difficult one; identification and symbiosis between therapist and patient become the engine of therapy, and from this 'dual' course, 'progressive' development may begin, enabling the patient to feel that kind of differentiation between the Self and the world which underpins psychic life.

Three important moments are envisaged in this course. The first is the establishment of a symbiotic bond with the patient that can be achieved through 'therapeutic phantasmatisation': the analyst must provide the patient with proof that he has understood his inner world without necessarily expressing so verbally. Through this process, the patient senses the therapist's willingness to make himself similar to him. In the second stage, the analyst breaks the symmetry created, positively setting out the patient's negative experiences, thus creating a contrast with the patient's negative image. This 'positive asymmetry' creates a way out of the autistic shutdown. A third stage sees the patient entering a mutual relation and identifying partially with the coherent and unified person of the therapist.

Given that the therapist does not seek to transform psychotic proto-symbols into concepts by interpretation but accommodates them as important communications, in the patient's asymbolic world, a process of symbolisation can originate within this dual communication. Every now and then, the therapist can give unconscious representations originating within the patient back to him, once they have been 'filtered'; taking due precaution, the analyst may also begin to communicate his own dreams, given that despite being fragile and fragmented, the patient is anyhow able to perceive the therapist's or his own family's unconscious processes.

Hallucinatory and delusion 'proto-symbols' may become symbolic nuclei if they can be presented in a representation that is broader and more positive than that of the pathology. Benedetti provided the example of a female patient who was convinced that Jesus and Barabbas were brothers as both were Maria's sons: in this case, the patient had discovered a maternal principle that placed together a good and a bad part that were no longer perceived separately. This is an example of a positively modified proto-symbol.

'Positive transformation of the psychotic experience' is an operation through which the psychotic experience is reflected in the therapist, from whom the patient captures a positive image of himself, as in a mirror. The intimate fusional experience that the therapist is able to establish with the patient leads to *intersubjective transitivism* that sometimes generates the death phantom in the patient within the therapist too: the therapist may dream the same anxiety-laden representations that are present in psychosis, such as finding oneself on the brink of an abyss, in a grave or in a bare lunar landscape, devoid of plant life.

According to Benedetti's experience, the patient, despite being shut away in his autism, is capable of perceiving a degree of strength in the therapist that can not only limit and contain death, but also present itself as offering life. In this case, too, the transmission of positive experience occurs through unconscious channels.

As can be noted, Benedetti took up the concept of the fusional forwarded by Searles, enriching it with new and original content. What is fashioned as therapeutic and the engine of transformation is not so much the interpretation in

28   *Part 1*

psychodynamic terms of what the patient 'feels', but fusional empathic identification with him to make him aware that his world can be shared. This occurs nonverbally and passes along unconscious channels. Benedetti believed that direct communication between two unconsciouses, the patient's and the analyst's, produces a progressive transformation of the patient's subjective experience and strips psychotic manifestations of their alienating character. This process does not come about through insight, which assumes separateness between the two, but by the patient assimilating outside awareness parts or functions present in the analyst's mind. Benedetti called this transformation process 'appersonation', a term that refers to the patient's progressive acquisition of human characteristics and functions through his incorporation of the analyst's psychological qualities, the analyst thus functioning as a developmental component.

Jacques Lacan

For its originality, I shall briefly mention Lacan's position on psychosis, which is discussed in many of his writings; it was through the study of paranoia that he actually came to encounter psychoanalysis (1932).

One of his most important concepts related to psychosis is *foreclosure*, which consists in the area of the signifier and therefore of symbolisation being impossible to access. Unlike the neurotic patient, the psychotic does not suffer from any symptom, but he processes a 'delusion' due to never having had any access to oedipal identification, or, rather, to the *Name-of-the-Father*.

For Lacan, the Name-of-the-Father is the sole position that enables the subject not only to take on meaning, but also to assimilate the specific nature of subjectivity. The Father, for Lacan, does not have real psychological features; it is a metaphorical figure whose foreclosure creates a 'hole' in the signifier (the *law*). The foreclosure represents a reality fracture that can stay that way until the psychosis breaks through. The subject who is destined to become psychotic is structurally injured and can remain so until trauma strikes; for example, he can maintain his rigid or mirror constitution until a third breaks his narcissistic structure.

The psychotic patient is unable to access the symbolic dialectic that organises the real and releases him from his condition of fragmentation. In psychosis, the Father cannot act to organise sense so as to lay down oedipal law; the possibility of reaching the symbolic function therefore remains foreclosed. According to Lacan, psychosis is one of the subject's possible responses to the oedipal situation. It is the position of an individual who has no symbolic field but builds a signifying void, which explains why the schizophrenic patient, with no access to imagination, equates words with things.

The delusion is an attempt at recovery that seeks to give meaning to language, an attempt that is unfortunately destined to fail for want of the Name-of-the-Father, the only symbol capable of identifying the subject as the sense around which the play of symbols rotates (Tarizzo 2003).

The subject thus remains without any paternal signification on the symbolic front, or corresponding phallic signification on the imagination front, that would allow access to the unconscious image of the body. The experience of a fragmented body is in fact remediated only by the image of the body that can occur in the mirror stage.

So, for Lacan, psychosis is the result of a basic defect, the effect of which is a failed structuring of the symbolic area, of the Oedipus, and the validity of the law. The symbolic should deal with the real and negativize the invasion of enjoyment, which instead explodes in schizophrenia. The foreclosure of the Name-of-the-Father means that a specular dimension with no bulwarks prevails, sustained by the presence of a powerful Ego ideal, the absolute keeper of imaginary dynamics (Bonifati 2000).

Among the various possible references, Lacan's considerations regarding the work of Joyce are particularly significant. Lacan claims that the 'Joyce case' is a clear example of untriggered psychosis thanks to containment via writing. Through real motivation towards writing, Joyce was able to fill the gap caused by a severely deficient paternal function; by pursuing his vocation as a writer, Joyce managed to 'make a name for himself' that served to compensate for his father's deficiency.

Note

1 Naturally, the technique described by Searles was not welcomed by the psychoanalytic milieu. Strangely though a similar technique has been put forward quite recently by several American intersubjective analysts who believe that the so-called self-disclosure of one's love fantasies to the patient is helpful.

3 Kleinian contributions

In the previous chapter, I have illustrated the therapeutic work of six authors who, in different periods, treaded the path of psychosis therapy unhindered by theoretical assumptions; these authors believed that psychosis was governed by laws that lay outside all previous theories, the illness therefore needing to be understood intuitively. As can be seen, their techniques were very personal and stemmed from each of their specific visions of the nature of psychosis. Their purpose was *restitutive*: starting from the idea that the illness was a form of regression to a primitive stage, they sought to recreate those psychological structures that had existed before the psychotic episode. Lacan should be considered separately as he incorporated psychosis into his particular theoretical model.

Melanie Klein insisted on the need to work only in an analytic setting without any external interventions, her contribution leading to an approach to psychosis that was anchored to theory. Next, I shall try to summarise the position of the Kleinian group, which gave impetus to the theoretical and clinical study of this mental state.

For the systematic models, I shall consider the therapeutic techniques that derived from Melanie Klein's thought. This great psychoanalyst created a theoretical system that rests on infantile anxieties that characterise primitive mental development and which, in her opinion, also help our understanding of psychotic symptoms. Her intuitions were subsequently developed and systematized, giving her pupils the chance to apply them to the therapy of psychotic cases.

These post-Kleinian authors, convinced they could analyse psychotic patients during both acute episodes and chronic stages, highlighted how specific pathogenic elements are active in the psychotic process, such as massive projective identification, loss of symbolisation, attacks on objects, the fragmentation of perceptive functions and confusion between inner and outer. Transference is *the* indispensable treatment tool with which to analyse pathogenic manifestations.

Melanie Klein

Dedicated to the therapy of severely ill children, Melanie Klein encountered the problem of psychosis at the very beginning of her analytic work; it was therefore easier for her to get a feel for the early illness, almost at onset. Regarding little Dick's therapy, Klein (1930a) described the main dynamics of the disorder: in addition to his love relation with his parents, the child had also developed a destructive relation; he attacked them in phantasy and consequently feared that they would do the same to him. His anxiety reached such high levels that he had to block out thought to avoid allowing further aggressive phantasies to take up even more space.

Klein believed that schizophrenic psychosis derives from an excess of sadism that then turns into persecution. In order to protect himself from this excess, the child resorts to many defence mechanisms, including splitting, denial, idealisation and various forms of identification.

Klein's most important work is *Notes on Some Schizoid Mechanisms* (1946), which saw the start of a specific therapy for psychotic patients. Here, Melanie Klein wrote of psychotic anxieties that appear during breast-feeding and which constitute fixation points for psychosis. In particular, she concentrated on how the child develops oral-sadistic phantasies towards the mother's breast to rob her body of its contents; these are the impulses that give rise to persecution anxiety, which underlies the development of paranoia and schizophrenia. Melanie Klein conceived anxiety as the result of the death instinct going into operation and being perceived as fear of annihilation; this destructive instinct is projected onto an object that becomes omnipotent and uncontrollable. Anxiety connected to being annihilated by an inner destructive force results in the fragmentation and splitting of the Ego: the more sadism predominates in introjection, the greater the fragmentation of the incorporated object, the Ego splitting correspondingly.

Another important process is object idealisation, which, on the one hand, defends from persecution, but on the other, it expresses the omnipotent desire to have a breast infinitely on hand. This process occurs in the infantile hallucinatory world and is created by virtue of the splitting of the object, denial of frustration and persecution. All this leads to psychic reality being blotted out. In this early stage, splitting, denial and omnipotence perform a function analogous to that of repression in more advanced stages of development.

Melanie Klein claimed that these infantile world primitive modalities are reproduced in psychosis, and here she connects back to Freud and his assertion (1924a) that, whereas in neurosis 'the loss' follows repression, in psychosis the more radical mechanism of 'disavowal' is in operation. It is not the drive that is repressed in psychosis but the perception of external reality.

An important contribution to understanding psychosis is the concept of *projective identification*. Melanie Klein sustained that when the infant projects destructive impulses into the mother, she is perceived not as a separate person but as part of the Self, often a persecutor. The splitting and projecting of parts of the Self onto objects concern the good parts of the Self, too, consequent confusion ensuing between what belongs to the subject and what to the recipient of the projection.

Melanie Klein spoke openly about the early origin of psychosis and the determining action of the destructive drive; in addition, as I have already mentioned, she considered child development and psychotic development as analogous, asserting that splitting and fragmentation, despite being physiological in the child, if overly

32   *Part 1*

frequent and prolonged needed to be considered as signs of infantile psychosis. In adults, depersonalisation and psychotic dissociation are nothing other than the manifestation of regressing to disintegration that was present in the infant.

In particular, when projective identification is massive, the impulses that control the object from inside him arouse fear in the subject that he in turn shall also be controlled and persecuted, and it becomes difficult to take back possession of the projected parts. When emotions and parts of the self are alienated and placed in other people, besides confusion between self and object, emotional voids form in the patient's inner world. The feeling of psychic death experienced by psychotic patients derives from the loss of important parts of the self and from the evacuation of the emotional world.

Another of Melanie Klein's contributions (1930a, 1930b, 1946) is having identified two phases that are also two mental functions underlying psychic development: the *paranoid-schizoid* position and the *depressive* position. The former is characterised by the impulse to react aggressively to any kind of frustration, the infant therefore hating the mother when she does not protect him or when she exposes him to frustration. In the depressive position, on the other hand, the infant lets the mother be a separate object, with her own needs and wishes, and he tries to repair the damage caused by his aggressive attacks. Such attacks towards the 'bad mother' will, if unresolved in childhood or adolescence, constitute the fixation point for subsequent illness. It is clear that for Melanie Klein, the psychotic process is nothing more than the exacerbation of infantile physiological states, and therefore in her vision the primitive is equated with the pathological.

With Melanie Klein began the articulated theorizing of psychosis linked to infantile phantasy events; indeed, in her cases of severely disturbed children, Melanie Klein (1929) highlighted extreme aggressive and sadistic phantasies as well as strong persecutory anxieties, to the extent that she came to sustain that the psychotic patient was imprisoned within his illness due to an excess of primary sadism. Her model, which sees the illness as deriving from primitive anxiety and corresponding defences, may be defined as *continuous*, as it links psychosis to primitive forms of mental organisation.

Her theoretical innovations allowed her collaborators to begin treating psychotic states in a setting identical to that of neurosis, as can be seen from the authors I have cited here.

Herbert Rosenfeld

Rosenfeld, one of Melanie Klein's most important pupils, left numerous accounts of his therapies undertaken with psychotic patients. In his book *Psychotic States* (1965), he described how both acute and chronic patients may be treated using psychoanalytic technique; specifically, with acute patients, the analyst needs to be guided by clinical experience with children. His assumption is that psychoanalytic method based on analysing the transference can be used to treat psychosis:

> In our approach to schizophrenia we retain the essential features of psycho-analysis; namely, detailed interpretations of the positive and negative

Kleinian contributions 33

transference without the use of reassurance or educative measures; the recognition and interpretation of the patient's unconscious material; and, above all, the focusing of interpretations on the patient's manifest and latent anxieties. It has been found that the psychotic manifestations attach themselves to the transference in both acute and chronic conditions, so that what one may call a 'transference psychosis' develops. The analyst's main task in both acute and chronic schizophrenias is the recognition of the relevant transference phenomena and its communication to the patient.

(p. 117)

Rosenfeld, who approached psychosis clinical work according to all of Melanie Klein's core teachings, thought that schizophrenic patients concretely experience the feeling of entering the analyst at the beginning of the session via projective identification, to then be expelled at the end. Splitting and projective identification at work in the psychotic state would explain the patients' lack of a sense of identity, their loss of emotions and difficulty using symbols.

In his first paper, 'Analysis of a Schizophrenic State with Depersonalisation' (1947), Rosenfeld described the case of Mildred, a young woman with schizoid symptoms. The traumatic event in her childhood had been the birth of a brother and her being distanced from her mother as a result; Mildred then stopped talking and walking, and in both childhood and adolescence, she presented other difficulties related to development and learning. As an adult, she often took to her bed, found it hard to get up, and withdrew from her friends.

The course of her analysis was complex and very difficult. Mildred often missed her sessions, or she would arrive late looking dim and sleepy, only half-conscious and stating that she was separate from the world, dead. Particular about her was that she would not accept transference interpretations, be they positive or negative. Of the many fantasies she had, Mildred related one that was connected to her difficulty to collaborate: it was about a devil that attacked good people, tied them up and gagged them, and if these people managed to free themselves just a little, the devil tied them up even more tightly; it was unclear whether the victims were killed because you couldn't tell whether they were dead, and there was no point putting up a struggle because the devil was the strongest of all. Rosenfeld considered this fantasy as a possible risk to there being a negative therapeutic reaction: in the transference, the analyst is the devil that personifies the bad father. When he tried to interpret her feelings of love and hate, the patient cancelled them by entering into a state of depersonalisation. At a certain point, a misunderstanding arose in the analytic relationship to the extent that Mildred began to suspect that the analyst wanted to push her into thinking along his lines. Rosenfeld's reflection was that when Mildred was little, she reacted sadistically towards her mother when she was expecting her brother and then omnipotently idealised and controlled her; part of the sadism was projected onto the father, who was transformed into a persecuting devil.

As can be seen, in this early period, Rosenfeld considered the fantasy of the devil not as an internal object – that is, as a pathological structure that dominates the patient – but as a transferential distortion of the paternal image caused by

34   *Part 1*

the patient's sadism. He also thought that the destructive impulses were directed against the patient's own self and were responsible for the depersonalisation and fragmentation of her personality: as opposed to attacking and destroying the object, the destructive impulses attacked the vital part of her personality. With events alternating between moments of vitality and phases of draining away, the analysis proceeded, with Rosenfeld always being directed towards interpreting the transference. The analysis finished when Mildred, who had greatly improved, got married and went to live abroad with her husband.

From the distance of many years on, we may say that Mildred did not seem to suffer from psychosis proper, but a marked psychic withdrawal that made returning to reality tiring. As a child, Mildred was certainly not sufficiently accommodated emotionally, and after her brother's birth, she was in fact looked after by a series of nannies and then sent to boarding school. There she excelled as a pupil. A self-destructive force then took the form of a devil that prevented her from speaking or functioning.

Another important point in Rosenfeld's clinical research on psychosis regards confusional anxiety. In 'Notes on the Psychopathology of Confusional States in Chronic Schizophrenia' (1950), he wrote that when destructive impulses predominate, mental states are created in which good objects can no longer be told apart from bad objects, and libidinal impulses and destructive impulses become mixed up.

The patient he gives an account of in this paper is in his second analysis: he is an artist who took a painting he had painted for the previous analyst to his session, the analyst having made a reference to the dark colours in the painting, connecting them to the patient's desire to soil with his faeces. The patient felt persecuted by this interpretation, and from that moment on, was convinced that he could no longer paint. Rosenfeld observed that the confusion derived from a sadistic-oral attack against the mother who was mixed up with faeces; the destroyed breast mixed up with bad faeces had become a persecutor who attacked and confused the patient from within. Rosenfeld's work analysing confusion between good and bad, between food and faeces and between parts of the body was to be extremely helpful to this patient.

Rosenfeld noted, however, that when interpretations were poor and imprecise (above all negative, I should add), the image of the analyst who is felt to be a persecutor becomes real. Persecution in the case of the painter derived from his perception of the first analyst as a persecutory and scornful Super-ego. Patients of this kind have internalised a Super-ego that constantly accuses and confuses them, and therefore wrong or negative interpretations help to project this internal object onto the analyst.

In his subsequent paper, 'Notes on the Psychoanalysis of the Super-Ego Conflict of an Acute Schizophrenic Patient', Rosenfeld (1952) wrote of the clinical benefit of forming a psychotic transference during therapy: 'The success of the analysis depends on our understanding of the psychotic manifestations in the transference situation' (1952, p. 65).

This position, as we shall see, would later be abandoned (1987), when Rosenfeld claimed that the psychotic transference is dangerous as the delusion can incorporate the figure of the analyst, thus paralysing his analytic function. For Rosenfeld, the schizophrenic patient has never overcome the earliest stage of object relations development; his dynamics, characterised by the splitting of objects and persecutory states, feature anxieties that are typical of the paranoid-schizoid position as well as unsuccessful attempts to gain access to the depressive position. Despite this inadequate level of functioning and symbolisation impairment caused by excessive projective identification, Rosenfeld felt it was beneficial to use interpretations in the acute and chronic psychotic patient alike: interpreting the projective identification tended to make it easier for the patient to understand the analyst's communications.

In order to understand how Rosenfeld worked in this early period, I shall cite part of an analysis undertaken in hospital, at five one-and-a-half-hour sessions per week with a patient suffering from mutacism, who at times would have aggressive outbursts and had found himself in a severe psychotic state for three years. Once, the patient had attacked a nurse and felt depressed and distressed immediately afterwards. According to Rosenfeld, the patient believed he had destroyed the world, had then taken it inside himself and needed to restore it; under the pressure of his guilt and the persecutory anxiety of the Super-ego, his Ego began to fragment, and it split into many men who perceived the anxiety and guilt. This situation also appeared in the transference: during the session, the patient showed how he had projected his own damaged Self not only onto all the other patients, but onto the analyst, too, transforming him into a damaged object. He became very suspicious towards the analyst and refused food, probably because he would have felt even more guilty had he eaten it. This was interpreted by Rosenfeld, and immediately afterwards the patient gave a grunt, but by the end of the session drank a glass of fruit juice that had been on his bedside table, his first sign of feeding himself after days of fasting. For Rosenfeld, it was important that this patient, despite being in a severe hallucinatory state, had been able to benefit from an interpretation that made him understand the relationship between his acute psychotic state and his feeling of guilt.

This short extract is just one example of how Rosenfeld constantly interpreted the fragmented, distressed and persecutory state in relation to the transference and to projective identification dynamics; in particular, he placed emphasis on the aggressive phantasies towards the analyst, on the Super-ego's corresponding death threats and on manifestations of primary envy. This patient's analysis was then abruptly interrupted upon his mother's arrival in England; she had decided to seek other treatment for her son, including a lobotomy. The analytic therapy had lasted only three months: the patient felt less persecuted, splitting lessened, his depression emerged more on the surface, and there were also periods of lucidity that lasted several hours, in which the patient was able to communicate normally.

An important problem though concerns patients' ability to receive and understand interpretations. As can be seen, these were patients who had been in a psychotic state with hallucinations and delusions over a long period of time and who moved in a sensory reality far from the relationship. Could these patients have understood interpretations, often containing symbolic meaning? It seems

36   *Part 1*

Rosenfeld was convinced that the patient would be able to restore his sense of Self if he could understand his mental functioning through interpretations. Rereading the writings of that time, one has the impression though that the patients who were in an acute stage of the illness, often having hallucinations and delusions, were exposed to an excess of interpretations. Rare were the descriptions of their inner world and their conditions prior to the analytic therapy; importance given to interpreting the psychotic transference and to projective identification content overshadow other clinical considerations.

Rosenfeld realised that much clinical experience was needed before acquiring the necessary skills to treat psychotic patients. On this he wrote:

> At this state of our research we shall not over-estimate the therapeutic possibilities of psycho-analysis in severe acute and chronic schizophrenic conditions. . . . At present therefore we can only hope to be successful in a minority of cases. However, this does not invalidate the psycho-analytic approach. Every acute or chronic schizophrenic patient, even if he is being treated for a short time only, enriches our understanding of the psychopathology and makes the analysis of subsequent patients easier.
>
> (1965, p. 127)

Wilfred Bion

Second Thoughts (1967) is a collection of Bion's papers on psychosis from the 1950s onwards, which integrates retrospective reflection with Bion's previous vision and shows extraordinary originality in the field of analytic theory and technique. Bion examined in depth and broadened several fundamentally important topics to aid our understanding of the psychotic state, such as projective identification (of which he gave a more radical description than that of Melanie Klein), the formation of the bizarre object, the psychotic part of the personality, the theory of thinking, the alpha function, the hallucination and so on.

The cases presented are patients with psychosis in the active phase. Bion did not provide information on patients' personal history, nor did he mention onset or the development of the illness; not even the patient's mental state before the session was taken into consideration. He confined himself to an *in vivo* presentation of the patient in the consulting room and to discussing the transference that develops with him. For example, he made no comment about a patient who was clearly hallucinating and almost delusional, who said he had ordered a coffee before the session but that the lady who served him had something against him, perhaps because of his voice and that coming through the mews the walls were bulging outwards but that, when he went back to check, everything was fine.

The importance of projective identification, which assumes a more destructive nature inclined to disintegrate the object, is central in his writings.[1] This process, when used indiscriminately, results in splitting the analyst in two (one positive and one negative and persecutory), in deforming and fragmenting language and in no symbolisation; consequently, it becomes indispensable to describe to the patient the process that is taking place.

Bion tried to shed light on the causes of frequent relapses that occur in the course of therapy and on the difficult nature of recovery. He hypothesised that when the patient improves and can think, he feels a psychic pain come so much to the fore that he shies away from his regained ability to understand, it being intolerable to him; by fleeing, however, he loses those tools that would permit personality integration and the employment of verbal thought. When integration is successful and the patient once again obtains consciousness of psychic reality, the danger is that he will begin to hate the analyst, who, in the patient's opinion, is to blame for having brought the disaster that occurred to his awareness. For two of the three cases considered, Bion did not speak of recovery, but of improved adapting to reality or, rather, of a particular kind of improvement.

Another important concept introduced by Bion here is the *difference between the psychotic and the non-psychotic personality*, which exists from birth and determines the subject's destiny. Bion highlighted four main features of the psychotic personality: the predominance of destructive instincts, hatred of inner and outer reality, the dread of imminent annihilation and a fragile and rash transference.

During the psychotic process, the child's sadistic attacks on the breast are directed against his perceptual apparatus that is connected to verbal thought, which is minutely broken up and then expelled. In the patient's phantasy, these parts of the perceptual apparatus, fragmented and expelled into external objects, continue to live autonomously and uncontrollably and are perceived as being full of hostility directed against the mind that expelled them. As a result, the patient feels surrounded by *bizarre objects*.

According to Bion, it is not possible to treat a psychotic patient if his destructive attacks against his Ego are not analysed and his perceptual distortions in operation via projective identification constantly clarified. Whereas the non-psychotic person uses repression and can therefore 'dream' the repressed content, the psychotic patient resorts to projective identification.

The technique Bion used was to directly interpret the destructive mechanisms by describing the patient's use of his own bodily organs. When sense organs are used to evacuate, hallucinations are formed. To a patient who was very detached during a session and said that perhaps he had heard incorrectly, Bion replied that his interpretations had entered his ears to then be transformed into a destructive mouth and expelled via the eyes. His exact words were 'You are feeling that your ears are chewing up and destroying all that I say to you. You are so anxious to get rid of it that you at once expel the pieces out of your eyes' (1967, p. 76).

Bion's interpretations were frequently so bold that they seem subjective, almost bizarre and quite difficult for the reader to understand; moreover, it is not clear how the patient could have taken them in and understood them. For example, in one case, Bion said to a patient that when he suffers, he wants to achieve anaesthesia to get rid of memory and pain, to which the patient, after having said his head was splitting, exclaimed, 'Maybe my dark glasses'. At this point, Bion remembered that approximately five months earlier he himself had worn dark glasses and that this image had been engraved on the patient's mind like an ideograph. For Bion, the glasses hint at a baby's bottle and the lenses being two, to the breast – the

38   *Part 1*

lenses are glass to punish him for trying to look through them when they were breasts; being dark means frowning and angry. They are dark also because they need to be in order to spy on his parents during intercourse. Bion told the patient that the dark glasses were like his sight and felt as a conscience that punished him for getting rid of them to avoid feeling pain and because he had used them to spy on his analyst and his parents (pp. 57–58).

The interpretation, as one may see, derives not so much from the patient's associations, but from the mechanisms that Bion places at the base of the psychotic process: hatred towards the breast, an excessive use of projective identification, the creation of bizarre objects, envy of the parents' intercourse, guilt and a persecutory Super-ego. So the dark glasses come to mean an agglomerate of bizarre objects due to an excess of projective identification and the resulting fragmentation of the Ego. What is interesting about this extract, which I have described succinctly, is that, according to Bion, the patient subsequently showed an improvement, which was confirmed by his use of verbal thought and more positive consideration for the figure of the analyst, who became a human being. Bion attributed the change to the fact that the patient managed to decrease destructive attacks against his own Ego and restore, at least partially, his use of repression in place of projective identification.

Another important concept is the *attack on linking* or, rather, on dependence, on the parents' relationship and on the link between words. In the sequence of a session that Bion (1959) cited, a patient said that a piece of iron had fallen on the floor: 'My interpretation, as far as I could judge, was felt by him as if it were his own visual sense of a parental intercourse; this visual impression is minutely fragmented and ejected at once in particles so minute that they are the invisible components of a continuum' (p. 309). 'I said that he felt so envious of himself and of me for being able to work together to make him feel better that he took the pair of us into him as a dead piece of iron and a dead floor that came together not to give him life but to murder him' (p. 310).

For Bion, the attack on the link is the main obstacle to progress: it is an attack on the analyst's peace of mind and originally on that of the mother. Through constant projections, objects (the breast, the mother and the analyst) are perceived as greedy, eager to devour the patient's projective identifications.

An important change was Bion's conceptualisation of projective identification. Up to a certain point, he considered projective identification as a negative mechanism belonging to the psychotic part of the personality that hinders development; later, he theorised a form of *normal or communicative projective identification* that, alongside introjective identification, constitutes the basis for mental growth and psychic progress.

Bion wrote that, in a session with a psychotic patient, he had interpreted his attempt to rid himself of death anxiety that was so powerful he could not keep it inside; subsequently, thinking again about the material of the session and the exchange that had occurred between the patient and himself, Bion realised that the patient had not used projective identification as a destructive mode, but had placed his anxiety inside the analyst in the hope that he could have modified it so that it could then be safely reintrojected.

The patient's associations in response to the interpretation demonstrated how Bion had not sensed the anxiety of his communication; the patient's subsequent effort to force the projections onto the analyst then became increasingly desperate, and the more violent his projections, the more the analyst, unable to accommodate them, became terrible in his eyes.

Bion hypothesised that an analogous event occurred at the start of life in the child destined to become psychotic. The violence of the attacks is greater when maternal receptiveness is lacking, whereas it is milder but never absent when the mother is able to introject the child's feelings without being overwhelmed. A normal degree of projective identification serves to let the child understand the nature of his own sensations through the effect produced in the mother once they are projected onto her. If the projection is prevented because the mother is unable to accommodate the child's communication, the link between him and the breast is destroyed, and curiosity is seriously compromised; following the destruction of the emotional link between mother and child, prerequisites for the destruction of emotional life are created.

Bion, however, thought that the mother's poor receptiveness to the child's communicative projective identifications was not the primary cause of psychotic disorders, despite its importance in producing the psychotic personality, and that congenital aggressiveness and primary envy bore more weight in this respect. In other words, Bion thought that psychotic disorders originated in an excessive congenital predisposition to aggressiveness, hatred and envy, together with the environmental factor concerning the mother, whose lack of emotional receptiveness prevents the patient from using projective identification as a means of communication.

In Bion's thinking on psychosis, two lines may therefore be captured: the first can be defined as *constitutional* and the second *environmental*, which, despite being conceived one after the other, continuously intersect. The constitutional component is predominant in the first part of Bion's work, which is more connected to Melanie Klein's thought. Bion believed that the psychotic part of the personality, a destructive mental state in which the death instinct and pride nourish *arrogance*, is present from birth. In the psychotic patient, attacking the link, envy and arrogance all destroy a convivial encounter with the object and deny access to the world of symbols and emotions.

The environmental viewpoint instead places emphasis on the poor introjection of fundamental functions for affective symbolisation because of a *container defect*: that is, a defect of the object originally destined to accommodate the nursling's projections. The psychotic part of the personality finds nourishment in a lack in the mother of the intuitive function that accommodates the child's communicative projective identification. Poor maternal receptiveness deprives the baby's communication of its value, burdening him instead with unbearable anxiety and thrusting him headlong into nameless dread.

Normal projective identification has entered post-Kleinian conceptualisation, many analysts using it widely. In my opinion, however, a veil of uncertainty surrounds the use of the term, given that two mental operations – one psychotic and the

40   *Part 1*

other normal – bear the same name. For Melanie Klein, projective identification represented a psychotic mechanism in which the patient projected unwanted parts of his own personality onto another person and stole others he desires: resulting from this was confusion between self and object and the perception of being spied on and controlled by the object into which the projection was directed. None of this occurs in normal projective identification, the purpose of which is to project onto the object not parts of the self but emotions that are difficult to tolerate so that they may be shared and understood.

Bion's intuition of projective identification for the purposes of communication is the basis of his conceptualisation of the relationship between *container* and *contained*, which is essential to understanding emotional growth and development.

Hanna Segal

In 'Some aspects of the analysis of a schizophrenic' (1950), Hanna Segal described her first psychoanalytic therapy with a young man who had developed a psychotic episode. The patient, Edward, had been diffident and hypersensitive since childhood; he had cultivated a long fantasy withdrawal populated by idealised women, often princesses whom he had to free from terrible fathers or rivals. While in India doing his national service, he had a psychotic episode. He was unable to carry out his superiors' orders and was then sent to work in a photographic laboratory, where he began to worry that his eyes no longer worked. Then persecutory delusions appeared that concerned a conspiracy by the Chinese who wanted to take over India and the threatening presence of a biologist who wanted to destroy the world. Once back in England, he spent six months in various military hospitals with a marked deterioration of his symptomatology characterised by delusions, hallucinations, a loss of identity and disorientation in time and space.

Hanna Segal met Edward in one of the military hospitals: he was apathetic, shut away in himself, had upturned lips giving a bizarre smile expression and was afraid that the world was about to be destroyed; he thought he had been transformed by who knows who, he seemed unable to tell the difference between himself and the world, he was hallucinated and heard that voices were in everyone else's head too. After being transferred to a private clinic, it was possible to begin analytic treatment. At first, Hanna Segal did not interpret the delusions and hallucinations; when the patient told her that prisoners in Germany were sending him the voices, she understood that Edward felt like a prisoner and not an ill person.

In the beginning, it was difficult to follow Edward's disconnected speech, but it could be made out that the delusion of being held prisoner became ever more structured. Edward was convinced his thoughts were produced by his stomach, or, rather, he himself was nothing more than a huge stomach, with arms and legs and a head, like tiny alien appendages; terrible distress was then felt because he thought that provisions would run out, and there would be no food left for anyone.

As early as possible, therapy was continued at the patient's home. Here, Edward's earliest childhood recollections emerged: anger over his mother's pregnancy, his brother having been brought into the world when he was four years old. Edward seemed to have identified with a pregnant mother full of babies (full of voices), and at the same time, he was also an embryo in the womb, all tummy and no limbs.

Edward did not accept the transference interpretations but remained attached to the analyst, who had become a protective figure; at times, however, he thought that the analyst was an agent working for the hospital and the doctors who had treated him there. Even during difficult moments, Hanna Segal maintained an analytic attitude and did not resort to advice, reassurance or declarations of friendship.

After approximately three months of treatment at home, Edward was able to go to the analyst's office, despite the fact that at times the delusional persecution included her too. The situation improved after a certain period of analytic work, and the patient seemed to move towards a neurotic way of thinking: he was able to recognise that others did not share in his delusions and hallucinations and that it was better to conceal them. Towards the end of the first year, all the delusions had disappeared at a conscious level; Edward was in touch with reality. He led an apparently normal life, enrolled at university and did some work in the countryside, despite being tormented by distressing fantasies about soil erosion. The only remaining symptoms were poor concentration and an annoying buzz in his ear.

Unfortunately, eighteen months after the beginning of treatment, the 'voices' returned. Hanna Segal reported a session in which she interpreted a psychotic oedipal conflict that seemed linked to the hallucinatory phenomena. Edward spoke of two relatives who had died a short time before then and of the fact that he had not felt sad at their passing away; then he added that the previous day, while doing 'eye exercises', which he counted, an echo in his head had kept track of his counting too. Hanna Segal connected his absence of emotions in relation to his relatives' death to his distance from the analyst during the weekend and his 'eye exercises' to watching his parents being united sexually, with the intention of killing them.

She examined this interpretation in depth using a subsequent dream in which a white figure became brown, and she said to the patient that when he did his eye exercises, he was trying to watch the analyst while she was having intercourse. Then he would angrily swallow her up and turn her into faeces; she then became a voice that persecuted him from the inside. At the same time, with a glance, he would fill the analyst with the same brown substance, faeces, and she would go from white to brown; at this point, one looking at the other, analyst and patient could not but exchange excrement, illness and death.

Edward's analysis proceeded with accurate interpretations of his anxiety regarding the female figure and his split between idealised and persecutory figures. The relation with the analyst gradually became warmer and friendlier; this was the first close relationship the patient had ever had in his life. Edward remained in analysis for three years, and then, open to his parents' persuasion and his own maniacal attitude, he interrupted his analysis to enrol at a prestigious university outside London. Segal reported that Edward was well after that; he married and pursued a professional career. Approximately twenty years later, however, he had another psychotic breakdown and returned to analytic treatment – not with Hanna Segal, though, as she could not fit him in, but with a colleague of hers.

42 Part 1

A second interesting paper that lets us understand how Hanna Segal worked with psychotic patients is 'Depression in the Schizophrenic' (1956), in which she claimed that the psychotic patient is unable to tolerate depressive anxiety and regresses when this looms large. The patient was a sixteen-year-old female who had suffered from hallucinations since the age of four and was diagnosed with hebephrenic schizophrenia. The severity of the illness was evident from the first sessions; she would jump and run about the consulting room, bite the sofa, rip her clothes, hear voices and at times scream with fear; from several broken sentences and the fact that she had scratched her neck, Hanna Segal deduced that the patient saw her as a vampire that sucked her brain and blood; at times it was the patient herself who was a vampire ready to suck the analyst's blood. The patient also had, however, a pleasant delusional world with highly idealised hallucinations: an 'ideal people' lived inside her, and in order to build this world, she would become a vampire that sucked the analyst's vital sap, and in turn, drained, the analyst would suck the patient's ideal world and take away her good hallucinations. The patient really feared being a vampire that could bring about nothing but death.

In one session, the patient had an insight and asked the analyst if by chance her problem happened to be that of constantly eating and taking things inside her without making any effort to build something good inside. For Hanna Segal, this was the moment of depression. After this session, in which the patient seemed more pensive and mentally healthy, she arrived for her next session with a dissociated, masturbatory and incoherent attitude, ignoring the analyst entirely.

Hanna Segal saw this behaviour as a negative therapeutic reaction: experiencing being solely destructive and draining the breast had made the patient feel unable to repair and reconstruct it. She was in fact depressed, but her solution was to project the depression onto the analyst, ignoring her and making her feel like a useless child; ridding herself of the depressed part, the patient became madder.

Hanna Segal's conclusion was that, as long as the patient had been able to keep her depressive feelings inside her, she could communicate healthily; when these depressive feelings became unbearable, she needed to project them onto the analyst, resulting in a loss of reality, a return to mad behaviour and the reappearance of persecutory feelings. In this case, the analyst had become the persecutor who carried inside the patient's depressive part, which she intended to push back inside her. For Hanna Segal, guilt and pain are intolerable to the psychotic, which is why they must be projected onto the analyst.

Yet another paper by Hanna Segal that lays out the vision of Kleinian analysts on psychosis and its therapy is 'A psychoanalytic approach to the treatment of psychoses'. Hanna Segal told us that psychotic illness has its origins in early childhood when the bases of mental functioning are formed: that is, during that time when the infant progressively acquires differentiation between the inner and outer world. Development occurs through projection and introjection, splitting the object into a good and a bad part, then their integration and identification with good objects. Simultaneously, the prerequisites for symbolic thought and language are developed. At times, something disturbing occurs in these earliest stages of development, the essential functions for growth thus being disturbed or destroyed, and the development of symbolisation processes hindered; the line between internal and external is unclear, and object relations become fragmented. Understanding the nature of psychosis is possible only if normal Ego development is considered and compared to the distortion undergone in the course of illness.

The fulcrum of mental stability is anxiety containment by means of an internal object that is capable of understanding: such an object is the product of the maternal function that receives and transforms the infant's anxieties. Mental stability can be destroyed for two reasons: the mother may be unable to receive and transform the child's anxiety, which then increases, reaching an unbearable level, or her receiving ability may be put to the hard test by the child's excessive destructive omnipotence.

Since the psychotic patient tries to project his terror, evilness and confusion onto the analyst, he develops an almost immediate transference, which is usually violent. After this projection, he experiences the analyst as a terrifying figure whom he immediately wants to distance himself from: this is where the fragility of the transference is created. Interpretation is perceived very concretely as a reverse projective identification, as if the analyst wants to push the unwanted parts inside the patient, leading him towards madness. The concrete nature of the experience of the patient, who feels that he is omnipotently changing the analyst and that the analyst is omnipotently trying to change him, is a fundamental point in analytic work.

The main themes of the psychotic patient's analysis, according to Segal, concern language, concrete thought, confusion between subject and object and the psychotic transference. She reconfirms the usefulness of the Kleinian model with the paranoid-schizoid position and the Bionian model with the mother who is able to contain the infant's projective identifications, these being at the heart of the analytic technique used by her group.

Segal offered the opinion that, in cases when conditions are favourable, psychoanalytic therapy is the best treatment as it deals with the psychotic personality disorder from the roots. Moreover, therapy of psychotics has a value that goes beyond the therapeutic aspect proper in that the study of thought, perception, symbolic thought and object relation disorders can allow processes outside consciousness that support and develop these functions to be examined.

Lastly, a very important concept is Hanna Segal's *symbolic equation* (1957), which is the psychotic patient's inability to symbolise or, rather, to distinguish symbols from concrete objects. In the symbolic equation, the paranoid-schizoid position prevails over the depressive position, which instead would allow the object to be perceived as separate from the Self.

Legacy of the past

Among the many who have been committed to the therapy of psychotic patients, I chose the work of those analysts I believe are most meaningful. Mentioned separately is Lacan, due to his original perspective.

I placed therapists into two categories. The first follow an *intuitive* and *non-systematic* approach, and the second may be defined as *theoretical* and *systematic*.

44   Part 1

In the first group, I mentioned Frieda Fromm-Reichmann and Harold Searles, who manoeuvred skilfully with rare courage and enthusiasm. No pre-existing theoretical system was there for them to refer to: they were true pioneers who relied mainly on their clinical intuition and were able to confirm that all the rules and guidelines deemed valid for the therapy of neurosis were unsuited to treating the psychotic patient. Their sensitivity and intuition led to their finding a different path into the relationship with this kind of patient. I also mentioned the original contributions by Madame Sechehaye, Federn, and Lacan, each of whom inserted their study of psychosis into their own unique theoretical system.

Different is the case of Melanie Klein and her collaborators. Taking the study of primitive infantile anxieties as her starting point, Melanie Klein was committed to constructing a theoretical system that could explain normal psychic development and its deviations. Within this theoretical system, psychosis had a place, too, or, rather, clinical data gathered on the study of psychosis even helped broaden knowledge of child development. Since it was a serious illness, it was logical to find as a starting point for psychosis the earliest stages of development, in particular the paranoid-schizoid position.

Melanie Klein's pupils then applied her theoretical frame to clinical work: projective identification, an absence of symbolisation, no repression, a difference between the healthy and psychotic parts and the psychotic transference are indispensable concepts for understanding and treating psychotic patients.

Technique then applied by Bion and Segal derived directly from these theoretical assumptions. In their opinions, psychosis stems from a child's early developmental stage and depends on his tendency for destructive phantasies towards the maternal figure. If destructive phantasies remain, without being transformed by processes of reparation, mental structures that contribute to the onset of the illness are created. Psychosis is considered a destructive process that originates in the death instinct prevailing over the life instinct. This makes integration, which could lead to recovery, extremely difficult. Segal clearly stated her idea that the recovery process can sometimes be complicated, as reparation becomes an extremely hard task in the face of such destruction. Bion, too, expressed a similar concept: over the course of improvement, the patient acquires the ability to understand psychic reality but cannot tolerate awareness of the destruction that occurred.

Neither author denies the existence of environmental factors that concur with the development of the illness. Bion put forward the idea that the mother's inability to act as a good container of the infant's anxiety projections is one factor contributing to the disorder. This hypothesis provides an understanding of psychosis development within a relational matrix, but his writings also include a hypothesis of the endogenous, destructive nature of the illness when the mother may be incapable due to the extremely aggressive nature of the nursling. Bion seemed more explicit when identifying the nursling's hatred towards the breast as the main determining factor in psychosis. Common to both analysts was their clinical approach, centred on constantly working on the transference. This regards patients in an acute phase (Segal) as well as those who have most likely been in a psychotic state for many years (Bion).

At that time, analysts from the Kleinian group believed that transference work was essential to obtain positive transformations in the psychotic patient, and only later, sustained by Rosenfeld, did the idea prevail that the delusional transference was extremely negative. When included in the patient's delusion, the analyst loses his analytic function, and the relational space that the analytic process needs consequently collapses.

Segal and Bion gave their patients very detailed interpretations on the omnipotent use they made of their bodies and organs. Rejection, expulsion, object destruction and projecting intolerable states of mind onto the analyst occur via the projective use of sense organs: mouths that swallow, ears that grind up, eyes that project.

Despite this broadening of the theoretical perspective by Melanie Klein and post-Kleinian analysts, we have not witnessed a corresponding and hoped-for development in clinical results. This might be one cause of the drop in literature on clinical work with psychotic patients over recent decades. As mentioned earlier, and as I hope to expand on later, psychosis therapy encounters knots that are difficult to transform. I do not have in mind so much the difficulty, even though it exists, of tolerating the depressive position, as was underlined by Bion and Segal. When these patients improve after having lived at length in a psychotic state, it is not rare to see that instead of even embarking on the path towards the depressive position and the sorrow and regret for what has been lost, they prefer to go back to denying reality and to the delusional state.

As I shall try to illustrate further on, other elements also make the recovery from psychosis arduous. One of these is certainly the nature itself of the delusional experience, which deeply encysts in the mind and seems to resist any kind of transformation.

My viewpoint

I shall briefly outline here some of my thinking on the psychotic illness and the difficulty in treating it.

It is my belief that psychosis has its origins in a dissociated world, an alternative reality that begins to form in childhood; in some cases, but not in all, this construction is fostered by trauma and abandonment that necrotise the child's personality, causing obvious splits in and damage to his mental functioning. The child constructs a new reality where he can live; at times the split-off parts are transformed into an aggressive internal presence, and from here hallucinatory and delusional phenomena, which may at times even start in childhood, begin.

In my opinion, it is not so much a case of the child destined to become psychotic being stimulated by aggressiveness as by a particular tendency to isolate himself from the relational world so that he may build with his imagination another dissociated world. Placed in the service of his fantasy, this dissociated world is appealing because there the limits of existence and frustrations of reality never need facing up to.

The destructive effect is not primary but the consequence of flight into unreality from which it is difficult to return. In order to construct a dissociated world, the

46   *Part 1*

patient must alter his sense organs and abolish his thinking capacity; given that this process is usually accompanied by a pleasant state, the subject is unaware of the dangers this operation can lead to, the withdrawal turning into a prison with little possibility of escape and the pathogenic structures, once set in motion, ending up looming over and dominating him.

What I have just described is similar to the story of 'The Sorcerer's Apprentice', the well-known ballad written by Goethe in 1797, set to music by Paul Dukas one hundred years later and played by Mickey Mouse in Disney's famous movie *Fantasia*.

The story is very simple: a sorcerer's apprentice, taking advantage of the temporary absence of the sorcerer, casts a spell to get out of doing chores he had been ordered to do. But at a certain point, the situation gets out of hand, and due to his lack of experience, he cannot break the spell that then turns against him. Luckily, the old sorcerer comes back, immediately restores normality and with a lash of his whip punishes his careless apprentice. In the therapy of a psychotic patient, there is no sorcerer who can restore order with a lash of his whip and cast his careless apprentice back to his junior role. In psychotic transformation, the patient does not act on a whim; unfortunately, his story goes back long before the signs and is nourished by longstanding mental functioning. The patient himself can no longer distinguish between psychotic and normal functioning: omnipotence is in command, and its first victim is the patient.

Therapy needs to begin from this point, and the analyst's task is to creatively understand how to strengthen the patient's healthy part in order to contain and reduce as far as possible the omnipotent part, which exercises great power over the patient; a complete change has taken place in the patient's mind, which is no longer a tool for thought but a sensorial organ that constantly produces impressions perceived as being real. The world of dissociated reality cancels out the mind's primary function: that is, its understanding mental processes and external reality.

The analyst is in a difficult position because he cannot expect to take the patient back to a previous stage of mental health with interpretative work, assuming such a stage ever existed; the analyst is not after all the sorcerer that can scale back a careless usurper.

This work requires much time and patience to discover the tools the patient uses outside awareness to distort his mental functioning; considerable imaginative effort is needed to enter into worlds so far away from our own. Even great competence acquired throughout the analyst's clinical experience may not be sufficient when having to deal with the field of psychosis.

The following pages aim to offer a picture of the salient points that are needed for the therapy of the psychotic patient. I believe that boosting research and clinical application in this field can be helpful for patients and can constitute a powerful stimulus for the development of psychoanalysis as a clinical and theoretical discipline.

Note

1 Only later did Bion introduce the concept of projective identification used for communication.

Part 2

4 The setting and transference in psychosis

The setting

The cases described in analytic literature, summarised earlier, mainly concern psychotic patients who spent long periods in hospital and were treated psychoanalytically, irrespective of the severity or duration of their pathology. These parameters are extremely important, however, for prognostic purposes as the psychotic process becomes irreversible once a certain threshold is crossed; this means that mental functions enabling contact to be restored with reality weaken, if they don't disappear altogether. Moreover, prognosis is more complex when the psychosis develops in childhood than in adolescence or adulthood.

Establishing a formal setting (times, the patient's position, frequency of sessions and so forth) that is right for that patient's treatment is important. Generally, the number of analytic sessions with a psychotic patient need not differ from that of any other kind of patient; that too high a frequency of sessions will destabilise the patient, something that is occasionally heard, is quite untrue. The result of treatment instead depends on how the analyst listens to and understands the patient's functioning and anxieties. A suitable number of sessions enables the therapist to enter into close contact with the analysand and understand his psychic dynamics; symmetrically, it allows the patient to focus his attention on the content of the session and to memorise and work through it. Furthermore, a suitable number of sessions reduces the frequency of relapses, given that for quite some time the analyst functions as the patient's auxiliary Ego, preventing the psychotic part of the personality from winning back its power.

Often, the optimal formal setting (number of sessions and position on the couch) cannot be prepared right from the start but must be built up gradually. Asking the patient to lie on the couch at the beginning would confuse if not frighten him altogether. The fact that he finds it difficult to stay in touch with reality means that lying on the couch, which reduces visual stimuli so that attention may be more focused on his inner world, would risk making him feel even more disoriented and confused. Besides, the analyst cannot expect the psychotic patient to follow the basic rule of free association as he is immersed in a world of sensorial images, disoriented and prey to confusional states.

As for the number of sessions, therapy can usually begin at one session per week face-to-face and then gradually be increased. More than any other, the psychotic patient needs to familiarise himself with the therapist, and this takes quite

50   *Part 2*

some time. As sessions are gradually increased, the therapist, when he feels that the time is right, can suggest that the patient lie on the couch, a position that enables both patient and analyst to communicate more freely. The patient must have built up trust in the therapist and feel that therapy is useful to him for this to occur. In some cases, such as when the patient is experiencing considerable anxiety or has just been through a psychotic breakdown, a higher number of sessions may be suggested from the start.

Establishing a traditional formal analytic setting is not always possible, nor, I shall add, is it always necessary. If the therapist has understood the dynamics of the treatment via the key elements he has gathered together, the patient can be helped with fewer weekly sessions and without using the couch. As mentioned earlier, the analyst functions as a strong ally to the patient's healthy part and can thus contain the action of the psychotic part; when this function fails, the risk of relapse is greater. The higher-risk moments are when sessions stop – at holiday times, for example – as the patient's healthy part is no longer supported by the presence of the analyst, and the patient can therefore fall victim to the psychotic part. Face-to-face therapies at one or two sessions per week do bring undeniable benefit and unexpected improvement, but it is harder for the therapist to restructure the patient's personality so that the emotional skills needed to carry out the more complex tasks of relational life can be developed.

With patients who have had a psychotic episode, patience and caution are needed to create and maintain the necessary conditions for therapy. I can remember a patient who did not come of his own accord but was persuaded by his parents and the psychiatrist he had seen after his hospitalisation. Given the clinical conditions, I decided to see him face-to-face once a week. I can recall that during the first consultation he was severely distressed, visibly delusional, suspicious and perturbed by 'voices' and was a victim of persecution in an international conspiracy. I remember also how difficult it was for me to understand his fragmented delusional speech and to gather together elements from his past, as well as intuit how he had entered the psychotic state. In particular, I remember his uncertainty when signing the cheque to pay for his sessions, which took him several minutes, his hands shaking all the while. Some years later, and after an obvious improvement (the analytic setting had stabilised at four sessions per week), it came quite naturally to me to remind him of how he had suffered during those first months of sessions, and I happened to mention his difficulty when signing the cheque. Much to my surprise, he answered that his awkwardness had not been due to anxiety but to the fact that a voice would tell him at that moment that it should have been me, the analyst, paying him because he was much more intelligent than I was. This is to show that the patient, despite having agreed to undergo therapy, had not at that point developed the subjective conditions to put his therapy to use, given the persistence of his omnipotent thought.

On a related note, it goes without saying how important it is in the psychotherapy of a psychotic patient to collaborate with a psychiatrist, who needs to see the patient regularly and intervene should there be a new breakdown; even when the patient has not had a psychotic breakdown and has never been hospitalised, this kind of collaboration is necessary. The referred psychiatrist must have trust in the analytic method and not interfere, even outside awareness, with the analyst's role. It is up to him to evaluate at a later stage of the analysis whether to reduce or stop the patient's medication. In their clinical practice, not all analysts keep psychotherapeutic and pharmacological treatments separate: for example, if they are competent in psychopharmacology, such as analysts who are qualified psychiatrists, they themselves administer medication when the patient gets worse or a psychotic episode is impending. Making this therapeutic decision is not easy, though: when the analyst resorts to medication, he runs the risk of a concentration lapse with regard to the analytic therapy and to understanding well the reasons behind a possible episode; his decision to resort to medication can be influenced by the countertransference and may also be understood by the patient as a lack of analytic skill at a critical moment during the analysis.

It is important to reconstruct from the start of therapy the 'history of the psychosis' in order to understand how it developed and prevent the risk of it repeating. Some information on how the original episode was triggered is provided by family members and additional information by healthcare workers, who can help us see how the patient, until a certain point in his life, maintained a balance, albeit unstable, between the psychotic and the healthy parts. Then an emotional trauma; the loss of a special friendship; frustration at being abandoned by a loved one, even only in fantasy or a serious conflict that thrust towards a state of imbalance may have occurred, which in turn propelled to a delusional experience. The patient usually tries to conceal his attraction to psychosis from the therapist, so it is imperative to do everything possible to make this tendency emerge and stop the healthy part of the personality from being invaded by the psychotic part. Together with the patient, the analyst must retrace the original psychotic episode to help the patient gradually broaden his awareness of his vulnerability.

When work first begins with a psychotic patient, the therapist cannot expect there to be dreams, associations, fantasies or transference development, through which conflicts and anxieties of neurotic problems are understood. The neurotic patient moves within the dynamic unconscious, uses repression and possesses a clear distinction between conscious and unconscious. In the psychotic patient, however, we find a totally different unconscious, without any symbolisation or repression; *repression* of emotions and awareness is not perceived in this kind of patient, and what we see instead is the *transformation* of psychic reality via the alteration of perceptive and thought functions; outside awareness, the psychotic patient creates a new world he painfully becomes prisoner of. The principal issue of treatment is, therefore, to discover how the psychotic patient transforms his perceptive world and self-awareness.

Transference

According to Freud, the analysand forms an image of the analyst onto whom he transfers his past childhood experiences, which is why transference work is important as it permits a return to the past; the nature of conflicts that featured

52　*Part 2*

in the patient's childhood and condition his present can thus be clarified. It was Melanie Klein who broadened the concept of transference, considering it not only a reproduction of the past but the result of the patient's projection of parts of his Self (unwanted or idealised) onto the figure of the analyst, who comes to represent them through projective identification: hence the analyst temporarily being an object of the present and the past in the neurotic transference, assuming, as a transferential object, an 'as if' position halfway between fantasy and reality. The conflict nucleus therefore needs to enter the transference so that it may be interpreted.

In therapy for psychosis, transference cannot be employed as a tool for quite some time because these patients are unable to symbolise or to represent their own history and think at a concrete level only. A psychotic transference risks being formed because of the delusion activity. This kind of transference is detrimental to therapy as it includes the figure of the analyst in the delusion, tending therefore to invade the space of the analytic relationship. This is why the psychotic delusion transference must be transformed as early on as possible.

There are two kinds of delusion transference: the *psychotic transference* and *transference psychosis*. The *psychotic transference* forms when the psychotic nucleus invades the patient's healthy part and destroys his intuitive and reflexive capacity. The delusion invades the setting and the analytic relation; the analyst becomes the subject of the delusion, his interpretative function can no longer be fulfilled, and the analytic process grinds to a halt. Excitedness can characterise the psychotic transference, as in the love-type delusion in which the patient believes the analyst is taken with a love passion for him, or in the persecutory type, when the patient experiences the analyst as an enemy that wants to make an attempt on his life.

As an example of this pernicious event, in the third part of the book, I have written an account of the analytic situation of Francesco, who had a very complex persecutory delusion. His psychosis began abroad after a conflict with a colleague, and from that moment on, the patient felt persecuted by a conspiracy on the part of that colleague's fellow countrymen, who were planning to kill him. Once, I happened to leave my office after one of his sessions and walked briskly to a nearby office; the patient saw me and interpreted my haste as proof of my going to report him to his enemies. In the following session, he very anxiously spoke to me about this perception, which for him was real. Worried about the direction that the analysis could have taken, I immediately began to talk to him about the reasons that had led him to believe I could have collaborated with his persecutors; he replied that I might have done so because I had been threatened by them or paid a huge bribe. While I knew that the psychotic transference bore early signs of the main elements of his delusional system, I made him reflect on the fact that he considered me an emotionless puppet in the hands of his enemies. I learnt then that the therapist can be incorporated into the persecutory delusion the moment he tries to demolish the patient's delusional belief; the patient at that point believes that the analyst wants to shatter what for him is reality, as he has come to some sort of arrangement with the persecutors. When trying to demolish the delusion, great care must therefore be taken.

The setting and transference in psychosis   53

As for the second kind of delusion transference, the *transference psychosis*, here the delusional ideation is purely about the analyst, and so it is a *psychosis in the transference*: that is, a psychosis limited to the transference. Before developing the transference psychosis, the patient is not delusional, and he continues not to be so, at least with respect to the outer world. This kind of transference usually develops after a prolonged period of incomprehension by the analyst, with repeated interpretations that are wrong or out of context; in other words, it is an impasse of a psychotic nature. The patient convinces himself that the therapist purposely wants to harm him and is fully aware that he (the analyst) is attacking him (the patient); the figure of the analyst thus deteriorates to the point of becoming persecutory.

That the transference psychosis can be due to iatrogenic intervention therefore requires vigilant awareness on the part of the analyst; should it occur, he must try to understand how it developed and then talk to the patient about possible distortions in analytic communication. Usually, if the analyst shows that he can go back to his wrong interpretations and acknowledge them as such, the transference psychosis may be overcome, and the analytic process can get back on course.

5 The psychic withdrawal and the psychotic part of the personality

The withdrawal

Analysts who work with children can observe that in several cases a process which may develop into psychosis is already up and running. These children, usually indicated by teachers as having learning problems or difficulty relating with classmates, are only apparently but not actually in touch with others. In reality, they live a secret life parallel to the real one, where they are shut away in an *infantile withdrawal* rich in sensorial qualities: that is, an alternative world to real life often populated by imaginary characters that at times are nourished by obsessively watching television cartoons. The most serious consequence of this life in fantasy is that the child does not structure a psychic apparatus capable of understanding psychic reality.

At times, when listening analytically to an adult patient, the childhood elements that triggered the psychotic state can be found, and early conditions that laid the foundations for vulnerability to the illness may be traced. It can therefore be assumed that detachment from reality began long before the clinical manifestation of the illness.

When Freud described the psychotic patient's isolation, he spoke of *autoeroticism* as a pathological process in which the newborn's primitive developmental experience, sensorially withdrawn into his body, is repeated. The term *autoeroticism* therefore describes both the psychotic withdrawal and the objectless stage of human development: that is, the primitive phase in which the infant, focused on his own bodily sensations, ignores the presence of his surrounding world. Freud's intuition is still useful in order to understand several aspects of the psychotic state: for example, when a patient who has totally detached himself from emotional reality then withdraws into his own body and produces perceptions from scratch. In this case, hallucinations originate in and have as their stimulus bodily sensations; there is no thought in the withdrawal, only dissociated sensory content that wipes out psychic reality.

My hypothesis is that the child who is prone to becoming psychotic may have had parents who were unable to accommodate his emotional communications or who invaded his mind with disturbing emotional projections; in this case, the withdrawal creates a dissociation from reality that serves as a defence against contact with the parents, but also against the relational world.

By dissociation, I do not mean a vertical split of the personality in which one part does not know the other, but rather that the world of psychic withdrawal is fed only by sensorial fantasying that is separated from the world of relations.

The psychic withdrawal is a mental organisation that can be a continual source of illness during an individual's life: not only is it a place for taking refuge from anxiety, as Steiner (1993) sustains, but above all it is a forge where worlds alternative to the real world are produced. Constantly creating an imaginary sensorial reality saps energy from emotional and affective development, hamstringing experience the individual needs for growth and compromising to various degrees the development of personal identity.

In this connection is the case of a fourteen-year-old girl indicated by her school as having difficulty studying and integrating socially: isolated from her schoolmates, she had an attention deficit, making it difficult for her to study. During her consultation with the therapist, she spoke about her malaise and the other world she lived in: in this fantasy world, where she spent most of her day, she had two children and was married to a very successful man. At home, too, when having dinner with her parents, she would get up and go to her room to enter this world that would summon her and continually seduce her: she had to tend to her children. This dissociated life, existing in parallel to her real one, eliminated her need to relate with peers and, when she was alone, made her believe she had a stimulating adult existence. In a case like this, it is foreseeable that the withdrawal will turn into a clear delusion when the imaginary world gains the upper hand and presents itself to the patient as being real.

It is extremely important not to underestimate the progressive and pathogenic power of the infantile withdrawal and to explain to parents the difference between withdrawal and other mental states of fantasy typically found in childhood: the child who spends most of his day at home alone, often in front of a television or computer without seeking the company of his peers, is not merely quiet and reserved but may not have developed a need for relations and have lost pleasure in social play.

When a child plays, he can distinguish between play (make believe) and reality; the child who lives in a psychic withdrawal loses this ability to distinguish between the two because fantasy assumes the quality of being 'real'. Whereas play enriches the emotional world, sensory withdrawal stunts the child's epistemophilic drive and captures him in a closed and autarkical reality.

O'Shaughnessy (1992) described this process well when she differentiated between the child who could overcome frustration using the precursors of thought (crying until the mother rushes to comfort him, for example) and the child who is less fortunate, who evacuates frustration (and reality) instead of modifying it. This second type of child does not cry but remains silent and focuses his attention on some sensorial detail; this is the beginning of withdrawal, which uses sensorial channels, creating a pleasant reality that removes the child from dependence that can foster his relational and emotional development.

Today, it is widely held that abnormal and maladaptive behaviour is formed when a child has not received sufficient sensory stimuli or competent emotional attunement

56   *Part 2*

during the critical period for the formation of the Self. If things go well and needs are met, sensory gratification comes to be included within an emotional context: physical tenderness, cuddling and kisses become typical relational exchanges.

But what happens when things go wrong? When emotional input is lacking on the part of the caregiver, the child uses his own body for the purposes of arousal; sensation, devoid of a relational quality that develops only within good affective caregiving, deviates. To combat a sense of disintegration, the deprived child clings to a series of sensations (a light, a voice, a smell and so on) that can serve to hold together the scattered parts of the personality, or he uses the body in masturbatory terms.

The sensorial world remains split off from the real world over a long period of time, and the individual can live in one world one moment and then in the other. The psychopathological construction of the withdrawal can be kept on an even keel indefinitely, but it usually tends to expand and dominate the rest of the personality. Several kinds of withdrawal, in particular those that lead to psychotic development, become the means with which to create sexualised, grandiose and persecutory omnipotent worlds.

The psychopathological structure of the withdrawal corresponds to the psychotic part of the personality (Bion 1957), the purpose of which is to conquer the healthy part: the more the process moves towards incorporating the individual's life in the withdrawal, the more he runs the risk of being conquered by the psychosis. Instead of developing thought and nourishing psychic reality, the mind is used as a *sensory organ*, which, in the advanced stage of the psychotic process, will cause hallucinations. Typically, the situation becomes evident when the sensory constructions that have been built up in the withdrawal but kept dissociated for a long time begin to invade the healthy part of the personality; it is at this point that the psychotic patient is brought to the attention of psychiatry, but it is important that the long preparation which got its start in childhood receives marked attention.

Meltzer (1979, p. 42) drew attention to the pathogenic significance of withdrawal in the development of delusion: 'We must in my view not lose sight of the worrying possibility that this tranquil and silent process may be present in anyone during the course of development and that, alongside the development with which we are familiar, the delusional system may therefore also be silently developing'.

This possibility is implied also in Bion's conceptualisation when he hypothesised that, in parallel to thought (the development of which he outlined in the grid), one can develop a delusional system (which he described in the negative grid). This 'calm, silent' world presents itself as an alternative to mental growth and communication with the world outside us.

Not by chance did Rosenfeld (1971) highlight that the patient perceives himself as living in a world or an object that totally separates him from the outside world. The delusional withdrawal creates the conviction of being able to find absolute pleasure in a condition of total anarchy; this is why the delusional nucleus ends up attracting the healthy parts of the personality, persuading them to distance themselves from the relational world.

A description of the delusion system's construction process can be found in the Schreber case, in which Freud (1910) outlined how the psychotic individual destroys the psychic world and uses the debris to reconstruct a delusional world he can live in.

Schreber was convinced he had destroyed the world and built another in contrast to the one wanted by God. He also believed in an external world where he could continue to live and publish his memoirs; this means that he lived simultaneously in a real and a delusional world. Meltzer (1979) wrote that the world built by Schreber had no connections whatsoever with reality and therefore could be situated anywhere at all.

And now a few words on the approach to adopt in order to help the patient leave the withdrawal. As previously stated, the patient is unlikely to tell the analyst about the existence of the withdrawal and the fantasies that animate it; usually he defends it as a secret and precious place, so it is up to the analyst to identify its existence and contents in order to transform it.

When the patient does begin to describe his life in the withdrawal, the analyst can then explain the purpose that this pathological organisation serves and show the patient how it makes his life deteriorate. Although the patient is *conscious* of leading a secret life in the withdrawal, he is not *aware* of the destructive effects caused by his retreat.

In addition to distorting emotional development, the withdrawal offers an alternative to the relational world, and it is no accident that in their social life these patients seem lacklustre, indifferent to their surroundings and unable to fulfil life tasks; every commitment in the real world becomes a source of fatigue and anxiety.

I would like to stress that what characterises psychosis is the construction of a *separate world*, usually in childhood: that is, an alternative world dissociated from real experience that corresponds not to a world of dreams and fantasies or 'make believe', but a psychic *withdrawal* in which the new reality created in fantasy is *sensory* and conveys the same perceptual depth as the real world.

Not all forms of withdrawal lead to psychosis or delusion. As I mentioned, some may remain silent throughout life without turning into psychosis. One of my patients, who presented a rich phobic symptomatology, always idealised life in fantasy at the expense of real life. When she met a man she liked, she would not seek a relationship with him but would use him to nourish her fantasy life: she would keep away from him and use him in her inner world as a character who would be with her always and love her passionately; then, once the fantasy began to fade, she would feel the need to see him again in the flesh to replenish the fantasy relationship.

In cases destined to become psychotic, the breakdown manifests when the sensory constructions created in the withdrawal dominate the healthy part of the personality. Silent energetic activity precedes the psychotic break: just as a wooden structure suddenly collapses, eaten away underneath by a colony of termites busy at work, so, too, is the psychotic breakdown sudden, after much long, constant labour.

58   *Part 2*

The psychotic part of the personality

This is how Freud put it (1940, 1938c, p. 201):

> Two psychical attitudes have been formed instead of a single one – one, the normal one, which takes account of reality, and another which under the influence of the instincts detaches the ego from reality. The two exist alongside of each other. The issue depends on their relative strength. If the second is or becomes the stronger, the necessary precondition for a psychosis is present. If the relation is reversed, then there is an apparent cure of the delusional disorder.

Rosenfeld (1969) commented that, despite having formulated the concept of the Ego splitting into a normal and a psychotic part, Freud did not further this intuition in his clinical work.

A new perspective on psychosis and the delusion opened up after Melanie Klein's (1946) writings on the mechanism of projective identification. In her opinion, the specific pathogenic mechanism of psychosis is projective identification: that is, the projection of aggressive and destructive parts of the self onto an external object. Linked to the paranoid-schizoid position, this mechanism consists in the infant's phantasy to project split-off parts of the self onto the mother's body in order to control her from within; these phantasies then become the source of anxiety related to being persecuted and imprisoned inside the object. Melanie Klein thought that when projective identification is massive and prolonged, the projected parts become difficult to retrieve.

We are indebted to Katan and Bion for their explanations of the difference between the neurotic and the psychotic parts of the personality. Katan (1954) described the pre-psychotic phase of the illness in particular, when one part of the personality is still able to control conflicts while remaining in touch with reality, albeit unstably; he referred to this part as the *non-psychotic portion* (parapsychotic):

> the delusion does not possess an unconscious. One may distinguish between a neurotic and a delusional projection. The neurotic projection serves the purpose of warding off the id. The delusional form of projection has a wholly different structure. To put it differently, although not entirely correctly: part of the id has become outer world. The delusion is a sign that in the prepsychotic phase or in the non-psychotic layer contact has been broken off, and the formation of the delusion is the result of the attempt to repair the break with reality.
>
> (p. 126)

Unlike Katan, who provided a clinical description, Bion (1957) proposed a dynamic reading of psychotic as well as neurotic functioning: the neurotic part operates according to assimilation, introjection and discrimination, whereas the psychotic part violently projects in order to eliminate psychic elements that it cannot 'digest'. Intolerance to frustration, which Bion connected to excessive envy, creates hatred towards all couple links: mother-child, analyst-patient, parts of the self etc.; attacking the link destroys symbolic language, which is what generates meaning.

I do not share the idea common to several Kleinian authors that the psychotic part is present, albeit only slightly, in normal and neurotic individuals; in my opinion, it is one thing to speak of psychotic functioning in some neurotic patients, but another to speak of clinically psychotic patients. With clinical work in mind, by the *psychotic part*, I mean a psychopathological structure that distorts psychic reality and produces hallucinations and delusions. If the patient begins analytic treatment after hospitalisation, then the psychotic part has already carried out its task of colonising the healthy part of his personality; when the patient has not had a psychotic break proper, has never been hospitalised or under the care of a psychiatrist, it is more difficult to bring the progressive action of the psychotic part to light. As mentioned earlier, patients frequently conceal their withdrawal into a psychotic world behind apparently good psychic functioning.

I therefore use the term *psychotic part* differently from Bion, who employed it to refer to that part of the personality where destructive instincts and hatred towards inner and outer reality predominate and which is nourished by an excessive congenital predisposition to aggression and envy. In my opinion, the *psychotic part* does not derive from destructiveness, but it identifies with that part of the personality that can create a world dissociated from human relational reality. Using the mechanism of psychic withdrawal is, I believe, more helpful in order to describe and understand psychosis and its dynamics.

Returning to the neurotic part-psychotic part contrast, it is not a case of their merely functioning differently, but rather being *antagonistic*, with one part (the psychotic one) trying to assimilate and colonise the other; opposing ways of experiencing psychic reality alternate between omnipotence of thought and the use of the mind to accept reality and related frustrations. In individuals destined to develop psychosis, there is an unstable balance between the two, the healthy part of the personality being conquered in the end by the psychotic part.

A female patient who suffered a psychotic episode brought this dream to analysis following several months of apparent remission:

> I'm driving my car in a narrow street, quite naturally, which surprises me a little. At a certain point, I decide not to follow the road signs any more, and I realize that I'm driving against the traffic coming towards me. This scares me but excites me at the same time. I think that I really need to take some driving lessons but then I decide that I don't and can just keep going like this. In the end, I feel very distressed, lose control of the car and end up in a desertified land, a Martian landscape full of cactus-like plants. I feel very alone.

This dream may be considered as a portent of the patient's capture by the psychotic part, represented here as an excited and transgressive state that pushes her to go against road traffic regulations in a mix of fear and excitement. In her mind there is but a vague awareness of being led by a dangerous and transgressive part; in fact, she asks herself whether she needs driving lessons and then decides that she does not. The psychotic part takes over and leads her to a desert land where each and every relation with a human being is erased. The psychotic part's functioning is well represented in this dream and is of great help to the analyst to prevent a new psychotic episode from occurring. As can be seen from the clinical material, it is almost as if in her dream the patient sees her healthy part (driving, which takes the rules of human coexistence into account) as a pointless habit that can be wiped out by the excitement coming from the psychotic part.

In these cases, it is important to describe to the patient the omnipotent, excited and seductive fantasies connected to the psychotic split-off part in order to prevent, within all possible limits, the patient's healthy part, with which the analyst has established his therapeutic relationship, from being overwhelmed. Not to be lost sight of is the fact that the psychotic part offers the patient no respite. Whereas the neurotic patient is not easily attracted to madness because he fears it, the appeal (often an offer of omnipotence) that the psychosis entices and leads the psychotic patient astray with is what actually dispels his anxiety. Frequently, the therapist is misled by the fact that the patient keeps his inclination for delusion to himself, and he ends up believing the patient's explicit communication without making any contact with his psychotic aspects at work below the surface. Anxiety emerges too late on, when the patient has already been conquered by the psychosis and at which point he realises that he can no longer leave the situation he himself has created.

The psychotic part of the personality, as mentioned earlier, is an heir of the infantile withdrawal, a place characterised by sensory fantasies that a certain kind of child builds in order to feel that he is the ruler of the world. Much time goes by before the delusion is clinically evident; Freud (1922) advanced this point when he wrote: 'it may be that the delusions which we regard as new formations when the disease breaks out have already long been in existence' (p. 227).

To develop the patient's awareness, the analyst must repeatedly describe the dynamics with which the pathogenic part entices him into the withdrawal, detaching him from his relationships, the analytic relationship included, and offering him the false benefits of a life alternative to that of reality. Clinical experience has led me to think that intrapsychic interpretations, those that describe the dynamics and mutual relationship between the opposing parts of the personality (in particular, the psychotic and the healthy part) are extremely useful for strengthening the patient's insight. In other words, it is helpful to treat the psychotic withdrawal, which corresponds to the psychotic part of the personality, as a drugging structure that tends to drain away the person's vitality and sacrifice his emotional growth for the power of sensory pleasure; a bond can thus be established between the patient's healthy part, which is always in danger of being weakened by the psychotic withdrawal's enticement, and the analyst, whose objective is helping the patient eventually draw a distinction between what is pleasant but destructive for the mind and what is good and constructive.

I have already mentioned that the psychotic patient does not speak openly about his psychotic part's functioning (rather, he conceals it), in particular the functioning of the delusion structure, which he sees as precious and does not wish to have

The psychic withdrawal   61

questioned by the therapist. Here, we find ourselves facing a typical problem of the psychotic state: that of *confusion* between the healthy and the sick part. The delusion can offer the patient the delights of a pleasant reality that is sensorially rewarding; it therefore seems not only useful but indispensable, so much so that it needs to be hidden from the therapist.

Even when the delusion structure is similar to a criminal organisation that blackmails the patient, it can be hidden from the therapist. A well-known example is that of Frieda Fromm-Reichmann (1959), whose patient revealed the content of the delusion during a session but the next day refused to see the analyst because she was terrorised by a voice that threatened her with death for having betrayed 'their' secret.

Besides these patients who do not disclose their withdrawal, there are those who do, either at the very beginning of therapy or at a later stage; the patient who does not reveal his delusional ideation to the therapist runs a greater risk of becoming completely dominated by the psychosis. The therapist must therefore intuit its existence and tactfully point out the dangers; otherwise a psychotic break may suddenly appear as if from nowhere, when in fact it was secretly in the pipeline.

I would like to underline that the ease with which a patient allows himself to be seduced is due to the fact that the psychosis presents itself with exciting and salvific features, and this exciting part that avoids suffering at the cost of perverting reality is considered by the psychotic patient to be good and positive; consequently, the part that is ill is seen not as dangerous, but as a source of well-being.

As shall be addressed in the next chapter, in order to bring to light the pathogenic work of the psychotic part, at times we can be helped by dreams.

6 Dreams and delusions in psychosis

Dreams

Earlier, I described how the preparation of a psychotic episode is dissociated from awareness, the ill part being considered healthy: it is as if the psychotic nucleus had the power to hypnotise the personality into being passive and yielding, thus creating the precondition for the delusional invasion.

This makes psychosis therapy particularly complex because the analyst is without those messages he needs in order to prevent, contain and transform the pathological course. In this respect, psychosis differs from other states of mental suffering: the depressed patient, for example, talks continuously of his malaise and projects his suffering onto the analyst. In psychosis, however, the analyst must resort to indirect signs: prolonged silences, skipped sessions or indecipherable speech that can alert to the danger of an imminent break.

One tool the analyst can use to prevent a possible break is the dream, which at times can show in advance the progression of the psychotic process as it moves forward. The dream can describe the break that is looming (or has already occurred), which is represented by the patient and therefore potentially becomes thinkable. The psychotic dream of this kind is helpful not only to contain and halt the psychotic course, but also to make the patient aware of how he yields to its charm.

Angela[1] is a twenty-one-year-old patient who had her first psychotic episode at sixteen, characterised by excitement and a mystical delusion, during which she was convinced she had intercourse with Jesus. After approximately two years of therapy, a second episode occurred in which the patient, convinced that she was the devil, begged the therapist not to look her in the eye; otherwise, she would be contaminated. The breakdown was managed at home with the help of a psychiatrist, and the patient's state of extreme suffering meant that she missed several sessions out of her evident fear of leaving the house and being killed. The therapist questioned herself at length on why there had been a new break and discussed this with me in supervision.

The analytic sequence that I shall now describe follows Angela's partial recovery of the psychotic episode and regular attendance at her sessions again. This, in my opinion, is the moment in which Angela may be helped to understand the

Dreams and delusions in psychosis   63

reasons behind her break and the charm that the psychosis exerts on her mind. In a session, she brought this dream:

> I'm on a train with my father, it's evening time. We have to go to a little town, and since it's evening, I expect we shall stay out overnight. During the journey my father is very focused on his paperwork and I feel ill at ease, alone. Then I'm in a car, my dad and I, and Mrs Franzoni[2] is driving. I recognise Mrs Franzoni and feel extremely uncomfortable in the car with her. I arrive at a boarding school surrounded by a high wall; it is a boarding school where they teach archery. In the evening I'm in my dormitory with other girls, and in the dark I can see a girl who is smiling strangely at me, and she has a phosphorescent bow. The next morning we all go to the swimming pool, and as I'm afraid that my bathrobe will be stolen, I swim the "dog paddle" and hold it in my hands above the water.

The patient's associations of the dream are that when she goes to the council swimming pool, she is always afraid that someone will steal something from her, so she puts her towel and locker keys near the edge of the pool. When the therapist suggests that the bathrobe is like skin, Angela confirms that what she is afraid of is losing her identity. Then she speaks about the bow and says that this girl's smile struck her; it was a smile that instilled fear in her really. Since her fear of being killed is also there, the good thing, of course, about the bow is that it is phosphorescent and can be seen and recognised. The session draws to an end, and the therapist says goodbye to the patient, giving a mutual commitment to think about this dream.

In the next session, perhaps for the first time since being in therapy, Angela brings what she herself has worked out:

P: Well, I thought quite a bit about what the bow in the dream might mean. I thought too that the girl who owned it might be me. I also remembered that as well as the strange smile that scared me, her lips were all moist . . .
A: So we can say that there was strong sensuality . . .
P: Yes, I thought so too, a big part of it is sexual. It was the light that evoked the bow, and so angels and devils came to mind. I become the light through the arrow hitting me.
A: Yes, this in fact is the delusional part, it is the part that hurts you, that lights you up and seduces you, making you believe that it is the only path to being superior, an angel.
P: [she giggles] Oh yeah, you're right, it's really crazy, I'm a human being after all, not an angel or a devil. I turn into them . . .
A: I wondered whether Mrs Franzoni too represented an omnipotent part, killing her son who fell short of her expectations. In fact, in the dream, she is the one driving. . . . Perhaps when you are isolated (your father is focused on his work) and far from the rest of the world, this exciting part conquers you more easily . . .

64 *Part 2*

P: Yeah, that's right. . . . And I feel like an angel . . . that can turn into a devil whenever.

A: Exactly, and therefore you are afraid that someone wants to kill you.

P: I still go to the dogs, you know [*Angela has stopped school for the time being and regularly goes to a city dog pound to help with the dogs*], and I think it's really important that I do. I thought about what you said to me last time, it's true that thanks to them I'm starting to learn about feelings, but not just by recognising them in the dogs, I realise that they also open up something in me, like a lung that fills with air. . . . I think it's the relationship.

I have reported this sequence to show how the delusional withdrawal (becoming the girl with the bow in the dream) can be a protective measure against solitude, but also and above all, it is a flight into a state of sexualised pleasure that Angela creates in order to take advantage of her father's mental distance (and that of the analyst).

The psychotic patient is taken with a kind of perversity that corresponds to a transgressive distortion of the mind; this practice, apparently pleasant and like a mental drug, will sooner or later turn out to be persecutory, (self-)destructive and catastrophic because it sets off a never-ending process that overwhelms the patient himself. The urge to coerce the mind with drugging pleasure-seeking reaches a critical threshold of no return, the psychotic anxiety then breaking through with all its might.

The patient needs to reach the point where he can *see* the psychotic construction, as in this patient's case.

As stated previously, dreams that psychotic patients bring to their sessions are enlightening because they describe, often very accurately, psychotic functioning and the exciting and befuddling power that keeps mental health in its thrall. During therapy, those parts that remain outside the system must be given support, prevented from being attracted to the system and helped to see clearly, so that the power of the delusion can be broken. Hence, the importance of guiding analytic work towards awareness of what the psychotic organisation means: that is, its tendency to incorporate the self and destroy the sense of reality. This is why, as can be seen from the clinical extract, psychotic dreams are helpful as they provide the analyst with an important message.

Accounts of this kind of dream are almost always without associations and should be thought of as a description of the dynamics between the psychotic and the non-psychotic part of the personality and of the action that the former exerts upon the latter. These dreams do not connect back to symbolic content but convey a message that is indispensable to working on the psychotic nucleus and on the patient's readiness to delusion.

In the dream, Angela describes in retrospect the episode she was hit by and what her involvement in it was. Usually, the psychotic dream *discloses in advance* the delusion that is brewing; when it follows the delusion, however, the dream is the patient's attempt to understand what happened in his mind. Hence, its value to the therapy as it can help the patient consolidate his efforts to resist future seduction by the psychotic part and better understand how it operates.

Since there is an awareness deficit in psychosis, the psychotic dream comes to *represent* a process in which awareness is lacking. Work here is complex and needs to be carried forward for quite some time; whereas the neurotic patient, after a useful interpretation, can integrate the content, the psychotic patient will continue to deny psychic reality. Irrespective of immediate effectiveness, psychotic dreams grant access to the area where the delusion formed; the analyst must therefore have experience of psychosis functioning to clearly understand the description of the transformation dynamics.

With regard to Angela's dream, the analyst needs to focus his interpretation on the description of the psychotic transformation that occurs when the dreamer finds herself in the car driven by an infanticide mother, who represents her psychotic part. The delusional reality (the swimming pool and the phosphorescent bow) is clearly represented here, and it appears when Angela's father leaves her alone because he is too busy working (which may also allude to insufficient analytic care). The analyst can assign meaning to actions in the dream, carefully describing the psychotic functioning and its exciting and befuddling power. It is clear in Angela's case that the psychotic part has seduced her vanity (and will seek to do so again), making her believe she is special, with the reappearance of the excited sexual part that she had delusions about in the past in her sexual encounters with Jesus.[3]

Themes that appear in the psychotic state are not many: the most common are those that describe the allure of the surreal and imaginary, sexualisation, omnipotence, megalomania, perverse excitement and drugging psychic experience. Without any form of disguise, these themes are described in *declarative* psychotic dreams. It is of utmost importance that analysts who accept a psychotic patient into care have a good knowledge of these dreams, which, when recognised and given back to the patient, can provide him with the opportunity to think and to begin to free himself from the psychotic ensnarement; should the analyst not understand the dream and trivialise it, he will not be in a position to stop the patient from proceeding towards psychotic colonisation.

Delusions

I shall now try to clarify the nature of the delusion and distinguish it from daydreams, myths and dreams.

In psychoanalysis, the term *psychic reality* means an individual's conscious and unconscious subjective psychic experience, and it includes fantasies, conscious and unconscious beliefs and positive and negative feelings that connect us to people and to all the knowledge gained from our life experience. Freud (1900) used this term also for the beliefs of hysterical patients who were convinced they had been subjected to sexual abuse in childhood: despite being untrue, their memories of abuse are real to them. Freud thus established that psychic reality or, rather, personal beliefs and actual reality do not coincide.

Generally speaking, people can distinguish between what is subjective and personal, such as ideas, thoughts and emotions, and what comes from external reality and interacting with others. With regard to psychosis, the inability to distinguish

66   *Part 2*

between inner and outer reality has rightly been highlighted, and the mechanism of projective identification described by Melanie Klein (1946) is certainly what creates this confusion between what is internal and what is external.

So what kind of psychic reality does the delusion represent?

How the delusional experience is conceptualised is fundamental to the success of therapy. If we consider the delusion a message, we should try to decipher its implicit meaning, as we do, for example, with dreams; if instead we consider it a construction built from scratch – in other words, essentially an obstacle to communication – our approach in the therapeutic relationship should be that of *deconstructing* it to enable the patient to free himself from its control, recover his intuitive thinking and establish contact with emotional reality.

Following on from Freud's (1910) comments on Schreber's memoirs, many analysts have considered the delusion something similar to the dream, a sort of truth that can be unveiled. Freud (1938a) himself, in *Constructions in Analysis*, confirmed the idea that the patient can disclose some of his history in the delusion.

From this viewpoint, the delusion may be considered to contain a hidden truth that was distorted by the defences and conflicts that govern the patient's mind. Indeed, Freud wrote that Schreber's complex delusion production as well as his sense of being persecuted by Professor Flechsig, his psychiatrist, both concealed a nuclear point of repressed homosexuality. Schreber's illness was the product of a homosexual conflict with his father, the libido remaining fixated at a primitive stage and anxiety projected outwards.

Many other authors, too, believe that in the delusion there is a kernel of truth. According to Niederland (1951), for example, what Schreber feared most was having to follow in his father's footsteps as he felt unable to live up to being a member of the Reichstag.

In his relation with Flechsig and in his delusion (God-Sun-Father), Schreber withdrew into the female position since taking on a male role would have been unbearable. Similar observations were made by other authors – Israëls (1989), for instance, who considers one of Schreber's complaints, that of his chest being compressed by 'divine miracles', as the consequence of orthopaedic apparatuses devised by his father to rehabilitate children; the introjection of paternal authoritarian and coercive methods returned as hallucinations and delusions.

As stated earlier, Freud (1938a) likened the delusion to the dream, and they do in fact bear many resemblances: both are nourished by a narrative plot comprising sensorial elements, visual images and auditory perceptions that lend a feeling of reality, but upon awakening, the dreamer, unlike the delusional patient, can compare the dream and reality and understand that the dream corresponds to an emotional narrative that is his, but which is not real.

For a psychotic patient, it is very difficult to distinguish a dreamed fact from a real one that has actually happened; when he dreams, he is uncertain whether it is a dream or reality, and when he is delusional, he is unable to think of the delusion as a dream in the awake state. That a 'voice' or an 'intuition' unveils a new irrefutable reality in the delusion makes the psychotic patient consider the dream a revelation of 'another' reality.

Dreams and delusions in psychosis 67

Freud (1910) recalled that President Schreber, at the time of his second psychotic episode, had dreamed that his nervous illness had returned and he had fantasized being a woman on one occasion during intercourse. According to Freud, in these cases the patient discloses in advance the same material that will then enter the psychosis, and in fact, Schreber was to communicate in his delusion that he had turned into a woman and been impregnated by divine rays.

Therefore, there are dreams and dream fantasies that announce the delusional reality in the making; such dreams have no symbolic meaning but describe the delusion structure that is preparing to conquer the mind (Capozzi and de Masi 2001). As previously stated, these dreams must be treated with descriptive interpretations that help the patient see that what is presenting itself as an unquestionable external reality is in fact his own creation.

Freud (1924a) also assigned a reconstructive value to the delusion that sees an attempt at recovery and the reorganisation of reality after the catastrophe; when the Id overrules the reality principle, as occurs in the psychotic episode, the Ego must find an alternative in a bid to replace the lost reality.

A first critique, although indirect, of the conceptualisation of the delusion as an announcement and an attempt at reconstruction comes from Federn (1952), who instead considered it a falsification of reality following the loss of the Ego boundary. One of his most important propositions was that whereas 'in neurosis we want to eliminate repression, in psychosis we want to restore it' (1952, p. 136). It is not a matter of 'making the unconscious conscious, but [of] making the unconscious unconscious again' (p. 178); therefore he recommended not giving symbolic interpretations of the meaning of the delusional experience because the patient, instead of understanding them, might think that the analyst is revealing the existence of a new reality.

A second way of understanding the delusion, based on the belief that there is a radical difference between neurosis and psychosis, is that of a totally new construction in an alternative, dissociated reality, which is my way of seeing delusional experience. The delusion is not the product of intuitive thought or unconscious activity, but the configuration of a new perceptive reality that is the exact antithesis of creative thought and self-awareness; that is, it is a separate mental experience, created by the mind's sensory activity, which cannot be understood using traditional psychoanalytic concepts of defence, repression, denial and so forth.

The imagination that creates the delusion does not take us back to an emotional reality or a repressed wish, but it 'unveils' a new world that tends to take root in psychic reality. The patient constructs his delusion content with the same sensory processes he uses to perceive external reality: the sensory imagination that produced the delusion gets engraved in his mind, and it becomes a real experience that can be reproduced. Processing the reality of a past delusional experience so that it may be considered a memory that is distinct from the present is what proves to be difficult; it is always brooding and potentially capable of recapturing the healthy part of the personality.

Using the imagination intuitively is a process that develops late on. Very young children are unable to represent their experiences: hence their inability

68   *Part 2*

to mentalise psychic experience; when they begin to play, they enter the 'make believe' stage where play and reality coexist simultaneously, and then at a subsequent stage, they form a theory of mind (Fonagy and Target 1996).

I use the term *imagination* to denote a mental activity that can make use of sensory images and that conveys wishes, curiosity and seeking experience and openness towards the world. Play and dreaming are both sensorially built experiences (visual and auditory images) that convey meanings, wishes and symbols that originate in the subject's emotional reality; the dream, in particular, has a communicative function that generates emotional experiences, comparable to that of artistic narration.

That psychic reality contains conflictual thoughts means that the same thought activity contains ambivalent impulses; however conflictual or egodystonic it may be, a thought remains a thought – it does not turn into a concrete perception, as unfortunately occurs in the delusion.

When the illness gives rise to delusional dissociated experience, it is not easy to foresee whether the patient will be able to recover the unity of his mind. Despite there being evidence of cases of spontaneous recovery, the psychotic delusion, even when it seems to have faded away, leaves traces that facilitate relapses.

Hanna Segal (1957) formulated the concept of the *symbolic equation* to explain the nature of psychotic thought, pinpointing one of the most serious complaints of schizophrenic thought, which is the inability to symbolise or, rather, to distinguish symbols from concrete objects. Segal discussed the case of a schizophrenic patient, a talented musician, for whom stroking the bow on the violin strings meant masturbating. He therefore refused to play in public because for him playing meant masturbating in front of strangers: the symbolic equation of psychotic thought.

For Hanna Segal, the symbolic equation, where no difference exists between the symbol and the original object, is used to deny the absence of the object. Symbolic activity, instead, originates when depressive feelings dominate paranoid-schizoid feelings: that is, when separation from the object, ambivalence, guilt and loss can be experienced and tolerated. The symbol is used not to deny but to overcome the loss. According to Segal, differentiation between self and object is necessary to maintain normal symbolic ability based on the introjection of objects experienced as separate from the self. With regard to the psychotic patient, one part of the Ego is confused with the object, and the symbol is confused with the object that is symbolised: an excess of projective identification is what erases the difference between the self and objects and creates confusion between reality and fantasy.

Segal (1974) was also interested in the artist's creative imagination and in how it differs from that of the delusional patient. In her opinion, the artist creates through reparation, allowing the birth of a new object; the delusional patient, on the other hand, is one with his creation. The moment the artist has finished a piece of work, he lets the created object be separate from him and can thus see his work from the right distance and with a critical attitude; he feels distinct from the parental couple, even though he identifies partially with them. The delusional patient places himself in his parents' stead, not acknowledging any of their functions. Lastly, the artist seeks to recreate an inner truth without mistaking his desires and fantasies for reality, whereas the delusional patient is unaware of the omnipotence the delusion produces.

In a piece of work published in 1971, Herbert Rosenfeld examined in depth the importance of projective identification and the splitting of the Ego in psychosis. In particular, he made a distinction between two types of projective identification: the first is used to communicate and the second to rid the mind of unwanted parts. This second form of projective identification is what the psychotic patient uses to transform psychic reality.

Edith Jacobson (1954) connected the delusional patient's identifications to the earliest infantile mechanisms of magical identification that make the child feel he is one single thing with the object or that he is the actual object regardless of reality. The link is clear between these forms of identification and the concept of projective identification proposed by Melanie Klein.

According to O'Shaughnessy (1992), the mind ceases to think when it uses projective identification excessively or differently from the way it is habitually used. Besides its communicative purpose, when an infant cries in order to be understood by his mother, for example, the mind can also use violent projections to evacuate self-awareness and object awareness; in this distortion, internal and external perceptions are not transformed into conscious and unconscious psychic elements that can then be repressed in order to enter dream work.

O'Shaughnessy reconnects with Bion (1957) when she says that the psychotic personality has its origins in fragmentation, which follows the expulsion of the means through which the Ego knows reality: that is, the senses, consciousness and thinking. In other words, there is an uprooting of what Freud called the 'reality principle'.

Several authors – Caper (1998), for example – think that the delusional construction can be worked through gradually until it transforms into a fantasy.

My clinical experience leads me to believe that there is a radical incompatibility between delusional imagination and fantasy and dream activity. As stated earlier, the delusion brings with it an anomalous transformation of psychic reality, and it is wrong to think of it as a defence: the defences, by changing emotional perception, create a mind-set that tends to be stable; psychopathological constructions such as the delusion, however, tend to deform psychic reality, transforming it continually.

I consider the delusion a psychopathological construction: that is, a belief that produces a falsification *outside awareness*, which acts at a *conscious* level via massive *distorted investment in sensory reality*.

The delusional experience avails itself of the psychotic mind's ability to *make imaginative thought sensory*. In this mental state, the psyche is employed not as a means to understand reality but to produce sensations and perceptions; that is, it is used as a *sensory organ*. What fundamentally characterises the delusion, as mentioned earlier, is its ability to construct an imaginary sensory world. At a certain point, however, this new pathological functioning of the psyche escapes the patient's control, and he is no longer able to distinguish between newly created reality and pre-existing reality: the patient is *conscious* of the delusional representation but *is not aware* of its falsified nature.

One of the most precise definitions of the difference between imagination and delusion is that provided in an interview conducted by Laurice McAfee with

70   *Part 2*

Joanne Greenberg, Frieda Fromm-Reichmann's patient and author of *I Never Promised You a Rose Garden*:

> Perhaps the most powerful thing I would like to say is that creativity and mental illness are opposites, not complementary. Mental illness and creativity are terribly mixed up. Imagination is, includes, leaves, opens towards and learns from experience. Madness is the opposite: it is a fort that turns into a prison.
>
> (Silver 1989, p. 527, author's translation)

The radically concrete nature of the delusional experience poses very knotty therapeutic problems. Unlike the dream, which can be understood and transformed, the delusion cannot; due to its predominantly sensory nature, it is extremely risky to formulate interpretations of its content for the delusional patient as they can lead to misunderstandings and mix-ups.

Pleasure in the delusion

I shall now briefly describe a clinical case that clearly shows how the delusional part takes control of the healthy part, luring it to exciting pleasure; specifically, it can be seen from the clinical material how several dreams portend the advance and manifestation of the delusion. We can understand that, once the episode has been overcome, the psychotic nucleus does not wither and die despite its branches having been severed as its roots and trunk remain firmly planted in the ground, ready to sprout again.

Alberta was hospitalised in a psychiatric ward after a psychotic breakdown with auditory and visual hallucinations and delusional thinking several months before the beginning of psychoanalytic treatment. The medical history gathered when she was admitted did not provide anything particularly meaningful; Alberta was an only child and always led an isolated life away from her peers. Her stay in hospital was relatively short because she regained contact with reality quite quickly even though not completely and was then entrusted to an outpatient clinic where the psychiatrist prescribed psychotropic medication and suggested analytic therapy.

The first months of therapy were face-to-face. Alberta, who came to her sessions regularly, accompanied by her mother, seemed interested in the therapeutic relation; she was almost amimic, fearful, at times absentminded and still immersed in a delusional atmosphere that she was trying to hide. She seemed sad and jaded, as if she felt empty and disoriented after the psychotic breakdown; at times she would try to speak about her family and the difficult relationship with her mother. After a while, the number of sessions rose from two to three then to four per week, and at a certain point, the analyst suggested that she lie on the couch. Regular contact was kept with the psychiatrist who was to check her therapy and intervene in the event of a break.

After the first few sessions, Alberta was able to come to her therapy on her own. As for her difficulty with her mother, she remembered that when she was fourteen, her mother had slapped her and forcibly taken her back home after catching her holding hands with and giving a small kiss to a classmate. Alberta said that

Dreams and delusions in psychosis   71

since then she had always refrained from going out with boys because she was frightened of her parents' possible reaction. In fact, during her adolescence she had never sought to become independent of her parents, never went on holiday with her friends and never had a boyfriend.

This episode of kissing her classmate when she was a teenager could be considered the first manifestation of the patient's love withdrawal, which then gradually took up more and more space. The delusion that had led to her admission to hospital had in fact been of an erotic nature, and concerned a schoolmate from early secondary school whom Alberta thought was in love with her; in fact, he belonged to a group that used to make fun of her. At this stage, Alberta no longer had any contact with this former schoolmate. In the delusion, however, his presence was everywhere; he would follow her and speak to her but never be visible, hiding from her. During Alberta's stay in hospital, her mental state was characterised by frenzy with visual and auditory hallucinations: that is, a string of delusional signals in which the boy would declare his love for her.

What follows is material from a session in the fourth month of analysis. Alberta came into the room smiling and a little frivolous:

> I'll tell you about a dream. I was living inside a video game; the walls would open and close at my command, when I said "open or close". When I opened them, some people wanted to come in, but they were dangerous. It was a constant opening and closing. I would have liked to go out but I was forced to close them to protect myself. I am always afraid. Even yesterday when I went to the city centre with my mother I was afraid, and when I got home I breathed a sigh of relief.

Through this dream, Alberta is describing her psychotic functioning: she can create a video game that replaces psychic reality, opening it and closing it at will. But then the psychotic system becomes threatening; Alberta can no longer control it and risks being locked up in a prison with no way out.

Several months later is this session just a short time before the summer holidays:

> I'm happy today because I had a nice dream, not an anxious one. I was with my friends from secondary school. We were at a school on the coast. I had a computer test to do, and my friends had a maths test. At a certain point I confided in them about what had happened in September [her psychotic breakdown]. Then I asked them to get the medicine that I have to take. They were very kind and understood me, but at a certain point Marco [her lover in the delusion] appeared, which was absurd; he didn't make fun of me and he wasn't unfriendly either, the opposite in fact; he told me that he would like to get along with me and go out with me as long as I stopped being standoffish. Then I woke up calm and peaceful.

In the first part, Alberta manages to talk to her schoolmates about her psychotic breakdown and even remembers the medication she has to take, but then Marco,

72   *Part 2*

the protagonist of her love delusion, appears. It does seem to be a peaceful dream, but a closer look shows that there is something ambiguous about it. Why does Marco appear suddenly in the dream? Why is the school on the coast? One might wonder whether the patient is trying to convince her analyst (as she does with her schoolmates in the dream) that everything is all right, and that she has regained her mental health, while in fact another delusional meeting with Marco is being organised, on the brink of the summer holidays.

In the next session, Alberta still seems peaceful:

> It's a time in which I'm thinking about the future; simple little things make me euphoric. I'll give you an example: I bought a cream for cellulite to use this summer, it's a nagging thought. I do nothing but think about the holidays. I bought a new swimsuit and spend forever in front of the mirror. It's a thought that makes me euphoric, it makes me feel really active. And I've been chatting online to Daniele [a peer] about everything, the cinema, theatre, sport.

The analyst says that her thoughts are pleasant but tend to be almost ill-like and uncontainable. Alberta replies:

> Yes, and I can only wipe them out if I take a sedative. Every time I go to the seaside I dream of meeting someone who will turn my life around, and might be the one I'll run away with.

The conclusion we can draw from these sessions is that a new psychotic episode is being prepared for the summer break when her analyst will not be there. The cellulite cream and the holiday at the seaside (the school on the coast) offer a glimpse of a new state of sexual euphoria. Within a short space of time, the same delusional atmosphere of the first psychotic episode is in fact recreated: Alberta begins to miss her sessions, preferring to wander about town while telling her parents she is going to her analyst. Early intervention by the psychiatrist and the resumption of regular sessions after the holidays, which in this case were short, were to prevent the patient's readmission to hospital.

This clinical material helps show how the delusion, once it is installed in the mind, tends to reappear. In this case, the allure of the eroticizing and ecstatic state is appealing and, at the same time, the approaching analytic separation tends to strengthen the psychotic part that will no longer be contained by sessions.

Alberta, precisely because she has always led a mortified and isolated life, tends to mistake freedom for the propaganda spread by the delusional part that portrays itself as an experience of exciting independence. When the dream about school is described during the session, the delusional part is already on the verge of conquering the healthy part. The dream describes how Alberta is once again allowing herself to be conquered, and, since she has lost awareness of what is happening, she is really delighted by this dream material. Here, the delusion has presented itself as a condition that will lead to a state of ecstatic excitement; mortified and weak, the patient's healthy part yields to the flattery.

Dreams and delusions in psychosis   73

In delusions, perception of reality is altered in such a way as to comply with the dominant theme: the persecutory patient sees enemies everywhere and interprets others' behaviour as threatening; the patient with delusional love themes interprets simple messages as being clearly erotic. The patient's alarmed reaction is rather typical when we try to cast doubt on the truthfulness of his delusional experience; it is as if we purposely wish to doubt his perceptions to make him look mad, given that he considers these experiences as real facts.

In the delusional state, the patient does not think: he 'sees' or 'feels' as if he were daydreaming. While dreaming, we consider the dream content as real, but when we wake up, we understand that it is an affective-emotive narration that is not real at all. The dream after all is a symbolic experience that connects back to the dreamer's emotional meaning, his wish, conflict or anxiety. The delusional experience has no awakening, doubts or distancing since it is not a symbolic narration but a concrete perception.

Another substantial difference between the dream and the delusion experience is that the latter continues to be 'a real fact' even when the healthy part is gradually restored. The delusion is forever something that really existed, with all the exciting or terrifying emotions that accompanied it; in this sense, it bears much resemblance to trauma, which, by its very nature, is not at all easy to work through. As is the case with the traumatised individual, the psychotic patient will frequently not remember the delusional experience out of his fear of once more coming under its sway.

The defence employed to avoid relapses is circumscribing the delusion, like a foreign body, and dissociating it; given, however, that its nucleus remains potentially active, often the delusion will form again. In Alberta's case, the love delusion is like an ecstatic state of excitement, a nucleus of pleasure, always there to capture her and rescue her from depressive feelings.

To explain better how two realities, psychotic and real, can coexist, I shall refer to some material from a colleague's supervision, that of James Telfer (2013),[4] which concerns Capgras syndrome, the pathology in which the patient lives with the firm belief that the people close to him have been replaced by alien replicas or imposters that are identical to them.

Elisa was a twenty-five-year-old young woman, shy and introverted; over a period of a few years, she became increasingly isolated and would run into problems at work, to the extent that her parents began to be worried about her. One night they found her in the garden, armed with a knife, ready to attack them if they came anywhere near her. Elisa confided in the doctor and nurse who had been called out from the Mental Health Service that her parents were, in fact, imposters who wanted to kill her. She gave her consent to be admitted to hospital and to take psychotropic medication. When discharged a fortnight later, Elisa seemed rid of the delusion but was unable to feel like a real, alive person, and so she accepted beginning psychotherapy. During her sessions, she spoke very little, was vague and disoriented and still convinced that her parents had been imposters even though they no longer were. The sessions were difficult because Elisa spoke monotonously, had no sense of time and gave the impression of living in

74   *Part 2*

her own private world like someone who was reared without parents. Gradually, over the following months, the live presence of the therapist seemed to shift Elisa from her passive state. At a certain point, Elisa spoke of her grandmother's death, which had occurred one year before the beginning of the delusion, a grandmother who had loved her so much that the patient thought of her as a mother. The loss of her grandmother was, in retrospect, the real traumatic event that had triggered Capgras syndrome because Elisa had been unable to work through the loss and mourning. Instead of 'dreaming her' to keep her alive in her inner world, as occurs in normal mourning, Elisa took the path of the delusion, refusing to acknowledge the role of her parents and turning them into dangerous imposters.

Relapsing into delusion

Alvise[5] came from a city a long way from Milan, and even though it was July, with the summer holidays in sight, he wanted to begin analysis immediately. His determination struck me, and perhaps this was what made me decide to see him. His analysis began in September at four sessions per week in an analytic setting, and Alvise moved to Milan. Alvise had been in a psychiatric ward for two months, followed by a short course of treatment with a psychotherapist who then sent him to me. He had had a severe psychotic break that culminated in attempted suicide: while on holiday, he hurled himself off a flyover, under the delusional conviction that he harboured a diabolical power that made him totally destructive. Other diabolical presences were at work, too, often in the shape of animals, such as black dogs, while, to the toll of bells or bursts of gunfire, the world proclaimed mass suicides. Alvise had felt that he could telepathically enter others' minds and bring about their suicides, and, thinking he was in touch with God (divine and terrifying voices declared catastrophic truths), he was convinced that his condemnation was final.

After seven years of analysis with me, the patient's condition had improved so much that his parents persuaded him to complete his university studies. (He only needed to pass one exam and do his thesis.)

Despite displaying discomfort with and intolerance to intellectual work, the patient accepted his parents' suggestion. In order to work on his thesis, Alvise needed to cut his weekly sessions from four to two; his analysis halved and the tension of preparing his thesis difficult to bear, Alvise had a new psychotic breakdown during the summer holidays. This time the auditory hallucinations were not experienced as perturbing, though (which they had been in the first breakdown), but as a special quality that made him unique, to the extent that he believed the CIA were searching for him in order to abduct him, take him to the United States and make him work for the American government.

Due to the new psychotic breakdown and a series of adverse circumstances, it was not possible to analyse his idealisation of his madness. Alvise and I both ended up feeling discouraged, and he did not come to his sessions anymore. Several years after this, I received news from his father that he had gone back home, was living a narrow life and regularly took antipsychotic medication. Ten years on, I received a telephone call from Alvise asking to see me again. We met up, and he greeted me warmly, but I had the impression that he still considered auditory hallucinations (this time centred on neighbours) as real facts. In the meantime, he had graduated, was looking for work, continued to take psychotropic medication and had put on a lot of weight.

When this analysis was over, I reflected a great deal on the case, and asked myself what had been lacking in my therapeutic approach. I had focused much of my analytic work on analysing the psychotic Super-ego that underpinned the hallucinatory state. Alvise had, in fact, improved and could tolerate awareness of the psychotic catastrophe that had happened. It is likely that pressure for a premature 'recovery', mainly sustained by Alvise's parents, had favoured a return to psychosis.

During the course of my reflections, I asked myself whether I had really understood the origin and dynamics of the delusion and if I had actually managed to get to the bottom of the original psychotic episode: that is, whether I had understood how Alvise had entered psychosis. In retrospect, I came to the conclusion that I had not done this; when I had tried to share and relive the sequences of the psychotic episode with the patient, I found he put up very strong resistance and tended to trivialize what had happened.

I understood that I had given up on carrying out a systematic analysis of the first psychotic episode because of the patient's resistance and my uncertainty about it and had instead focused on his need to repair the psychic damage in order that his mental functioning could be restored. I understood late that the original psychotic episode had been there between us like a third wheel.

I would like to recall two important thoughts that, after Alvise's case, have always stayed in my mind. The first is by Arieti, who stated in his book *Interpretation of Schizophrenia* (1955):

> An important point to be considered is the relevance of the original episode. It is not just a precipitating event; it is a very important dynamic factor, without which the patient would have been able to check, or even compensate, his psychotic propensity.
>
> (p. 909)

The second is by Searles (1979):

> Schizophrenia cannot be understood simply in terms of traumata and deprivation, no matter how grievous, inflicted by the outer world upon the helpless child. The patient himself, no matter how unwittingly, has an active part in the development and tenacious maintenance of the illness and only by making contact with this essentially assertive energy in him can one help him to become well.
>
> (p. 22)

If the first psychotic episode enhances a patient's readiness to be delusional (and the structure of subsequent delusional episodes is similar to that of the first), the analyst, as best he can, must go back to the past and rebuild the way in which

76   *Part 2*

the patient entered the delusion construction for the first time. It must be borne in mind that the first psychotic breakdown leaves an indelible mark on the mind, and it is onto this matrix that subsequent delusional experiences will be built.

Delusion relapses may occur for various reasons. When the delusion produces an excited state of pleasure as, for example, in the love delusion, the state of ecstasy, like a drug, gets lodged in the individual's memory as an experience of vitality, which is why it can recapture the patient. We have seen this condition in the case of the patient Alberta.

Something very different occurs in the persecutory delusion, in which the patient is in fear of his life; in this case the psychotic experience is tantamount to something traumatic that remains fixed in one's memory, like anxiety that cannot be worked through. The sensory and concrete quality of the psychotic experience makes it a true traumatic event that is ready to reactivate when the same configuration that triggered it happens anew. It is an *endogenous trauma* in this case, produced by the delusion that reawakens; just as traumatic experiences suddenly re-emerge as sensory, acoustic or visual flashbacks, the delusion, apparently forgotten but never completely dispelled, tends to reproduce itself.

I have already mentioned that the patient is easily colonised by the delusion formation, which poses a complex problem for the therapist. Somewhere in the mind is a place, not easily accessible to the analyst, in which the psychosis is constructed. The delusion has an undeniable hold over the patient, who neither averts the danger it poses nor understands its pathogenic significance; I cannot stress enough how helpful the message contained in some dreams is, as the withdrawal and the colonisation of the psychotic part are clearly described there, without any form of disguise, helping the therapist to intervene before the delusion suddenly explodes.

I would now like to examine analytic material on a patient who seemed on the verge of repeating a psychotic episode.

This case[6] regards a twenty-six-year-old male patient who had a psychotic episode that 'illuminated' him. The pope informed him that he, Gianni, had invented 'morkema', a language that would enable the deaf and dumb to communicate with each other and with the rest of the world. Immediately afterwards, though, this illumination turned into persecution: a 'voice' would tell him that he was not a genius after all and that the devil had lured him into a trap to kill him. Gianni said that this 'voice' incited him to kill himself because after his death, he would be able to achieve something extraordinary. After working for several months on the delusion, Gianni began to feel less distressed and understood that he had gone from a state of grandiose excitement to one of persecution, in which he felt like the devil, who had destroyed the order of the universe.

Gianni: I felt distressed when I woke up. I dreamt I had a big tummy because I was pregnant and it moved like a book that had a child inside it. I felt good in the dream.

Analyst: What is your opinion about the dream? It seems as if you have everything in this dream, a penis and a womb. You got pregnant all by

Dreams and delusions in psychosis 77

	yourself, as if another's presence were unnecessary: 'I can do every-thing by myself'. I do not need my parents to feel grown up.
Gianni:	Yes, I see now that I have good parents. My best friend, Chiara, a lesbian, asked me to have a baby with her. But I don't know how to. I don't like her as a female, and I don't think she could arouse me.
Analyst:	'I can do it without a female' seems to be the message in your dream. 'I have everything inside me'.
Gianni:	(laughing) Yes, maybe. I'd really love to live as I did in the past. Maybe in Berlin [the city he idealised as a place of sexual pleasure]. But now I know it would just be me escaping, and I'm a bit scared to go.

Besides the delusional content in this clinical extract, I think it is important to highlight the contrast between the distressed state upon awakening and the merry and aroused condition that characterises the dream. (The pleasure of begetting a child corresponds to the omniscient individual Gianni thought he was during his delusional experience.) It is precisely this that differentiates the psychotic part from the non-psychotic part of the personality. Distress upon awakening is the perception of danger that the non-psychotic part senses when the psychotic functioning appears. By analysing the emotions that the dream content arouses (anxiety and pleasure), the analyst can show the patient that there is fascination with delusional omnipotence, but also alarm and distress coming from the healthy part. Dreams of this kind are cause for alarm for the analyst, who must interpret the seduction performed by the psychotic part.

Specific to the psychotic illness is its progressive and generally unstoppable nature: the delusion nucleus possesses such force that it can maintain lasting power over the patient's mind.

That the clinical condition of psychosis has radically changed today does not mean that the illness is no longer progressive and dangerous. The numerous chronic psychotic patients who populated asylums and, because of institutionalisation, were destined to spend their whole lives in these places, are no longer common, but the pathological force of psychosis means it still needs to be fought against tenaciously.

Thanks to psychotropic drugs, the most dangerous expressions of the illness can be limited and the most clamorous symptoms kept under control, but stopping the process once it is set in motion still requires great effort.

During the course of the illness, mental paths are activated that function as predetermined delusion routes, where thought gets directed and distorted. Even when there is visible progress, the therapist cannot delude himself that stable improvement has been achieved; if anything, in some cases, the perception of having made progress actually creates a state of triumph in the patient, pushing him towards grandiose and maniacal mental experiences. Generally speaking, it may be asserted that the delusion experience settles in the mind like a mark, ready to reactivate in circumstances that are difficult to foresee: it is like a hot ember under ash that never burns itself out.

Naturally, there are more benign forms, limited to a single episode without relapses, but psychosis is a danger to the mind as cancer is to the body. It would

78 *Part 2*

therefore be fruitful to work with patients, especially children and adolescents who are predisposed to the pathology, before the illness visibly manifests with a breakdown.

What gets lost in the psychotic condition, as mentioned earlier, is the difference between the psychotic parts and the non-psychotic parts: that is, between the healthy and the ill parts. Often the delusion and hallucinations are not considered by the patient as dangerous distortions to thought; what he believes is that he has acquired special qualities that place him above the rest of humanity.

This is how the *idealisation of madness* is brought about: the ill parts are perceived as good and healthy and providers of power. In the perversions, too, a similar phenomenon occurs, which is circumscribed, however: the perverse patient confines himself to glorifying perverse sexual pleasure and his superiority in relation to normal mankind.

Awareness of the illness, a diagnostic element in traditional psychiatry, is still a dividing line today between neurosis and psychosis for this reason.

When we have a psychotic patient under our care, before us is an individual who lives in a world of dissociated sensory perceptions that alter thought and prevent him from understanding psychic reality; we must intuit the innermost way he distorts thoughts and perceptions, altering his very instruments of knowledge in the process. If the patient's sessions are close together, we can monitor his progress and setbacks; whatever course the therapy takes, our participation, observation and reflections must be consistent. In particular, when we witness regression (an extremely frequent occurrence in the course of treatment), we must go back to understand why it has occurred.

The case of Philip Dick, the well-known American writer who fell victim to a psychotic episode late in life, shows us how the dissociation that regulates psychotic experience does not allow delusional reality to be easily integrated with psychic reality.

In this particular case, it is not easy to establish the extent to which his abuse of drugs, barbiturates and vitamins played a role in his psychosis.

Dick called psychosis *anamnesis* and spoke of it as a fact that could not be forgotten; in his subsequent literary work, he sought to understand and rationalise it, and in his writing, it is evident how his hallucinatory visions were indelibly fixed in his mind, going on to constitute a complex and protean mixture in which true and false, perceptions and hallucinations, continuously blend together.

Dick most likely pushed himself so far into unreality that there was no turning back.

Carrère (1993) provides this description of Philip Dick's psychotic episode: the writer, aching for days after having a tooth out, rang his doctor to have a painkiller prescribed, which was delivered to his home by a woman wearing a necklace with a gold fish-shaped pendant. Dick was mesmerised by the sight of the golden fish, which for him represented a way of being saved from oblivion and a means with which to activate intuition that would unveil reality. The girl was a secret Christian who had been sent to him to make this revelation, wearing the symbol that could uncover secrets. Like many characters in his novels,

Dreams and delusions in psychosis 79

who believe they live in one life and then discover they belong to another era or a different civilisation, Dick sensed that the shroud keeping human beings in slavery was being lifted.

At this point, he knew that he was in 70 AD and should not back away from the revelation of the truth; above all, there was no need for him to protect himself with reassuring explanations, telling himself that what was happening to him was a hallucination. He was a Christian, persecuted by pagans. During the nights that followed, he dreamt profusely and was certain that he had dreamt these dreams to make his delusion intuitions complete. Open books often appeared, perhaps written in foreign alphabets, the pages of which turned over so quickly that it was impossible to read them. Dick understood, however, that all the information in there was being hidden from him for security reasons.

Several days later, as soon as his wife went out, he approached his young son Christopher, who was looking for his bottle, poured chocolate milk in the shape of a cross on his forehead while reciting a religious passage in Greek and gave him the new Christian name Paul.

Several nights later, his wife woke up terrified because Dick had hurled to the floor the radio that he loved to keep on even at night: a song entitled 'You're No Good' had been playing, which he had understood as *You're no good; you're bad and must die*. The anxiety of being killed took control of him. The enemies of Christians, recruited by the Romans, wanted him dead; he, a secret Christian, had been found out and would have to die. Again at night, the radio broadcast in a deep voice insults and obscenities against him, interspersed with death threats.

In the morning, Dick believed that his enemies had put the radio programme on the air to drive him to suicide, but he had managed to thwart their plan. He thought that his brain, activated by the golden fish, had become like a radio receiver bombarded by contradictory information in a continuous flow of signals.

From that moment on, Dick produced various delusional fantasies, such as that of being a Christian in a cage at the Coliseum, with giant lizards trying to get him. At times, he would see writing engraved on a vase dating back to the eighth century BC and would agonise over the thought of not being able to reconcile this date and the historical period in which he was forced to live. Fantasy led Dick not only to produce delusions but to seek to explain them too. He would spend whole nights looking with fright at coloured marks on the wall that were dangerously spilling over, as if they were an infinite series of Kandinsky's or Picasso's paintings blending together. He would wonder whether the messages he was receiving came from inside him or from some outside agency. An excess of medication and vitamins might have brought about a change to his neuroreceptors, or perhaps he had become the subject of a telepathy experiment by the Soviets, given that these paintings were on display at the Hermitage in Leningrad.

One can see how the writer pushed his mind in two directions: the first by continually conceiving other worlds from which he drew inspiration for his novels and the second by reaching new levels through substance use. It is possible that the mind, when pushed 'beyond', produces phenomena that we call psychotic, but which others may call mystical.

80   *Part 2*

In order to understand what happened to his mind, Dick left us a series of notes that have been gathered together in an extremely interesting book, *The Exegesis of Philip Dick* (2011), published after his death. In his reflections, one can see that he was sometimes able to diagnose his own psychotic episode but would stick to his belief more often than not. Idealising his state of alienation, he wrote:

> In Feb. of 1974 I momentarily withdrew assent to the reality of this world; a month later this world underwent visible changes, and its true nature became perceptible to me: it is, as the Gnostics said, a prison. . . . What each of us must do is repudiate the world, which is to say, deny it "while at the same time" affirming a sanctified alternate reality, which I did vis-à-vis the golden fish sign.

(2011, p. 400)

Notes

1 This case of Dr Marina Medioli was also cited in my book *Working with Difficult Patients* (2012) to illustrate the transformation the analyst undergoes in transference. Here, other aspects are considered.
2 A mother convicted for infanticide.
3 As can be seen, the first episode is always ready to reappear.
4 This work was presented at the APAS Conference in Melbourne in October 2013.
5 I described this patient in my book *Vulnerability to Psychosis* (2006).
6 I discussed this material with Dr Rosana Russo.

7 Hallucinations[1]

A contribution similar to the one presented in this chapter is uncommon in psychoanalytic literature, given that the analyst is unlikely to find himself treating a hallucinating patient, something that is more likely to be observed by psychiatrists who regularly have patients with psychosis or anatomical brain lesions in their care. Although hallucinations may involve any of the senses (sight, hearing, touch, smell and taste), the most studied and commonly occurring are auditory. Of the patients who suffer from hallucinations (for example, epileptic, traumatised and Alzheimer's patients), I shall confine my discussion to psychotic patients whose hallucinations tend to be an expression of a delusional system.

Important in the study of hallucinations is the judgement of reality: How does the patient assign reality to stimuli that, beyond all reasonable doubt, originate in his mind?

Some points that help us understand this complex subject are provided by Mark Blechner (2005), who has asked himself how we know that something is real or imagined or dreamt. Blechner makes a reference to Kosslyn's (1994) work on the functioning of a subsystem that, in the awake state, polarises attention on the stimulus to be perceived and renders it as real. It is unclear whether this subsystem assigns this same quality to the dream and the imagination: it has been suggested that in dreams, since the dreamer knows that it is a dream, at least two subsystems that can set one against the other are needed.

Blechner reports the rare case of a patient undergoing psychoanalytic treatment who dreamt of his father, who had been dead for some time. The patient dreamt that his father was alive and continued to think of him as so even after he woke up. On previous occasions, he had imagined that his father was alive but knew that this was just a figment of his imagination. When he awoke from this dream, however, his conviction that his father was still alive remained. This might suggest that the patient had a hallucination in the dream that persisted even after he woke up.

Blechner sustains that intense emotions, mourning in particular, can bring about alterations to the attribution of reality as sometimes occurs to widows who hallucinate their dead partner. This would demonstrate that reality assignment is based not only on our perception of the external world, but also on the brain ascribing to it a particular emotional experience.

82   *Part 2*

An interesting neuroscientific experiment has demonstrated that the judgement of reality is deceiving, and its alteration depends on brain structures that can influence the mind (Schacter et al. 1996). An interviewer read aloud a list of words that corresponded to objects. After hearing the words, the subjects read another list in which some of the words in the previous list were included (and had therefore been previously heard), and others were the same as the objects in the previous list but named using a different word (for example, 'pudding' instead of 'cake'). The subjects were then asked whether a certain word was part of the first list or not. Sometimes the participants mixed up the names in the second list with those in the first, whereas at other times they remembered the names in the first list correctly.

Using neuroimaging techniques, the researchers observed that the hippocampus activated when the subject remembered correctly and incorrectly. The difference was that when recall was accurate, the auditory cortex, the seat of auditory memory, activated too (the first list was heard, the second seen); when instead recall was inaccurate, regardless of the participant's belief, the hippocampus activated but not the auditory cortex.

The researchers concluded that the activation of the hippocampus provides memory with the impression of reality, regardless of whether the event really happened. This explains why, in cases of false memories of abuse, the person can be convinced that the fact really happened, even though it never actually did (Pally 1997).

The psychoanalytic viewpoint

Freud examined the subject of hallucinations from many perspectives that, at times, were difficult to integrate. Initially (1894), he explained hallucinations through repression, regression and the return of the repressed: given that pieces of reality are connected to the incompatible representation, in order to distance itself, the Ego detaches itself from reality, similarly to throwing the baby out with the bathwater. When Freud (1910) described the case of President Schreber, he asserted that his hallucinations were the product of his unconscious conflict connected to repressed homosexual impulses. On the subject of regression, Freud (1915c) wrote that under normal circumstances, reality testing leads to forgoing hallucinatory wish fulfilment, whereas in psychosis, the older hallucinatory mode is reactivated.

Later Freud (1924b) formulated the interesting hypothesis that psychotic reality derives from feelings in one's own body: that is, the patient comes to consider proprioceptive perception as external. Entering psychosis occurs in two steps: first the Ego rejects reality, then it creates a new one via a delusion and hallucinations; this new creation is the Ego's compensation for the damage inflicted upon it, and anxiety is due not to the return of the repressed, as in neurosis, but to the re-emergence of the part of reality that was rejected.

Quite surprisingly, in his mature theorizing, Freud (1938a) returned to the subject of hallucinations, linking them to memory and asserting that non-psychotic

Hallucinations 83

hallucinations contain memories of remote events, something that the child heard or saw before he was able to speak:

> Perhaps it may be a general characteristic of hallucinations to which sufficient attention has not hitherto been paid that in them something that has been experienced in infancy and then forgotten returns – something that the child has seen or heard at a time when he could still hardly speak and that now forces its way into consciousness.
>
> (p. 550)

And psychotic hallucinations, placed within the delusion systems, likewise carry meaning of past memories that strive to emerge from nowhere, albeit in a deformed fashion.

I had always considered this statement by Freud as a purely theoretical hypothesis until I found Audrey's account in the book *Living with Voices* (2009), which I shall briefly summarise.

Audrey's illness began with hallucinations of crows inside her room, and then one day, they also appeared in the kitchen where she worked as a chef; she started throwing knives at them and needless to say got the sack. Her auditory hallucinations were heard as inner voices; some would criticise her thoughts while others would be supportive. Many years later, when she was in partial remission, Audrey managed to remember that the vision of crows was connected to sexual abuse she had suffered when she was very young under a tree full of crows. Clearly, this was a dissociated traumatic memory that reappeared initially as a hallucinatory perception.

The psychoanalytic contribution

According to Bion, hallucination is the result of a mental operation that destroys alpha elements (symbols), reducing them to fragments that can only be evacuated but not thought. This evacuation occurs through sense organs whose functioning is reversed so that undigested beta elements are expelled into the external world together with traces of the Ego and Super-ego, thus giving rise to *bizarre objects* (1958, 1965). *Transformation in hallucinosis* is, for Bion, an evacuative phenomenon too, but it involves less disintegration of the projected material, and consequently, what is expelled are sensory elements with shreds of meaning attached. Unlike hallucinations, transformations in hallucinosis do not involve the perception of non-existent objects in external reality but the perception of non-existent relations (Meltzer 1982a, 1982b). From this we may infer that for Bion some patients use omnipotence implicit in the hallucination as a way to gain independence from any object through the use of their own sense organs as evacuation tools in a world they themselves have created.

An original understanding of hallucinations comes from Lacan (1981), who stated that the structuring of psychosis is the outcome of an original lack of a signifier capable of polarising signifieds; the absence of this signifier is what causes

84　*Part 2*

the individual's bewilderment, depriving him of stable reference points. As we know, Lacan distinguished between three orders: the imaginary, the symbolic, and the real, which he saw as linked by the function of language. When *foreclosure* occurs, as in psychosis, language can no longer fulfil its linking function; confusion ensues between the real and the symbolic, which is clearly visible in hallucinations. For Lacan, the hallucination is the return of what was not processed at a symbolic level but foreclosed; that is, a real fragment is dissociated from consciousness. The content dissociated from the individual's personality thrusts its way in as if it were an experience coming from external reality, the unconscious word in the hallucination therefore appearing as pure Id (Miller 2000).

The authors mentioned next have studied the phenomenon of hallucination as a primitive form of perception: hence, their interest in sensory phenomena observed in autistic children.

Meltzer et al. (1975) and Meltzer (1983b) sustain that the autistic patient has a bidimensional mind in which the Ego perceives only the sensory nature of objects. It is a world that makes no room for introjection, where the perception of the object and the sensory quality of its surface are tightly bound and the Self is but a mere sensitive surface. The autistic child breaks the object down into single sensory components and is consequently unable to give meaning to stimuli from the outside world, experienced as bombarding the senses.

Frances Tustin (1986, 1991) described sensory phenomena, her so-called 'autistic shapes', which she regarded as the precursors to hallucinations (visual, auditory and so forth). In her view, such phenomena are present in both autistic children and autistic adults. Autistic objects are bizarre creations bearing coarse auto-sensuous properties, and they derive from self-induced body sensations that are stimulated by hard, solid objects such as toy cars or trains.

As can be seen, analytic literature on hallucinations provides differing hypotheses on their origin. These go from the primitive conflictual origin, which leads to denying reality via massive projection onto the outside world (Freud) to hallucinations as the result of a destructive attack on the sense organs (Bion); Lacan saw them as resulting from the dissociation of various mental functions by means of foreclosure and, for Tustin, they originate in a kind of excited, primitive, epidermal perception, similar to that in autistic disorders. They are sensory forms that are unconnected to thought and serve to distance the patient from the anxiety of the void and of non-existence.

A neuroscientific contribution

Advances in neuroimaging mean that brain structure and function can be studied *in vivo*, thereby paving the way towards new findings in the study of human psychopathology.

The most significant neuroscientific data on hallucinations can be found in 'The hallucinating brain: A review of structural and functional neuroimaging studies of hallucinations' (2008) by Paul Allen and colleagues, which gathers together the most important studies from 1990 to 2008. Researchers have observed that, in the absence of brain damage, activation occurs in the brain region that corresponds to the type of hallucination (that is, auditory, visual or tactile). For example, during psychotic episodes with auditory hallucinations, activation was found in Broca's area (McGuire et al. 2003), involved in speech function; the anterior cingulate gyrus, which plays a role in attentional processes and the temporal cortex, involved in auditory perception and memory; these same areas are inactive when the patient is no longer hallucinating. In addition, the sensory areas that produce hallucinations activate only when the neighbouring language areas activate.

There is therefore verbal preparation of what the patient will express sensorially during the hallucination (Hoffman et al. 2008). Relevant is the fact that even before the hallucination is produced, intense preparatory activity is going on, which is thought to demonstrate the individual's complete unawareness of his involvement in his disorder. There is a change to brain activity six to nine seconds before the onset of verbal hallucinations in the left inferior frontal cortex, the cingulate cortex and the right middle temporal gyrus. This is believed to demonstrate that the cortical regions mediating internal language prepare hallucinations and activate before those that give rise to hallucinatory perceptions. For several decades this was already known in psychiatry from recordings of neuromuscular activation of the vocal cords and pharyngeal muscles, which activate several seconds before the patient produces the auditory hallucination.

Another interesting finding (David et al. 1996) is that when the subject is hallucinating, the brain regions involved in the hallucinatory phenomenon are engaged and are impermeable to the reception of external stimuli that they normally respond to; external sensory perception and hallucination therefore compete with one another.

As for the complex problem of reality attribution – that is, how the patient assigns reality to stimuli that originate in his mind – neuroscientists believe hallucinations can change the sense of reality due to a complex imbalance between top-down and bottom-up circuits. Bottom-up processes concern sensory information and perceptions that move from the lower to the higher levels of the brain and are more complex than top-down processes, these latter being involved in control and monitoring that process from the higher levels down to the sensory brain regions.

Hallucinations can form due to a malfunction in the top-down system or to a bottom-up dysfunction; this latter is related to hyperactivation in areas of the secondary somatosensory cortex involved in experiencing vivid perceptions in the absence of sensory stimuli. These, together with a top-down impairment, can give rise to hallucinations and delusions. Cortical and subcortical centres that regulate emotions also activate during hallucinations, which would account for high emotional arousal in the hallucinatory phenomenon.

Interesting is Kenneth Hugdahl's (2009) work on this subject. Using neuroimaging data and a battery of tests, he found a difference between patients who hear inner voices and recognise them as such and those who attribute them to external sources and therefore hallucinate. For example, in subjects who recognise voices as being 'inner', the connection between the temporal lobe, where voices are generated, and the prefrontal cortex, implicated in higher cognitive

86 *Part 2*

functions, is retained, whereas in psychotic patients with auditory hallucinations, this connection is lost. In the former case, the prefrontal cortex monitors the sensory experience and rightly considers it as coming from inside, not outside. In psychotic hallucinations, therefore, the function of prefrontal cortical regions that assign meaning to our perceptions fail; specifically, these regions help distinguish between what is subjective (created by the imagination) and what appears real (because it comes from the outside) but is not. For the patient, the 'voices' are *real*, whereas for an external observer, they are not *true*.

The hypothesis that psychosis is a progressive and irreversible dissociated withdrawal from the world could perhaps find support from neuroscientific studies that can account for the neurobiological bases of this process, which involves a change to connections between perceptual brain regions and those of thought. In the course of the hallucinatory process, sensory perceptual brain regions become hyperactive, and higher functions, whose task it is to monitor the judgement of reality, are hypofunctional. Therefore, in order to produce hallucinations and dominate the rest of the personality, the psychotic process must inhibit higher functions and simultaneously activate sensory perceptual regions. As Kenneth Hugdahl and colleagues have shown, when the connection with prefrontal regions remains intact, voices are not projected externally but are perceived as internal.

I believe that there must be a similar disconnection during sleep, when the higher cortical functions, whose task is to assign meaning to the individual's experience, and the purely sensory ones that are monitored by the former, lose contact with one another. As a result of this connection being lost, the dream seems *real* to the dreamer, who, however, understands it as something *dreamt* upon awakening as the connection between the upper and lower functions is restored. In the psychotic hallucinatory process and in the delusion, given that the disconnection persists, the two perceptions – that of the dream and that of the awake state – cannot be compared, as would normally occur. From a *neurobiological* viewpoint, this is the *difference between a dream and a delusion*. It also explains why the dream can be interpreted and therefore transformed, but the delusion, encoded as a real fact, is stubbornly fixed.

The mind's eyes

Psychosis develops via a gradual process of regression in which the individual disinvests from relational psychic reality and withdraws into his own personal, bodily and sensory space. The contrast is not between external and internal reality but between *psychic reality and sensory reality*, the latter developing at the expense of the former in psychosis. This leads one to think that, in order to create the psychotic process, mental functioning must be restricted, the more evolved functions being locked out so that they can no longer give real meaning to the surrounding world and our psychic experience.

In order to do this, the patient must disconnect himself from cognitive brain functions that discriminate between what is created internally and what exists outside him. This process, to a limited extent, could be at the base of autosuggestion, ranging from milder to almost hallucinatory forms. During the psychotic episode, the patient lives in a dimension within his body that hostilely separates him from the rest of the world.

The patient 'feels' thoughts but cannot think them. When the higher functions, located in the prefrontal lobes, are inhibited, attention towards the outer and relational world narrows, shrinking the individual's mental space. An important phenomenon is that during hallucination, sensory areas involved in this process are always engaged, meaning that messages from the outside world cannot be received.

The appearance of hallucinations bears witness to a psychic withdrawal that has developed to the extreme, where preformed inner reality gets exteriorised with all its contents of anxiety and violence. The reality of the delusional experience is so because the patient uses his mind's 'eyes and ears'; in other words, his mind internally builds an image, which it then 'sees' externally. Since hallucinations have a 'sensory' and concrete quality, they can easily deceive the patient as they are similar to perceptions that, under normal conditions, describe the surrounding world. Put differently, visual hallucinations arise from seeing with the mind's 'eyes' and auditory hallucinations from hearing with the mind's 'ears'.

This is the case of one of my patients who felt persecuted by a group of enemies plotting to kill him. For a long time, his sessions were filled with anxiety-laden descriptions in minute detail of all this criminal organisation's diabolic actions; the patient was convinced that his enemies had installed microphones and surveillance cameras in his home to monitor his every move. Since he insistently spoke of this hard fact, I asked him to bring one of the video cameras to the session so that we could look at it together, but he said that this was impossible as the video cameras were so tiny that they were virtually invisible. When I asked how he was able to see them, he told me that he saw them *with his mind's eyes*.

In the hallucinatory state, spatio-temporal organisation and self/outer-world differentiation are obliterated; fantasy loses its 'as-if' quality of the imagination and becomes concrete thought. Psychotic hallucinations are of a specific nature, differing from all other mental states: they take shape in close connection with the delusion, which usually occurs first, and once they appear, the psychotic process goes from an *ideative* delusional level to one that is more specifically *sensory*. The hallucinatory symptom originates in such clear and indisputable sensory perceptions that any recourse to normal experiences that confirm reality would be in vain. In other words, hallucinations are 'prepared' by the psychotic part that seduces and intimidates the patient.

Perceval (Bateson 1961), an author/patient who wrote an account of his illness after his recovery, illustrated with particular clarity his gradual departure from the hallucinatory world. Perceval remembered that towards the end of his confinement in an asylum, as he began to recover from his psychosis, he managed to distance himself from the 'voices' that for many years had dominated and tormented him. Often these 'voices' originated in his body: in his wheezy breathing, for instance. One day, while listening to a voice that was speaking to him, he realised that it vanished if he focused his mind on something external to him; if

88 Part 2

instead he recreated the same absence of mind, he went back to hearing the voice. He realised too that his breathing was clad in hallucinated words and sentences, especially when he was agitated. These accurate observations led him to conclude that the voices originated in his head, even though they seemed to come from above, from the air or from the ceiling cornice. Perceval came to understand that hallucinating and directing attention towards the outer world were antagonistic: if the former prevailed, the latter vanished; acknowledging the existence of the outer world deprives the hallucinatory fantasy of its power. Therefore, in order to create the hallucinatory state, it would seem that a mental state of submissiveness is needed.

My clinical hypothesis is that hallucinatory phenomena are the result of a distorted use of the mind practised over a long period by the psychotic *outside his awareness*: instead of being a tool for relating with others – that is, an organ of *knowledge* – the mind is employed to create a sensory world dominated by a special, regressive type of pleasure. And this is how the primitive infantile withdrawal into the world of sensory fantasies is created. Naturally, this is not the only process through which the illness is produced, but I believe it is a principal one.

Usually the psychotic hallucinatory experience is positive and seducing in the beginning, with gentle, charming voices, but it then changes, with critical, contemptuous and terrifying voices coming onto the scene, and the state of grandiosity gradually turns into a condition of persecution.

One of my psychotic patients said that before his breakdown and consequent hospitalisation, he, unlike his friends, had been able to get high endogenously without taking drugs. Later, however, this 'pleasant alienating' operation turned into a terrifying world for him. What occurs during the psychotic process is that the newly created sensory reality begins to run out of control at a certain point, dominating and invading the healthy part of the personality; auditory or visual hallucinations become malevolent, and delusions of grandeur turn into persecutory states.

We have seen how neuroscientists using neuroimaging techniques have been able to document what happens at a neurophysiological (brain) level when the psychotic process advances in the psyche (mind). The psychosis conquers the mind because it disables discriminatory functions of thought, located mainly in the prefrontal regions, paralysing them in the process. A psychotic sensory withdrawal – that is, a tool capable of cancelling reality – results. The patient can stay in the sensory withdrawal only if he inhibits the brain centres that assign reality and receive emotional input from the environment; thought functions are replaced by sensory perceptions so that the world perceived by the patient is kept within sensory channels whose expansion gives the appearance of the entire world, separateness between inner and outer being lost in the process. Said differently, sensory stimuli do not reach the cognitive centres where they could be analysed and filtered but are 'held' in sensory areas, where they dilate and are employed autistically.

That hallucinations and delusions in the psychotic patient result from using the mind as a sensory organ is indirectly demonstrated by the positive effect of psychotropic drugs, which reduce or stop the sensory production of the psychotic mind: hence, their necessity when treating psychotic symptoms.

Thanks to research findings in the field of neuroscience, we now know that mental transformations in psychosis are reflected in changes to the neurobiological substrate. This terrain shows a body-mind encounter in the form of one single interface. I am of the idea that, as opposed to speaking of a biological base, it might be more fitting to conceive mental illness as being biologically mediated.

From my perspective, psychosis may be considered a bio-psychological transformation, a *psychosomatic illness* in which the 'mind' is able to bring about transformations to its biological substrate, the brain. In this regard, neuroscientific findings concerning changes to sensory brain structures and connections between various regions, when stimulated or when active during a hallucination, represent important acquisitions that help us to establish a link between clinical symptomatology, subjective experience and the neurobiological substrate.

The psychotic illness is the result of a transformational process that involves the whole personality: human relations and awareness of the self, body and mind are annihilated. Once set in motion, the transformation is difficult to stop because it presents itself to the patient as a stimulating enhancement of perceptions and self-awareness.

In this connection, Bion (1967) wrote:

> The patient feels imprisoned in the state of mind he has achieved, and unable to escape from it because he feels he lacks the apparatus of awareness of reality which is both the key to escape and the freedom itself to which he would escape.
>
> (p. 39)

This means that when the psychotic patient becomes prisoner of his hallucinatory and delusional experiences, he no longer has at his service the apparatus for consciousness of reality that could help him rebuild his real identity.

Note

1 This chapter draws on subjects of a paper I published with Davalli, Giustino and Pergami in the *International Journal of Psychoanalysis*, 96(2): 293–318 (2015). The text here has been summarised and changed somewhat.

8 Trauma and the Super-ego in psychosis

Trauma

The relationship between trauma and psychosis is complex and controversial and understood from numerous perspectives. One perspective considers the beginning of the psychotic process to be a consequence of repeated infantile traumas, often accompanied by abandonment and neglect. In addition to the violent traumas, all problematic factors in the child's earliest dependence relationships during emotional growth play a part.

On this subject, Paul Williams (2004) has described the experience of *being invaded* by external forces that some severely disturbed patients speak of in analysis, and he has hypothesised that this feeling stems from an early containment failure of their projections, as well as from the forcible introjection of disturbing aspects of the person who is supposed to take care of them. Incorporating the *invasive object* hampers the development of self-regulation and pushes the child to expel into others his own mental states that are unbearable to him; the use of violent projection in the individual's mental functioning thus gets its start, preventing normal identification and the construction of a cohesive sense of self.

A similar concept was expressed by Piera Aulagnier (1975), who connected the origin of the psychotic illness to *maternal violence*, that kind of violence which the mother normally uses on the child to structure his sense of reality. In the case of the psychotic patient, excessive violence acts in the same way as an intrusive object that establishes itself in the child's mind, and in a bid to escape the chaos, he tries to violently construct a representation of the Self outside the relationship with the mother. This violence employed by one mind on another is relived within the psychotic process: the patient feels forced to believe in the delusions, and the analyst feels invaded by a distorted and alien way of thinking.

Considerations by Piera Aulagnier and Paul Williams have in common the numerous observations of the ways in which parents manipulate their children outside awareness, using them as parts of the self and in so doing violating the psyche. Parents' intentionality, be it conscious or unconscious, which often does not correspond to open violence, influences the child's growth and potential development. What can psychopathologically condition the infantile mind is the *emotional trauma* that stems from the pathogenic relation between parent and

Trauma and the Super-ego in psychosis   91

child as it favours the formation of psychopathological objects and structures that will continue to function as parts of the future patient's Self.

Violent traumas suffered at a young age need to be considered separately. A large body of data exists on this subject, which confirms the relationship between early trauma and psychosis (Read and Ross 2003; Read et al. 2005; Schäfer and Fisher 2011). The literature documents a high rate of trauma, including physical and sexual abuse, in individuals destined to become psychotic in their lifetime. Read et al., on the basis of the 180 cases studied, believe that many symptoms of psychosis, hallucinations in particular, could be connected to abuse and abandonment. Severe infantile traumas are at any rate an important risk factor for any type of adult pathology.

Extremely interesting accounts from this viewpoint are in the aforementioned *Living with Voices* (Romme et al. 2009), which contains approximately fifty cases of patients with hallucinations. Not only do the patients described present with hallucinatory symptomatology, but some are affected by the psychotic process proper, which not infrequently leads to their being hospitalised. The authors, whose intention was not that of providing therapy, saw these patients in group sessions to help them reflect on the nature of their hallucinations; the aim was to take the edge off their condition through sharing with others who suffer from the same disorder. According to the authors, this experience was helpful as many patients from the group came out of their distressful isolation, where they had chosen to stay in order to conceal their symptoms for fear of being hospitalised against their will. The 'voices' they heard were described as commentary on thoughts or actions and had in common that they were initially friendly and comforting, but then turned aggressive if not downright diabolical.

Of the fifty or so cases considered, eighteen had suffered sexual abuse, eleven emotional negligence (three also with sexual abuse) and six adolescence problems. Two were victims of bullying, two others suffered physical violence and sexual abuse and seven were without a clear cause. Naturally, these figures are insufficient to establish causal connections, but they are useful to hypothesise that many people who have suffered severe infantile traumas are more vulnerable to psychosis.

A very interesting case is described in the book (mentioned in Chapter 7), which presents hallucinations with crows. It is the case of the patient who had heard voices since she was a child; this was totally normal for her, given her conviction that she had an implant in her head which produced hallucinations: that is, until she was hospitalised at the age of twenty-four. After many life events, hospital admissions, psychotropic drugs and episodes of depression, she was able to establish that the voices that spoke to her were seven in number. One of these was the voice of the boy who had abused her when she was eight, which she had begun to hear when she was thirteen; it was a vulgar and aggressive voice. She had not spoken to anyone about her abuse, and when she began to hallucinate, she forgot all about it. Among the other voices was one, for example, that she named with her hypocorism and whose job it was to comfort her. After joining the group, the patient felt less terrified and began to accept the voices; then, thinking back

92   *Part 2*

to the hallucinations about crows, she remembered the sexual abuse, which had happened in a wood under a tree in which there were dozens of crows. The abuse had been forgotten, but the hallucinations about crows had contributed to making it re-emerge, like pieces of a jigsaw puzzle that all fit together.

In some cases of sexual abuse, the hallucinatory manifestation is directly linked to the perpetrator. I have supervised two cases of adolescent girls who had been abused and had interiorised the perpetrator as a voice that intimidated and dominated them, creating uncertainty and making them doubt their own free will.

A trauma that occurs in early infancy interferes with those functions outside awareness that allow mental and emotional life to be represented, and it prevents the development of a mental structure capable of understanding psychic reality. When the infantile trauma is severe, it is clear that emotional functions involved in personality integration will be weakened: the stress, anxiety and loss of faith in others and in oneself generate an oppressing sense of non-existence. In these cases, hallucinations present themselves as seducing or intimidating voices; many hallucinations are organised around a powerful psychotic Super-ego that instils terror and humiliation. In infantile trauma, we may say that the voices issuing orders and making scornful remarks are like parental blame that gets registered in procedural memory and remains dissociated from the whole personality.

Psychosis as a trauma

A second point in the relationship between trauma and psychosis is that of considering the psychotic breakdown as a real trauma for the psyche: the traumatic event of the psychotic episode produces nameless dread and annihilation anxiety that upset the mind, biologically even more so than psychologically. Van der Kolk (2014) has described the case of Marsha, a participant in a group study on the long-term effects of mental trauma. Marsha involuntarily caused the death of her young daughter in a car accident due to her absent-mindedness. Using neuroimaging, the researchers were interested in changes to her brain activity while she listened to an assistant read an account of the accident, which had occurred thirteen years earlier. At the end of the test, once out of the scanner, Marsha was worn out and frozen, with dyspnoea and eyes wide open, the epitome of vulnerability. The scan had recorded activation in the emotional brain (the limbic system, especially the amygdala). These data confirm that when the individual is exposed to images, sounds or thoughts connected to the traumatic experience, the amygdala activates a state of alarm, as occurs in panic attacks (intensified blood pressure, heartbeat and breathing), many years after the event. This case studied by Van der Kolk confirms my belief that the psychotic episode is like a trauma for the mind, similar to that of violent traumas, and as such it is dissociated and stored in the psyche, ready to re-emerge and reoccur.

In her book *The Centre Cannot Hold: My Journey Through Madness* (2007), Elyn Saks describes her psychotic illness in detail, and for her, a psychotic break is like being in a war zone or being involved in a dreadful car accident. In fact, when psychosis is produced, it generates *nameless dread*, and the traumatic effect continues even when the psychotic episode has been overcome. The split-off delusion nucleus, which cannot be *forgotten* or transformed, always remains active and threatening. This is why the psychotic patient finds the breakdown difficult to remember; just the memory of it triggers unbearable anxiety, as in the case of severe trauma victims.

The psychotic Super-ego

The Super-ego was defined by Freud as heir to the Oedipus complex, an introjection of paternal authority and prohibitions, but also as a destructive entity whose origins lie in sinister forces.

Overcoming infantile omnipotence and gradually accepting the paternal figure's regulatory and protective function result in a normal or oedipal Super-ego. A melancholic Super-ego, whose origins are rooted in a traumatic relationship with the mother, is instead destined to become a strict internal object that the Self and the object are criticised and attacked by. It was Abraham (1924) who stated that a melancholic Super-ego, fraught with hatred towards the Self and the disappointing object, forms when early trauma encounters the primitiveness of objects.

When Melanie Klein equated pathology and primitive mental states, she connected the ruthlessness of the Super-ego with the degree of aggressiveness in the primitive Ego, claiming that the struggle against the Super-ego, or first bad object, happened very early on: afraid of punishment and reprisals, the infant fears and hates the mother, who is experienced as an extremely severe Super-ego. Only a stable introjection of a good object can tame the Super-ego's implacability and harshness. Once, and only once, the persecutory primitive Super-ego has been worked through and transformed can the child reach the oedipal experience; this failing, the peculiar paternal regulatory function of the oedipal Super-ego described by Freud cannot be interiorised.

If we are to understand the nature of the Super-ego in psychosis, we must first set down what differentiates it from that in other forms of illness. Contradictory and befuddling in nature, the psychotic Super-ego totally dominates the mind, advancing as seducing and then threatening. When this is taken into account, it is no longer feasible to consider the psychotic Super-ego as a primitive agency of the mind, but a pathological structure with no link whatsoever to the primitive Super-ego, despite it bearing some resemblance to it.

Whilst the primitive Super-ego observes the law of an eye for an eye, a tooth for a tooth – that is, punishment for the sin committed – the psychotic Super-ego is perverse and deadly: what dominates the rest of the personality is not so much primitive ruthlessness but intimidatory propaganda that comes over as moral truth and justice. What this Super-ego is engaged in is distorting mental growth: manifesting as an internal voice that intimidates the individual, it stunts his sense of freedom and his curiosity to learn from experience.

Therefore, *in place of the normal Super-ego*, a similar structure develops, one that cannot evolve into more highly developed forms but which corresponds to a psychopathological construction similar to destructive narcissism (Rosenfeld

94   *Part 2*

1971). The normal Super-ego, the primitive Super-ego, and the psychopatho-logical structure may frequently be encountered in the course of the psychotic patient's analysis, all operating simultaneously in different areas and at different levels. Whereas the primitive Super-ego can be gradually transformed through the analyst's work of containment and interpretation, the pathological organisa-tion is resistant to transformation: on a par with the delusion formation, of which it comes to be a part, it needs *deconstructing* so that its power over the rest of the personality may be weakened. Not to be overlooked is that during the psychotic process, the Super-ego is often party to hallucinatory and delusion phenomena, wielding its power via intimidatory accusations and orders.

Befuddlement marks the superegoical psychopathological organisation of the psychotic. As mentioned earlier, an exciting and thrilling Super-ego frequently manifests during the first stage, and it convinces the patient that he has reached a superior, omniscient and pleasurable mental state. Here, the Super-ego acts as a force that can change the mental state for the better, providing it with a feeling of excitement and well-being. Under the influence of this propaganda, the patient convinces himself that he is equipped with special powers sustained by divine guidance, divinity often being a theme in delusion constructions.

A second stage sees a transformation in the opposite direction: the patient is convinced by one or more voices that his state of well-being, superiority and omniscience is not a divine gift after all, but a destructive, diabolical disposition; at a certain point, he convinces himself that he is like Lucifer, who challenges God in order to seize his powers (see Chapter 6) and that having now become dia-bolical, he rightly deserves punishment. This transition from superiority/goodness to negativity/destructiveness is an extremely frequent occurrence: the delusional accusation of being diabolical becomes unbearable, and feeling destructive, the patient thinks he can annihilate the world, including the people he is connected with, to the point of being killed himself or driven to suicide.

The Super-ego's befuddling action is clear also in the hallucinatory state. Typi-cally, hallucinations are initially positive, pleasant and seductive; only afterwards do they become negative and aggressive, constantly plaguing the patient with accusations and intimidatory comments. At times, the friendly voices switch all of a sudden to aggressive voices, like psychic splinters gone mad, all jumbled together; each piece belongs to a part of the patient's now dissociated and frag-mented personality. The voices come forward as separate entities that converse but that also fight or get into arguments with one another. Dialogue of this kind increasingly leads to confusion and to the healthy part being held captive within the psychotic structure.

On occasion, the psychotic Super-ego's accusations convey truths, however distorted they may be. The voice that accuses the patient of being diabolical casts light destructively on one truth: the patient, believing that he is God, has actu-ally managed to subvert the order of the mind and destroy the rules of thought. Accusing, scornful hallucinations stem from the same Super-ego that prompted the megalomania; the patient therefore finds himself bombarded by disparaging invectives: the *voice* accuses him of being a failure or a homosexual or a loser, and these hallucinatory accusations are projected onto the world around him. In thrall to the psychotic Super-ego, the patient sees normal human weaknesses as proof of cowardliness or unworthiness. Dominated by a mad unopposable voice, he projects hallucinations onto everyone, including those who accidentally enter his life.

Worth noting is that several past scholars postulated a kinship between schizophrenic psychosis and manic-depressive psychosis, sustaining that they were possibly one and the same illness. Although never confirmed, it can be seen that the psychotic Super-ego most certainly often assumes manic-depressive features, going from maniacal exaltation to melancholic destructiveness.

Part 3

9 A psychoanalytic therapy

I thought at length about whether to present here various other clinical cases or give a detailed account of this one single case, a patient I had in my care for a long time and who, despite an obstinate and dangerous attachment to psychosis, made good progress. In the end, I opted for the latter, as it seemed more suited to conveying progress and regression in long-term psychoanalytic therapy and to showing how important it is not to become discouraged by the many difficult moments. I hope that my account of this analysis allows the clinical material to be connected with the concepts I have sought to discuss in the previous two parts of the book.

Beginning of treatment

When Francesco came to me, he was about thirty years old. He had been abroad doing an in-company master's programme and while there, had a psychotic breakdown and was hospitalised; once back in Italy, he was under the care of a psychiatrist and took a medium dose of psychotropic drugs for several years from then on. Even before going abroad, where the psychosis exploded, there had been worrying signs. Francesco had gone to the south of Italy for a short holiday, and in the resort he had been staying at, he was afraid of being kidnapped by the local mafia: he had seen clear signs of danger and was sure that a helicopter hovering above was there to kidnap him. His stay became unbearable, so he rang his parents and went back home. This instance was not a cause for worry for Francesco or his family. No one had felt the need to consult a specialist, and so Francesco went abroad to do the master's programme, but even there he thought he was being followed and monitored by individuals who looked like Italian southerners belonging to the mafia.

I must state here that the very last part of Francesco's undergraduate studies in Italy had been difficult for him: throughout university, he had been euphoric, was a success with his peers and, having joined a student drama group, was convinced he would become a successful actor. But then, when he finished his studies, he took a downturn, lost his enthusiasm and found himself all alone. He fell into depression for a while; a friend he had had an important bond with started to keep his distance, and Francesco began to worry that he would not find work while he watched his university friends manage to do so. This period of uncertainty saw the euphoria he had felt at university deflate.

100   *Part 3*

Then he received a call from a big multinational company, and he left for Germany, where he began an in-company master's programme. At this time, he was convinced that a brilliant career lay ahead of him: the breakthroughs he was to make would make him a saviour of mankind in others' eyes. To prove to himself how great he actually was, he felt he needed to win girls over; on one occasion, a girl, perhaps irritated by his insistence, left a small party he had organised and went away with an Arab peer. The following day, Francesco went to express his objections to this person who had 'stolen' his girlfriend. In order to seem more threatening, he took an Italian from Sicily along with him to make the Arab believe he was backed by the mafia.

Sometime later, once he realised that the Arab was no longer at the college, Francesco thought that this person had fled because of the threats, but he also remembered that when he had confronted him, the Arab had not even batted an eyelid and said that the matter concerned the girl and Francesco, and that, if he wanted to try to go out with her, he could do so no problem. This chap's apparent indifference really seemed threatening to Francesco: during this period of calm, who knows what he was plotting to do?

The delusion proper exploded several weeks later when Francesco, while at a conference in another city, realised that three Arabs were there. Immediately, a conspiracy came to mind: the three Arabs were there to kill him and avenge their fellow countryman. A persecutory delusion proper manifested at this point, with death anxiety to the extent that the organisers of the master's programme were so concerned that they had Francesco hospitalised. From that moment on, the delusion flourished and invaded every minute of his days. Once back in Italy after this short stay in hospital in Germany, Francesco kept on seeing enemies everywhere; he was sent to a psychiatrist who suggested analytic therapy, and, given that his mother had undergone analysis, this was willingly accepted.

When he came to me, I immediately had the impression that he was in an advanced psychotic state and thought I could not begin an analytic therapy there and then because of his mental condition (he was plainly delusional and hallucinated) and because of the great effort it took him to come to my office. I therefore decided to see him once a week to try to understand what could develop between the two of us and how in that case I could help him.

During his first sessions, Francesco, deeply distressed, gave me an alarming and fragmentary account of his persecutory perceptions. Although I was only trying to listen to him without interfering with what he was saying, I found it extremely difficult to follow his speech but understood that the persecution was expanding right there and then: his enemies were everywhere and were conspiring to make an attempt on his life using every diabolic trick in the book.

For example, he could not go to the coffee bar because he was sure that the waiter would lace his drink with poison; he suspected everything and everyone. The doorman's wife, bribed by his enemies, could have allowed them to poison the drinking water at his home; mysterious figures would constantly appear in the street to spy on him. He was suspicious of me, too: he would not tell me where he spent his weekends and kept secret the location of the country house his father

A psychoanalytic therapy   101

invited him to. Implicit was that I could have given the address to his enemies. I would listen to him carefully, knowing that if I doubted the reality of his delusional experience, I would jeopardise my neutral position, and Francesco would certainly think that I was denying the danger to make his persecutors' task easier.

I continued to see him once a week; I was interested in how the psychotic breakdown had arisen and in reconstructing it chronologically. In addition to telling me about the delusion, Francesco also told me, albeit quite patchily, about his life – some episodes from his childhood and youth, for instance. I came to learn that before the persecutory delusion that had led to his undergoing therapy, there had been two other alarming episodes. The first was when he had tried to sell his car: the potential buyer, a southerner, seemed strange to him, making offers that did not seem so transparent, and Francesco immediately thought that he was from the Camorra; he was so frightened that he asked his father to see to the sale of the car.

The second, which was more serious, happened, as I have mentioned, in the south of Italy when he had decided to spend a week's holiday there before leaving to do the master's programme. As soon as he disembarked from the plane, he saw a chain in the boot of the car belonging to the driver who had come to pick him up at the airport. What was the chain for, if not to immobilise him in order to kidnap him? Suddenly, in his mind, the driver had become a delinquent, and Francesco felt so small, helpless and shaky in his presence. In the resort where he was staying, strange, threatening individuals who frightened him roamed around. His holiday had become so difficult that he hardly ever left his room, and when he risked doing so, he interpreted the staff's kind exchanges as dangerous invitations that he absolutely had to decline. His persecutory terror reached its peak when he saw a helicopter fly over the resort: he immediately thought it was a means of transport sent by the local mafia to kidnap him. It was in fact merely a spectacular means of transport used for a wedding taking place in a nearby town. Terror stricken, Francesco rang his family, described what had happened and was persuaded by them to return home. For many more months to come, even when he was abroad, just the sight of any individual with dark skin and a moustache struck fear into him: he was sure that mafia spies were following him because he had uncovered their secrets, and they therefore had to do away with him.

All these facts were of course narrated in fragments during the first months of therapy, which were filled with his distressing accounts of delusion threats that were clearly everywhere all day long. He circumspectly looked at each and every object around him to identify what hidden danger to his life lay in it. While at his part-time job, he would spend much time trying to understand whether a colleague with a black moustache and piercing look was part of the 'gang'; he believed that his persecutors had trespassed his property to leave poison there, or, rather, he was quite sure about it as he had found traces of the powder. The patient no longer lived in reality but was projected onto something that he himself had built outside awareness and which seemed to bear a quality of indisputable reality; it was as if he had projected himself into a film plot where he was the main character, and things could happen such as an ordinary sandwich in a café being wrapped in a toxic paper napkin, put there to poison him.

102   *Part 3*

I then began to see the patient twice a week at his request but still face-to-face. Approximately six months after beginning therapy, during the summer holidays, he took the initiative to go to a tourist resort again, and there his delusion grew out of all proportion. It was clear that Francesco had denied the precariousness of his condition, feeling that he was better and certain that he had overcome the psychotic episode.

I willingly agreed to his request for two sessions per week. I thought that his coming to sessions would allow him to deposit in me the anxiety that constantly tormented him, which was a good thing: Who else could he have spoken to about it in order to have some respite, albeit temporary? And in addition to any apparent improvement, it was useful for me too in order to understand his delusional system: that is, how it formed and persisted. Several months later, Francesco asked if he could come three times a week, and at this point I suggested lying on the couch, which he did without any difficulty; subsequently, we increased the number of sessions to four per week.

During this period, I continued to listen to him carefully; I only gave some meaning to his experiences, to his feeling of terror and above all to the megalomaniacal, omnipotent and murderous character that his persecutors had. Fear was always present: in one session, he told me that he had had a good English lesson, which had cheered him up, but then a friend had told him that there was a website on the internet where you could see bodies being butchered. The peaceful English lesson was replaced by a secret place full of hatred and mortal danger, and the terrorising and persecutory world was once more set in motion, making him feel in danger. He told me that ever since he was a child, he had been tormented by macabre visions; he remembers he dreamt that he had tried to put back together again a young cousin of his who had been dismembered and chopped up.

After the summer relapse of the first year in analysis, during which he had gone back to being delusional, Francesco would not distance himself from Milan: far away from his home and his analysis, he feared being easy prey to persecutory anxiety when faced with the unfamiliar and the unknown.

Revelations

At times, I was able to describe to Francesco how his persecutory visions consisted of actual *revelations* of hidden truths. I had realised that Francesco did not use thought but functioned by means of constant, sudden revelations. Things and people around him were not free of preconceived ideas but placed on a set path. Francesco realised that first came his idea of a conspiracy, and then all his perceptions were organised around this original idea: the *revelation* shaped everything and acted to manipulate his thought that became an anti-thought, a place already saturated with content that expected facts to adapt to his revelation and not vice versa. The delusion perception presented itself as if it were reality, an unquestionable truth that asserted itself through absolute perceptions.

During this same period, when I could, I would underline his transformation of the persecutors into inhuman beings with unimaginable cruelty, a kind of absolute wickedness. It was like an endless struggle between good and bad for Francesco, in which he believed he represented being good, honest and not at all aggressive, whereas others – the persecutors – were greedy, domineering and vindictive. It was significant that his persecutory delusion had been preceded by self-idealisation: in his exaltation during his master's programme, he had convinced himself that he would have become like Gandhi and eradicated world poverty and inequality.

Francesco's delusion about the *Mafiosi* traces the life of the main character in the novel *Dream Story* by Schnitzler, in which fluctuation between reality and delusional fantasy is described:[1] the main character feels persecuted because he goes to a party, discovers that it is an orgy that must be kept secret and fears having seen things he should not have. Francesco, too, had come into contact with a mafia organisation and had 'seen' things he should not have. The content of the persecutory delusion had then expanded to include the whole Arab world. From that time on, a narcissistic entity aimed at killing whoever dared challenge it settled in his mind; this grandiose entity, hating whoever threatened its power, was similar to that which could be harboured in an omnipotent child's mind.

It could stand to reason that the persecutor corresponded to a split-off and projected narcissistic part, which Francesco knew existed, given that he had felt omnipotent in the first stage of the delusional expansion. This kind of interpretation, advanced several times, was, however, unable to halt his tendency to continuously build delusional content.

During sessions, Francesco did not even trust me; on one occasion, I was included in his delusion. It was when, once our session was over, I left the office quickly, and, sitting in a nearby bar, he noted that I was in a hurry. The next day, very hesitantly and visibly distressed, he told me that he had seen me walking quickly and thought that I was going to report him to his persecutors, who were waiting for me in a small nearby shop. Aware of the danger that the analysis might be in, I tried to help him transform the delusion transference, and luckily, I was able to. This circumstance confirmed that the organisation of delusional thought was like a vortex that, with all its swirling might, swallowed up and destroyed everything that came into its orbit. The death threat was omnipresent.

I began to note that the invasion of the delusion happened verbally: words, verbal assonance and contiguity links took the place of things and created connections that endlessly dilated his delusional vision. For example, the father of one of his female friends, who had been to the German city where Francesco had attended his master's programme and an engineer who worked in the oil industry (Saudi Arabia being a major producer) immediately became potential assassins and were therefore feared and avoided. Identifying his friend's father with the persecutors occurred via a geographical coincidence and that of the engineer via verbal association (Saudi Arabia-oil). The persecutory black hole attracted and contaminated people and places, who became bearers of terror merely through proximity and verbal assonance.

My speech, too, when not carefully calibrated, met the same fate. One day I said to him that he was like a character doomed to the death penalty, and I quoted a film in which the main character was on death row in the United States, waiting

104   *Part 3*

to be executed. He replied that the company that had called him to do the master's programme, which became included in the persecution when he was hospitalised, had its headquarters in the same region as the prison in that film, which meant that I too was in contact with this company. Naturally, I took advantage of this opportunity to describe his way of connecting facts and news to linguistic links that provided his delusional imagination with a quality of reality: words in place of things.

Another example was an episode in which a girl he had gone out with spoke to him about a friend of hers who lived in Strasbourg, and Francesco then felt that she too was part of the conspiracy, given that the Arab had told him that he had been invited to a party in Strasbourg. Francesco's thinking functioned by creating contiguous associative links, as in phobic constructions in which the terrifying object contaminates other contiguous objects.

In that period, sessions were full of distressing references to everything that happened to him throughout the day and to how diabolic his enemies were in their constant efforts to devise means of striking him: messages on the internet, waves coming from his computer and conspiratorial dialogues all intertwined in his mind.

The delusion would enlarge every time Francesco undertook a new initiative. He decided to enrol on a postgraduate course, but this decision then began to frighten him: it was as if he felt projected right into the middle of a dangerous conspiracy. The first time he ate in the college canteen, he was in fear of being poisoned; he had to check the pile of paper napkins the waiter was using because he was sure that those destined for him had been poisoned. He then decided to take food with him from home but thought that this would have exposed him even more to his persecutors. I too – his analyst – was capable of reporting this to his enemies. Conversations his fellow students would have seemed full of intentions to kill him. Extremely discouraged and frightened, Francesco decided to drop out. This distressing atmosphere of persecution was attenuated when, back home again, he met people who were his friends; he saw a cousin of his who had come back from abroad, and he was once more able to find a safe haven.

In Francesco's opinion, the Arab had shown that he was selfish and wicked by wanting to take the girl away from him. Francesco really believed that this person had dropped out of the course because of his alleged threat and also because of the Sicilian's presence; the Arab was the son of a very wealthy family that had made its fortune in oil, and, since he was unable to bear defeat and had enormous wealth, he had taken bitter revenge. Francesco was really the one who had been unable to tolerate the stinging disappointment at failing to win the girl over; he was so confused by his endless fantasies and the delusion construction that he was unable to understand who had offended whom.

Grandiosity

It became increasingly clearer that the delusion explosion had been prepared by the grandiose mental state which had driven Francesco to clash with megalomania. Aspirations of a brilliant career had led him to cut ties with the meaningful people in his affective life: he had left his home and friends without feeling much regret.

A psychoanalytic therapy   105

Frustration at not winning the girl over was unbearable as it had occurred at the height of the megalomaniac expansion, and having transformed the rivalry into a clash with omnipotent, vindictive enemies, he had become an angry victim. We may say that his grandiosity was projected onto the rival who, furious about the narcissistic wound caused, was ready to draw on enormous wealth to seek his revenge.

As you may remember, the euphoric excitement at doing the master's programme came after Francesco's downturn, when he had not found work and his feeling of being successful was waning fast. Francesco mixed up being great with being grandiose: being great for him meant being superior, as opposed to being able to tolerate frustration and life experience. Francesco remembered that once when he was little, and faced with frustration while at the beach, perhaps due to being told off, he had tried to bury his head in the sand; another time, the only time in his life that he had been smacked (by an uncle – his parents never smacked him), he had beaten his head against a wall for hours afterwards.

What was particular about this therapy was that even though my interpretations on his grandiosity were accepted, the situation did not change: the delusion continued to influence the main aspects of his life, and he was unable to retain the insights gained during his sessions. At times, I was able to make him see how his projecting evil onto his persecutors represented a major falsification; the reason he had seen himself as the victim of his Arab peer was that he had considered the girl as his: that is, a possession that could not be taken away from him. It was a display of his power, success and grandiosity. Even the fact that he had been called by an important multinational company in Germany had represented his merging with an omnipotent object, which then turned into a state of persecution.

The big company was after him now: Francesco was sure that an elegant gentleman he had seen leaving my office was an agent from the multinational company, who had come to spy on him. First, he had identified with the multinational, which represented an omnipotent object; then, however, he understood that the multinational commanded a secret organisation to eliminate all those who strayed. The big multinational did not tolerate frustrations either and felt challenged in its omnipotence.

Delusion projections were everywhere. For example, Francesco was convinced that his university professor (he had been appointed to teach college lab courses), certainly in league with the group of persecutors, had asked him to teach a lesson on his own with the aim of making him get it wrong to humiliate him and triumph over him. He always felt at war with his enemies, like a soldier that had been dispatched to hostile territory, with no protection whatsoever and enemies all around. His mother and aunt, who said it was better for him to continue living at home, were experienced as reassuring and protective figures; had I proposed the benefit of moving out of the family home, I would immediately have been considered someone who was going to expose him to his enemies, with whom I was in cahoots. In one session, he told me about his grandfather dying in a city hospital. I replied, trying to anticipate him, that part of him might have believed that his grandfather had perhaps died not of natural causes but at the hands of his enemies; he firmly denied having thought this, but the next day, he came to his session distraught at the fear of having to go into hospital and dying, just like his grandfather: that is, poisoned. I was amazed at this sudden change of opinion.

He told me that he had gone to renew his expired identity card, and, since the clerk had made him sign various different forms, Francesco thought that he wanted to duplicate the document for illegal purposes and place the blame on him. It was during this period that the aforementioned psychotic transference had developed, and Francesco was terrified by the idea that his persecutors had coaxed me into reporting him through bribes and blackmail. When I asked him why in the world I, his analyst, would report him and hurt him, he replied that anything was possible, and thirst for money could win anyone and everyone over. I replied that that was not how things were: some things were possible, others improbable and others impossible and that everything was possible only in omnipotent thought and in an imaginary world. The omnipotence of thought made him believe that anything whatsoever imaginable to him was actually possible.

I frequently realised, as mentioned earlier, that new persecutory themes could emerge out of simple contiguity or verbal assonance links of everyday occurrences. Psychotic terror was like a black hole that Francesco feared being sucked into by the sheer volume of associative links; he was also convinced that his persecutors acted with no restraint whatsoever, using great means to harm him; for example, the Arab was not just any chap, but the son of an extremely wealthy emir who had made his fortune in oil and therefore had the power to do anything he wished. Francesco showed readiness and submissiveness towards the delusion also because of the size of his persecutors, who loomed within him. Anything whatsoever that was unexpected, such as when he had seen me outside my office, unleashed persecution. Once he had gone to a party for young people of his own age, but he saw an elderly person there, and immediately, the persecution exploded. What was that person doing there? Had he come to spy on him? Or an anonymous email was without a doubt sent by his persecutors, or a modest nosebleed was a clear symptom of having been poisoned.

I also analysed his tendency to consider good objects weak and corruptible: he, Francesco, was good and fought pure evil, but he felt threatened by wicked persecutors who were everywhere. The split between good and bad, however, was not invariant: there were rapid changes of what was good and what was bad; even his analyst could become bad.

During this period, which corresponds to the end of the second year of analysis, Francesco spent much of his time at home under the bedcovers because he felt helpless and perceived the world as a jungle full of malicious beings. My impression was that his megalomaniac competitiveness had torn his mental skin, letting the hated world get beneath it, where it could hate and attack him.

Now and again his distrust of me would reappear; if he sensed during a session that I knew something that, in his opinion, he had not told me, he would immediately think that I belonged to the organisation that was persecuting him. Once, when he came to his session and had not seen the previous patient, immediately he went into a panic at the thought that I had reserved a little time in order to get some persecutory ruse ready. During his session, he then made the association that ever since he was little, he had developed profound distrust of his parents; he thought of them as people who did not speak openly to him and secretly kept an eye on him.

I had never seen his parents, to whom I would have liked to speak at the beginning of Francesco's therapy; I had, instead, met an aunt Francesco got on well with. Only once, when Francesco had a very acute delusional break, did I meet his father, who came with the aforementioned aunt.

Francesco was sure he could pick up on his persecutors' intentions at a mere glance; with this divinatory skill, he only needed to look at the position of their hands as they spoke to understand what their hidden intentions were, and he would cite books that confirmed that this was possible. From my point of view, the omnipotence he exercised was certainly connected to his childhood, when he categorised people as good or bad without even needing to speak to them.

Francesco was very alone, and complained that no one, not even his old friends, ever contacted him; for this reason, he had decided to organise a party and invite various people, some mere acquaintances. It ended up being a disaster, as Francesco found himself in a conspiratorial ambience organised by the CIA and the KGB. His anxiety was so acute that it prevented him from staying at home (a studio flat he had moved to), and he was forced to flee to his parents', where he felt more protected from the risk of conspiracies. It was on that occasion that his father and aunt asked to speak to me.

During that period, at the end of the third year of analysis, I was striving to help him think of his anxiety as a subjective problem. I felt that if Francesco understood that his anxiety was created by his mind, he could have tolerated it better, but he would tell me that the danger was there before his very eyes, that it was real and not a product of his mind. He told me that before going to Germany, he had worked in France, where he had met a married woman who had two children. She liked him and would invite him to her home to spend time with her and her children. At a certain point, he began to fear that the woman's husband, who worked away from home, would have suspected a secret affair between his wife and him and would therefore have tried to kill him. I expect that a colleague, perhaps jokingly, had told him that the woman's husband had already killed a rival.

Even this short episode followed the same pattern: the persecutor was a male whom Francesco had challenged, either in or outside awareness. This character resembled an overbearing and vindictive father, almost paranoid, and this was also the image that Francesco partially had of his own father: in his opinion, his father dominated his mother, who would bow to his will. He too, following in his father's footsteps as a child, would make a younger female cousin obey his every command.

The middle period

In the fifth year of analysis, a period began in which insights were more frequent, and Francesco's childhood experiences could be assessed and the infantile origin of his psychosis reconstructed.

108   *Part 3*

During one session, when he had several minutes of clarity of mind, he plainly saw that his fantasy world had been created through omnipotence; he even sensed that his parents, whom he dearly loved and admired, had been mentally absent, consequently making him feel uncontained from a very young age and letting his imagination wander freely. Thus, he had been unable to learn anything from real experience.

He told me of a meaningful experience he had had in his adolescence: he had wrapped up a notebook on sex in which there were many pornographic images but then was no longer able to find it; he was sure that his parents had found it and confiscated it, but neither of them ever mentioned it in the slightest.

During this same period, Francesco brought a very meaningful dream. He was at the cinema with his parents and some friends of theirs. During the film he needed to poo, which he did immediately with great pleasure. The adults smelt the odour and complained out loud, and at the end of the film they cleaned the excrement. Not one of them asked him about it or merely said in passing that that sort of thing was not allowed. Francesco connected this dream to the fact that his parents never confronted him but let him live as freely as he wished; for example, as a child, when he spat at his grandfather, he would not be told off by his father, who would just turn it into humour by saying that he would become dehydrated if he kept it up. In the dream, what struck him was that none of the adults commented on him pooing, and he associated this silence with that of the Arab, who had been silent when Francesco objected to what he had done. That silence, and the fact that this person did not look him in the eye, bothered him afterwards to the extent that he feared revenge.

I told him that perhaps his parents' silence made it impossible for him to understand their emotional states, which might have induced him to develop a tendency to interpret things he did not understand and to imagine them as being threatening. His persecutors plotted against him silently, and it was up to him to interpret what their intentions were. Naturally, this genetic hypothesis, despite Francesco listening to it and taking it into consideration, could not in itself produce any substantial change to his tendency to be delirious. And although he had begun to consider his megalomaniac fantasies with a critical eye, his propensity for delusion, as I shall later illustrate, would not let up: a new delusion would come hard on the heels of those that had preceded it.

My work consisted in making constant comparisons between delusional thought and healthy thought in a bid to differentiate them and strengthen the healthy part of the personality in order to examine the psychotic functioning. Whenever possible, I would re-examine the psychic conditions in which the delusional experience had developed. This was a difficult task because Francesco, as soon as his distress had been overcome, would forget all the connections we had found. Once, while we were working together on his 'little worm' (this is what he called his aptitude for reality transformation) and on how it acted inside him, Francesco told me that he realised he tended to forget the work we did together: when he left his sessions, he immediately forgot everything we had analysed.

There were also times when Francesco was free from psychosis. For example, he told me of a film he had seen about some Spanish anti-fascist actors who had

A psychoanalytic therapy   109

gone to work in Nazi Germany during the Spanish State and had been subjected to a series of checks by the German police; he said that he was calm when he left the cinema, relishing his freedom and placing persecution in the past. On that occasion it almost seemed as if Francesco had managed, helped by the film, to reacquire the ability to distinguish between the dream and reality. I drew his attention to the fact that he had recovered his ability to think and to rediscover his identity. At other times, however, films were like powerful evocative machines that caused him to lose his identity.

He reflected genuinely on the period that had preceded his psychotic explosion and said he understood that his flight into megalomania had been his only expedient to create distance from the pain he felt when he realised he had fallen behind and lost contact with his university friends. It was as though the delusional construction resulted from his fall from the maniacal state; the confrontation with his Arab peer, together with losing the girl, had threatened to throw him back into his previous feeling of failure. It became clear too that his delusional wish to be adored because of his fame corresponded to his wanting to restore the ecstatic state of the little child who was venerated by his parents.

In part, this had been Francesco's real childhood experience as he had never received the frustrations needed to structure the mind in order to deal with life and its vicissitudes. When frustrations arose, he experienced them as unjust: he was just; his rival was unjust. Gradually we were able to establish continuity between the state of infantile excitement, which was neither modulated nor contained by his parents, and the development of the delusional dream; Francesco admitted that ever since he was small, success had been like a drug to him and that he had sought only to receive continuous gratification from others.

Islands of clarity

At times, some 'islands of clarity' would emerge, followed, however, by moments in which Francesco's insight would vanish. His failure to pay constant attention to the emergence of delusional intuitions meant that they constantly recurred. Being captured by the delusion, which was understood as a force that could change reality, fascinated but then terrorised him. This is well represented in the following dream: He is in a tunnel similar to the ones in the Underground. He is trying to get outside and so has to climb up a long, fanciful flight of steps, similar to those in Mirò's paintings. Once outside, he sees a man who shows him a threatening message; someone from behind sprays liquid all over him, and he is then grabbed by other men who jump on him and start kicking him. The words of the stranger's message are: 'These last five minutes will be the worst of your life!'

This dream helped to understand Francesco's construction of the delusion; his way of constructing persecution can be traced in the manifest content. The delusion preparation is represented by the Joan Mirò-like fanciful flight of steps: that is, by the action of fantasy dissociated from reality. Transforming reality, which corresponds to creating new forms as in surrealist painting, is idealised by Francesco.

We worked a lot on this dream which enabled us to understand the difference between revelation and intuition: the former appears as such and asserts itself beyond all doubt; the latter is immediate but is followed by questions and answers that substantiate and confirm it. As represented in the dream, the delusion has two phases: the first is exciting, the second distressing. Francesco had always said that he would hear a click in his head, and when he did, there would be no escape as he would then fall prey to the delusion.

Each time the delusion appeared, Francesco having learnt to speak about it openly by now, I would seize the opportunity to tell him my observations on its construction and on the difficult task of coming out of it. It was a time in his analysis when he would come to his session and tell me about his being delusional the previous day, or he would describe a dream that he defined as psychotic; during the session we would be able to *deconstruct* the delusion, and the session would end with a sense of relief. However, transforming the delusional experience during the session, which was similar to working through a dream, was not stable, unfortunately: our work brought Francesco relief from anxiety connected to the delusional experience, which would constantly recur, though, because after each session Francesco would end up forgetting all the work we had done together.

The delusion constructions were thus only apparently transformed by the analytic work, remaining etched in his mind, ready to be reactivated. Francesco temporarily rid himself of the delusion, but he was unable to transform it. I understood that the delusion fantasies were not transformable as they were *real* constructions based on upheaval to perceptions and thought.

Francesco's persecutory projections were aimed at people unknown to him: strangers and potential enemies, not family members or friends, and no longer at me, given that our bond by this stage had been strengthened; emotional bonds functioned as a barrier against the expansion of the delusion. Francesco's delusional anxiety had even activated physical illness, ulcerative colitis, which manifested as a loss of mucous and blood in his faeces. In part, he denied the illness, and in part, he attributed it to his persecutors who were poisoning him; it took him quite a while before deciding to go to the doctor, who then prescribed medication. This illness, at times mild, at others severe, lasted for quite some time, disappearing only when the analytic therapy had produced a substantial improvement that brought a reduction in anxiety.

From a certain time on, at the beginning of the sixth year of analysis, I saw that Francesco had begun to reflect more on his own mental processes and was aware of having an alter ego that distorted his real world. The delusional experience no longer had that immediate and automatic quality about it. My function continued to be important though; Francesco would begin to worry at holiday times because he feared being unable to fend off the return of the delusion.

I considered the reappearance of a certain vital aggressiveness as a sign of improvement. The following dream bears witness to this change: There is a ferocious cat that goes into his house and torments him; he grabs it and hurls it from the fourth floor. He feels relieved when he sees it flat on the ground.

During this phase, he had learnt how important it was to be helped to understand one's emotions, and so he began to write a book on the subject and bring one chapter after another to me. He seemed convinced that he could classify emotions on a single chart, where all the various feelings combined could form others as if they were chemical elements that reacted, generating yet other compounds: that is, other emotions; he also had in mind to form a work group with a female friend of his who was studying psychology and then go around primary schools teaching children how important emotions were. Although I knew his wish was nurtured by omnipotence, I thought that the well-being deriving from it together with the chance to have persecution-free experiences would make it worthwhile. I knew that Francesco was repeating with me in the transference the childhood experience of the adored father he had tried to imitate; I therefore sought to keep this space open so as not to dampen his enthusiasm, kindly commenting on his ideas. In addition, and in spite of the fact that I had tried to make him see the difficulties, he enrolled at university to study psychology in order to then work as a psychologist, but after two years, during which he just barely passed two exams, he dropped out. The line between fantasy and reality was still quite fine, and often grand projects destined to peter out would supplant reality.

Although Francesco's relational world was improving, his psychotic world was not regressing to the same extent, and many random stimuli could reactivate the delusion. Once he had gone to the theatre to see a play set in the slums of Tokyo, about a depressed alcoholic whose wife was detached and cynical. He felt afflicted by the evilness in the world as this representation had become real; it had lost its imaginative and symbolic quality and become a concrete experience of a frightening reality in which he was the main character.

He had met some girls and arranged to see two of them, one of whom was foreign, but they did not show up; he felt distressed at the rejection and immediately went to the swimming pool where he noted a suspicious individual who had certainly opened his locker; perhaps this person had gone to the two girls to convince them to stand him up. Unforeseen setbacks definitely depended on some persecutor; at the bottom of this belief was the idea that someone was competing with him, envied him and wanted to make him fail.

During the summer of the seventh year of analysis, Francesco had a severe psychotic breakdown during his holiday abroad with the foreign girl mentioned earlier, whom he had started to go out with. The delusion preparation had begun before their departure. What follows is how I was able to reconstruct it after his return to analysis.

Francesco had idealised the relationship with this girl, thinking that they were a perfect couple and wanting their relationship to last forever. The girl, who had come to Italy through work and whose return home was scheduled, wanted to meet people while here who were interesting to her personally and professionally. Before going on their holiday, the girl had been invited to a party and asked Francesco to go with her, which he did unwillingly. During the party, he noticed a man, clearly sexually aroused (Francesco had seen his erection!), who began to chat to the girl. While on holiday, Francesco was convinced that this girl was in a sexualised mental state and that she masturbated and had sex with other men when she got up at night to go to the toilet. Francesco kept this idea to himself until one

112   *Part 3*

evening, while they were having dinner in a little restaurant, it became so clear to him that the waiter, who seemed rather intrusive, had been hired to kill him.

Once back in Italy, he remained in this delusional situation for approximately one month, during which time he refused to see the girl as the delusion had flared up the only time that he had tried to meet her; what had happened was that the girl had suggested listening to a song, and Francesco had taken this as a clear warning of death. The girl, too, worried and disheartened by Francesco's condition, preferred to keep her distance after this.

While reconstructing this episode, I thought of the euphoria-persecution sequence I had come to recognise: far from his analysis, his improvement and the new relationship turned into a state of mental expansion that made him feel superior and in conflict with other men. Francesco, who had not wanted to go to the party, transformed his feeling of exclusion into a terrible condition of sexual betrayal: he thought of the girl as a sex addict who wanted to rid herself of him with the waiter's help.

When considering with me the onset of his psychotic episode, Francesco remembered that his girlfriend, before the delusion flared up, had seemed detached and much too interested in going out with her Italian colleagues. A non-psychotic individual in this same condition would have had a dream in which he saw himself being betrayed by his partner.

Francesco, who was unable to 'dream', *saw* the girl sexually aroused and the guy with an erect penis while at the party. In the face of this emotional delusion, he demonised the person who had frustrated him and substituted the concrete reality of the delusion for emotional reality. Had he been able to dream the same scene, he would have understood his emotional state and been able to work through it. In order to do so, though, he would have needed to have an inner emotional space where he was in contact with the complexity of his emotions; instead, he was captured by his need to triumph and had idealised the relationship with this girl, which he turned into a triumph over other men that he then feared being ousted by. In the delusion, the rival appeared with his erect penis (the image of a phallic father) and defeated him with the help of an unreliable girl who wanted him dead.

I mentioned to Francesco that he lacked a mental apparatus that could enable him to tolerate frustration and that he would go from megalomaniac excitement to persecutory anger because of the humiliation he had endured. He replied that, throughout his life, he had always tried to avoid conflict. At university, he was kind and everyone's friend so as not to be at odds with anyone; after university and after he and his best friend had fallen out, his ascent began towards a state of superiority in a bid to stifle his suffering at the hands of others.

His return to a severe psychotic state made me see firsthand just how fragile and unsteady his apparent improvement had been; it was clear that Francesco could not yet deal with a romantic relationship, given all the doubts and uncertainties that ensued. This short romance turned into a maniacal state that inhibited Francesco's ability to think and to perceive emotions: Francesco even came to believe

A psychoanalytic therapy   113

that this girl was in Italy to seize his wealth (which was not his but his parents', who even paid for his analysis), a delusion theme he often had.

Reflecting on the megalomaniacal fantasies, Francesco admitted that they could possibly be unlikely, but he entertained the idea that being megalomaniacal and crazy meant being original; for the first time, he told me that he thought of this mad part as his 'secret private garden'.

Following that, another romantic bond towards the eighth year of analysis unleashed the same delusional pattern: Francesco began to think that the woman in question, a professional who incidentally earned handsomely, was only interested in his money, was cold and devoid of emotions and was also determined to kill him. Besides Francesco's tendency towards delusion (this was not an acute episode), other issues made the relationship with this woman quite difficult; Francesco felt very motivated by her on an intellectual level, but he was also very disturbed by her intemperance.

When he decided to split up with her, it seemed as though he had reached a clear and rational level of thinking. During the session in which he had spoken to me about his decision to break off the relationship, he had shown no sorrow. But the following day, he told me he had been delusional: they wanted to kill him, and a pain in his groin was his proof. I told him that he had once again plummeted into the cruel, persecutory world because he had wiped out the world of affects so as not to suffer. As an explanation for Francesco's maniacal inclination, I began to think that perhaps he had suffered great infantile pain and that in order to tackle it, he had become a megalomaniac child withdrawn into a fantasy world. Wiping out the emotional world, which it seemed he had done, had not eliminated the trauma; rather, it had created the preconditions for it.

Sometime later, he told me that he had found out from his aunt that when he was nine months old, his parents had gone away and had left him with someone he did not know; he lived at this person's home quite some distance from Milan for a fortnight, and when his parents returned from their trip, they found him run down, inappetent, and unable to recognise his mother.

Had he feared dying, abandoned by his parents?

For sure, since then he had never been sad, but quite the contrary: that is, a cheerful, maniacal child. His parents' behaviour is hard to understand, given that they were very attached to him. The hypothesis I formulated and kept to myself was that this abandonment was due to his mother's depressive state; perhaps she was too worn out from looking after her son.

His father

I often asked myself whether the delusional threatening figure could somehow be connected to the past or to his father; at times I felt that in childhood Francesco had experienced the paternal figure as threatening and vindictive, perhaps feeling small and helpless and always at risk of being crushed or intruded upon by him. And yet, in his childhood story, it seemed there had been no events to that effect, even though the father had sometimes defeated and humiliated him in his teenage years when he had taken him on at games or sport.

At certain times, it was possible to analyse his pathological identification with a domineering father towards a good, submissive mother. His father had certainly contributed to the construction of Francesco's infantile megalomania, nurturing his sense of omnipotence through rewarding him and treating him like an adult and turning him into a sort of confidant in the process. Frequently, Francesco would imitate his father, trying to dominate girls younger than him – his young cousin, for instance – just as he had seen his father do with his mother. Moreover, his father, who was unable to understand Francesco's problems and share in his distress, tended to behave in a way that made the child get mixed up with him. When Francesco the child told his father that he was afraid, his father would reply that he had to behave like a hero, or he would tell him stories in which the main characters defeated evil without ever giving in to fear, encouraging Francesco to be strong since the world was a bad place.

Francesco remembered that when he was little, he had intervened to break up fights between his parents; he would take on the role of an adult who reproached other adults. One evening, for example, after waking up because his parents were fighting, he got out of bed, shouted at them and went back to bed, convinced he had settled their dispute. It is likely that his parents had instead understood that it was better to put their fight off to another time so as not to disturb him. Francesco had not introjected his parents as protective, structuring figures because they really were quite absent psychologically.

Worthy of mention is the fact that Francesco's episodes of persecution appeared more often when he improved, as though a domineering figure who hated his vitality had lodged in his mind. Francesco's only solution was to remain passive and submissive, also because he was unable to distinguish between growth and maniacal expansion. I thought that in his eyes personal emancipation was dangerous because it would turn into a competition against an omnipotent and testy father. Clearly, in his delusion he felt threatened by a despotic and arrogant father who considered his growth an attempt to oust him; this threat resulted in Francesco becoming small and helpless and therefore even weaker still when facing his persecutors.

Even at an advanced stage of his analysis, as I shall relate next, Francesco suddenly became afraid at an exhibition where he had sold two of his paintings and had heard references to as well as actual death threats against him. It was as though he thought that when he was successful, he invoked the wrath of the gods, offended by his superciliousness, almost as if he had defied God to dethrone him. It was clear to me that his persecutory ideation strengthened when he achieved success; there was an immediate reactivation of the antagonistic power of a vindictive part that threatened him for his resourcefulness. Once, for example, he had a short fling with a girl, and then, afterwards, he felt dangerously exposed to the rays that came from his computer.

In a dream during this period, a tendency to disown the megalomaniac part began to appear. An important figure offered him the opportunity to be part of a grand trafficking ring in radioactive material. He was afraid to turn the offer down for fear of retaliation, but, in order to overcome his subjection, he decided not to accept, telling this person to find another partner.

Challenging authority had been a constant factor in Francesco's mental life ever since his childhood, when he would run away from school to defy his teachers and parents; his hyper behaviour, particularly on those occasions when he ran away from school, must have caused his parents concern. Francesco remembered somewhat vaguely that he had been taken to a psychologist.

Later, around the ninth year of analysis, Francesco began to be more aware of his maniacal state. In his dream, he was riding his bicycle and realised that he was doing sixty kilometres per hour. He pedalled even faster and reached seventy, then had to go downhill and went even faster again. At a certain point he saw a traffic light and some cars that were coming from the side; he didn't want to brake as he was doing something extraordinary. He leaned sideways and rode across the junction frightened that he may fall off and crash to the ground. Francesco's association was his being able to feel special by manipulating reality; in fact, in the dream, he reached a very high speed because he was pedalling downhill.

In a subsequent dream, excitement and falsification were once again represented:

I was playing pinball and realised that by tipping the machine a little I was able to get higher and higher scores. I was excited because of my success, but above all for being admired by those present. I was winning and could have continued to do so for hours on end.

After these dreams, we were able to connect the state of excitement, obtained through falsification, to his childhood attempts at seducing his mother. Being the eldest out of a whole host of cousins, he would organise contests in which, considering his age, he was sure to win; at times, he would magnanimously concede to sharing the prize with one of the younger ones. When he was young, Francesco was, in fact, idealised by his mother who, even when he was unable to do things because of his psychosis, would continue to sing his praises.

Clearer reflection on the father's personality began in this period when Francesco started to see his limits, his intemperance and his high opinion of himself; now he thought that his father too had a truly narcissistic component that came through in his work and in the family. He was, however, also aware that his father kept his feet on the ground (his father was a property developer), whereas he would take off with his head in the clouds. When he was little, Francesco had identified with his father and believed himself to be a little genius; for example, he had asked his father to explain binary logic to him, thought he had understood it and boasted about it in class.

During his adolescence, Francesco's father had become interfering and argumentative, to the extent that Francesco admitted having wished him dead on several occasions; when they played each other at games, for example, his father would systematically beat him and humiliate him to the point of exasperation. His mother, on the other hand, was always very gratifying, but uncritically so, and in

116   *Part 3*

one of Francesco's dreams he captured this flimsiness by making her whirl around in the air without any gravitational pull.

Despite still being conquered by delusional thought, Francesco was developing greater intuitive abilities as well as a new approach to assessing human qualities in people. In a dream, as a journalist, he was covering a running race and watched the fastest with admiration as they ran past the others. He sent a helicopter to collect two women, perhaps his mother and aunt, who were among the last ones. Much to his surprise, he realised that the two women were not interested in competing in the race but only wanted to be in others' company.

Unlike the dream in which his mother was floating in the air, here he realised that the two women were interested in other human beings, and they most likely also represented his parts that were developing in analysis. This occurred in parallel to his keeping a distance from a competitive, dominant father figure and to his appreciating the maternal figure's qualities, now seeing her as an intelligent and cultivated woman who was not interested in competing in order to succeed. In the dream, the excited and megalomaniac part – the helicopter that should have taken the two women to the positions out in front – was unable to capture Francesco's human and relational part.

Thinking the delusion

In this period, it was not uncommon to see Francesco reflecting more deeply on the dynamics of the delusional construction. In his opinion, the delusion was built in two steps: it began with a fantasy, such as when he thought that someone could have pointed a laser device at him to strike him while going down into the Underground; at a certain point, this fantasy left consciousness but was on hand should there be any unforeseen circumstances or 'anomalous' events, ready to re-emerge with all the force of the delusion.

The fantasy served as the cast to give shape to the delusional theme, which could appear suddenly because of purely random events. For example, he heard a young man on a tram say to his friend that he had been to the casino with his father: immediately Francesco felt persecuted; he detected, in his revelation, that this person was bad and could commit crime out of his attachment to money.

Thinking about his persecutor, imagined as a furious and murderous individual, Francesco connected this figure to his childhood tantrums at his frustrations. In his opinion, his persecutor was mad in a certain sense, too, believing that Francesco had committed sins even though he had not. Something of this sort had happened in France, when he thought he was being persecuted by the lady's husband; this man was going to kill him because he was convinced that Francesco had had an affair with his wife.

Francesco believed that betrayal was common practice; the first girls he had briefly gone out with had betrayed him; he had caught them in the act. In fact, as we then reconstructed, Francesco would believe he had seduced a girl when what he had actually done was extort a sort of consent, just to feel more at ease. This is what had happened in Germany with the girl the Arab then ran away with; she had said yes only to appease Francesco's insisting but then ran off with the Arab guy as soon as she could.

Francesco told me that when he was twenty, he felt fairly happy and peaceful; he played on the computer and saw some friends. Then he looked for love and sexual relations. He was attracted to a female friend of his who told him from the start that she had promiscuous tendencies, and in fact, she betrayed him right from the very beginning of their relationship. Francesco was indifferent to this. He adapted to her ways so as not to lose her and to keep going out with her; clearly, he was proud to be able to say that he had a girlfriend. When she left him, he suffered terribly and began to have relationships without becoming emotionally involved; he was sure that once he became a powerful man, he would have lots of women at his feet.

Once he said that he was struck by a comment I had made that concerned his being unable to defend himself; he was referring to my comments on his behaviour when he had accepted his childhood friend's attacks without reacting, a child he saw at his parents' insistence. Usually, he would be unable to handle conflicts with vital aggression, getting excited in fantasy instead and ending up feeling empty and fragile. At other times, he would project hate onto the other, who was experienced as an enemy who wanted to harm him, but he was never able to defend himself.

A small event made us see clearly how persecution followed Francesco's state of excitement. He told me he had spoken to his aunt and uncle, whom he was very close to, and who were having a heated discussion; his aunt, annoyed with her husband, remarked that Francesco, unlike her husband, understood her. He immediately felt a thrill of excitement at this acknowledgement, but then just as immediately, he was afraid that his uncle would be deadly furious with him. On this occasion, too, the same pattern was set in motion: Francesco challenged an omnipotent rival who became a persecutor. This episode certainly draws attention to an oedipal situation and to wanting to take the father's place; it is a psychotic Oedipus, full of violence and deadly revenge. Francesco did not feel guilty about having eliminated the father (in this case, his uncle) and consciously triumphed over his defeat. The male figure was not, however, transformed into a castrating father but a murderous one. Receiving acknowledgement, in Francesco's mind, unconsciously equalled gaining the upper hand over a rival that he subsequently felt hated and persecuted by.

Working with Francesco totally convinced me that a persecutory delusion cannot exist without being preceded by megalomania. My impression was that Francesco had experienced his parents not as a couple but as two psychologically separate people. He had certainly been worshipped by his mother, and he returned this by deeply idealising her; he thought of her as his true partner and, despite never having been aware of this, it is likely that he feared his father's resentment. He probably believed that his father thought of him as a brother, not a son, and perhaps this is why he experienced his mother and his father separately, as opposed to one united couple.

Francesco now realised that he had never had the feeling of being treated like a child, but as someone special, worshipped by both parents. He had grown up always believing that he had great creative talent; even during his analysis, he loved painting and was convinced that sooner or later he would become a famous artist, exhibiting his work in the world's most prestigious art galleries. He was always inclined to overestimate his abilities: once he made ice cream that his girl-friend really liked, and immediately he was sure that he was good at it and could therefore open a successful ice cream shop in Milan. Not considering my observations, it took him almost one week to understand that this kind of project required financial investment and working in conjunction with others. Francesco's grandi-ose side would not yield easily; it would doze and then wake up again for other enterprises that were destined to fail or be left unfinished.

Emancipation from the father figure proceeded arduously. In one session, Francesco spoke of a Chinese girl who lived and worked in Milan and sent all her earnings to her parents in China. Comparing himself to her, he felt really guilty: his parents paid for his analysis, his father worked very hard, whereas he still had no job; he was also sorry for the fact that, of late, he had been at variance with his father. I underlined that he had to learn to distinguish love and gratitude towards his father from possible conflicts that might arise along the path of differentiation. At this point, Francesco remembered that when he was a child, he thought he had to be perfect to comply with the wishes of his father, who often made him feel inadequate.

A double reality

At this point in time, now in the tenth year of his analysis, an important stage in Francesco's life began. He met a girl, Anna, who seemed to have many good qualities. After getting on well for several months, they decided to live together. Anna had a good impact on his life: she motivated him to be more active, pushed him to look for a job and took him out of that cloud that had kept him withdrawn and at home.

'Free intervals' were longer, and generalised persecutory anxiety had disap-peared, allowing him to relate more competently. Francesco began to reconstruct his personality and no longer lost his self-boundaries. After a while, he began to work part time.

Naturally, at a certain point, the relationship with Anna started to be contami-nated by the delusional distortion. Francesco became very suspicious and thought that Anna was with him only for his money. When Anna told him she was preg-nant, he heard gunshots coming from the street and convinced himself that they were a signal from his persecutors, who were celebrating their triumph. This girl had managed to trick him by getting pregnant in order to take possession of his wealth and would then kill him with the help of her relatives. (He had just seen a film in which the main character was assassinated.) His delusional anxieties aside, Francesco did not want a child and tried everything to persuade Anna to have an abortion; then, since she refused to, they decided the pregnancy should go ahead, and when the child, a boy, was born, Francesco grew fond of him and willingly took care of him.

A psychoanalytic therapy   119

I would now like to give you a clear picture of this last delusional experience centred on Francesco's family life, the woman he lives with who bore him a son, and her relatives. I must explain that this woman is Sicilian and has very close ties with her brothers and sisters, who moved to Milan, as she did, a long time ago; the fact is that it is a very close-knit family. Francesco never tried to conceal his difficulty with these in-laws, whom he did not really understand and who made him feel ill at ease; they belonged to a more modest social and cultural environment than his, which prevented him from developing an empathic relationship with them.

Usually, when Francesco found himself in any group context, he expected to be the centre of attention, in tune with the rest of the company so that he could boast about his talents. This expectation came to disappointment, even for socio-cultural reasons, and Anna's relatives behaved kindly and formally towards him without there being a particularly spontaneous or close exchange; as a result, Francesco felt marginalised from the group. When in their company, he would be passive, trying not to go beyond their cultural and social differences, and therefore social exchanges in order to get to know these people better were minimal.

At a certain point, these mysterious and distant relatives became the characters of a conspiracy against him: they had decided to kill him to seize his 'wealth', and what greatly perturbed him was that Anna was in on it. It seemed that, at this point, Francesco was able to live two separate realities, the delusional one and the normal one. This would begin by his healthy part being frightened by the delusion as it burst in, threatening to overwhelm it:

> Doctor, it's frightening. I started to think that Anna had taken sides with her brothers to rob me and knock me off. When I looked at her, the power of the delusion was so strong that I didn't recognise her and no longer felt anything for her.

His conviction that Anna was leading a double life, one that she shared with him and which he enjoyed and another that was secret and diabolical, lasted for quite some time.

Francesco was sure about his partner being involved in the conspiracy: he had caught her giving him a strange smile and once, on the phone, had heard her say that the time had come to do a certain thing. And the previous evening, he had heard his brother-in-law, a great steelworker, tell a nephew behind his back that he was going to buy a new car 'when . . . the time was right'. That evening, he had tried to be friendly with them; he had made a great effort to be kind, but then all the scaffolding came away, and the delusional terror shot to the fore.

He admitted to me that he was unable to sleep at nights, that he was afraid of being killed and that he constantly examined his partner's face, like an entomologist, to understand whether she was a murderess or a caring mother who took good care of her child.

At the height of his anxiety, he asked if he could have a fifth session before the weekend, and I said yes. The Easter break was coming up, and I was worried

120   *Part 3*

about him; with one extra session, I hoped to help him get over this distressing situation. I had my serious doubts, though; whereas in the past I had analysed many times the dynamics of the delusion, this time I felt I was without any means to help him.

Besides the terror that was overwhelming Francesco and the unpleasant surprise that it was for me, the delusion bore its usual recurring pattern: one or more figures, unfriendly and male, whom he experienced as powerful, could do whatever they wanted to him. This time it was the girl's family's turn: Sicilians, so closely knit as to form a true clan, in which, to Francesco's dismay, there were some very powerful people (a lawyer and a coroner!). Given Francesco's inability to distinguish delusional perceptions from real ones, while I listened to him, I asked myself which criterion I could use to help him tell the difference. After giving it some thought, I made this comment: In his delusional world, there were no emotional bonds that held people together, and life was a jungle governed by power and greed. (That was how he portrayed his persecutors.) Without an emotional bond that can keep people together, I said to him, thoughts, no longer contained in a human dimension, became unmanageable, like wild horses; the real world, however, unlike the delusional world, was full of solidarity and emotions. I told him that when he spoke of his partner as someone who took care of their child, he had in mind a real emotional world, but he would then create another delusional world in which she became inhuman, a murderess who was thirsty for money; I added that there was a constant passing from one world to another so that two opposite and incompatible perceptions existed together (the good mother and the killer partner). The difference between the real human world and the delusional inhuman world may have served to help him distinguish between delusion and reality. I shall not go into whether Francesco used this attempt of mine to distinguish between the delusion and reality, but in the following session, he told me that he did not go to the bed where he had been sleeping alone but returned that night to his partner's side and that of his child to feel some human warmth.

In the following sessions, I took up the point I had always considered important: the simultaneous existence of two incompatible realities. On other occasions of delusion, I had insisted upon this point with Francesco, but I now went back to it with greater firmness. During these sessions, Francesco said he realised he had a *bi-ocular* vision of reality. I noted that he expressed himself with great precision: he did not say *binocular* but had used the term *bi-ocular* to signify that his vision lacked integration, and thus the two visions, delusional and real, remained distinct and separate. Both, however, retained the same sensorial quality of reality.

We worked together to bring out the steps in the delusion construction process: usually Francesco would be disoriented when he was with people who were different from him, and this made him experience them as dangerous. In the case of his Sicilian relatives, there was a real difference in their histories, habits and mentality, but there was also something else: before the delusion exploded, Francesco, outside awareness, had disparaged his partner's relatives, who then became the persecutors. With an attitude of narcissistic superiority, he had judged them as being inferior and envious and therefore well placed to relieve him of his

A psychoanalytic therapy 121

privileged position. A constant feature in the delusional construction was that, in a world dominated by evil people, there were no institutions for protection and justice or for defending the weak against oppression by the violent; in his emotional world, he could not find a parental regulating function, an absence that brought to mind the psychological and emotional absence of his parents, who had left him over a long period in his omnipotent infantile withdrawal.

Many times in the past, I had been able to reconstruct the course of the delusion and recognise its constituent parts, but at this point, I realised that my work had not removed its readiness to recur; it was as if it had left an indelible trace that would form again and again. Instead of being erased, the delusion was encysted and coexisted with normal mental functioning. When it returned, Francesco was unable to sleep because of the terror he felt; death anxiety was so overwhelming that, as you may remember, he became ill with ulcerative colitis. His illness was most likely a psychosomatic consequence of his terror, and when Francesco improved, his illness eased and then cleared up completely.

I felt that during these sessions, Francesco was fighting the power of the delusion with more resolve. He would say to me that when he was with me, he would be aware that it was something 'invented in his mind', but then, as soon as he left, the power of the psychosis would influence him again, making him believe in the reality of the persecution. The voice of the delusion would convince him that his vision was superior to mine – it was sharper than others' vision. And this same voice at times would suggest that I, his analyst, wanted to demolish his conviction because I had taken sides with his enemies to make it easier to kill him.

Several weeks later Francesco skipped a session, something quite rare for him, and the following session he apologised for not coming and said he had really forgotten to come. I pointed out that this was very unusual since the times of the sessions had always been the same over the years, but he was unable to explain why he had forgotten; then, however, he remembered that that day he was so busy doing a job that the rest of the world, his analyst included, had vanished from his mind. He said that this self-isolation was very similar to the way in which the delusion was created: in these conditions, his mind functioned in a *monotasking* not a *multitasking* mode (his words); it was as if mental space shrank and he found himself shut in a 'mono-space' mind, where all communication with the outside world and with himself disappeared. When he was delirious, he was unable to launch other thoughts in his mind, and precisely because of his being so self-absorbed, the delusional thoughts recurred endlessly. In other words, it was as if the delusion were like a maelstrom that sucked in all other mental activity, nullifying it.

Never before had Francesco seemed so interested in unlocking the mystery of his delusional transformation; in every session he would take up the theme of the delusion without dropping the subject. I felt that this time he really wanted to rid himself of the seduction and colonisation of the psychotic part for good. He was determined to work hard in his analysis until he gained more awareness of the mechanisms, both internal and external, that gave rise to the delusion and which were an intrinsic part of his personality that needed to be transformed.

122   *Part 3*

In the meantime, he had become better at speaking to and cooperating with his parents; he helped his mother manage their real estate, and, when he could, he assisted his father. He brought this dream: He was in a car with the foreign girl (the one he had had the psychotic episode over). He was driving, and after a while he wanted to park the car but realised that the girl's mind was elsewhere, and she didn't give him any help. It seems that, in this dream fragment, Francesco recovered his ability to see what he had not seen before the onset of his delusion: that is, his partner's emotional distance. At this point, Francesco was able to distinguish his 'true' dreams from his 'psychotic' dreams, which expressed delusional themes.

Once he said to me that he had been able to go against being colonised by delusional ideas about several strangers in a bar, normally a typical sign of a conspiracy against him. This was very important because Francesco was now beginning to differentiate between healthy thoughts and mad thoughts. During childhood, he had been unable to do this, given that, in his opinion, he had been allowed to do and think anything; his mother did everything he asked her to without ever saying no and without understanding that he had already been captured by a withdrawal of grandeur. It seems that the mother's mental absence and obligingness, together with paternal grandiosity, had played a significant role in the development of Francesco's infantile megalomania.

He dreamt that he had to get married in a castle that belonged to the family of a friend, but he realised that his parents were absent and he got angry. Francesco commented that, for the first time in a dream, he had been angry with his parents. Although the dream contained the grandeur of the castle and no bride, the patient's emotional reaction towards his parents' absence was significant.

Yet another important transformational feature appeared in a dream in which he was able to distance himself from his mad part. He is in a group of people, tied with an elastic band to a kind of carousel that projects them into a space where you can perform any kind of acrobatic move. At a certain point, the elastic snaps, and a girl falls to the ground. The group, himself included, hesitate at length over whether they should keep whirling, and he talks about this to the owner of the ride, who is trying to persuade them to continue. The fraudulent portrayal of the ride's owner is evident here, representing the exciting psychotic part that wants the wild display to go on. His association was his having been an omniscient child, a little dictator who thought he knew everything and believed that the world should revolve around his wishes.

In this period, he began to have clearly transferential dreams: He came to his session, and I asked him whether he could have his session with some girls. He said yes but was not terribly convinced about the whole thing; the girls spoke to each other about schoolwork and after-school tutoring. The session was held outdoors, and at the end, the girls thanked him and even wanted to pay him. Represented in the dream is a parent who had no specific place for him or for girls his age. His mother had actually been a teacher; therefore, I imagined that her son could have seen her working with other boys and girls. In the dream, Francesco is unable to communicate his displeasure at having to share his space with the others.

A psychoanalytic therapy   123

In another dream, I (the analyst) was with him and his female cousin. I caressed and cuddled him while slides with the writing 'I love you' were being projected. Francesco said to me that he was a little disconcerted or, rather, surprised by the affection between us. Apart from the current of love and gratitude that Francesco was beginning to feel towards me, the dream highlighted once more that privileged affection he had always had for his mother.

In two subsequent sessions, he brought dreams that referred once more to his parents. In the first, his father had organised a big party, but in the wings of the house, several guests were making a mess, spitting on the ground and flicking ash on the floor. He was angry and argued with them. In the dream, Francesco was describing a father who was unable to judge or set out rules, thus favouring his son's excited and aggressive parts.

In the second dream, Francesco was masturbating outdoors while looking at pornographic magazines. His mother passed by and saw him, said hello and apologised for her interference. In the dream, he felt anger at the fact that his mother looked the other way and did not reproach him.

In this period, hints of the delusion were still there, but discreetly, like passing clouds. For example, once Francesco told me that while he was speaking to his mother on the phone about his father going into hospital, he heard some interference on the telephone line and thought that it was a delinquent listening in to obtain information so as to kill his father. A girl from his gym he had given his telephone number to had not come back to the gym, and perhaps she had given his number to his enemies.

The problem remained of understanding how the delusion exerted power on his mind despite our efforts. In one session, Francesco said there was a sort of *threshold functioning*: he explained that, as with neurons, firing was all or nothing. The delusion was triggered when this threshold was crossed, and he could no longer do anything to stop it; he could not use his reasoning to turn back. It was not like a dream that you wake up from and understand that it is virtual reality.

I agreed with him but thought that what caused this threshold to be crossed was his tendency to suspend his attention and become passive; then, when the delusion burst in, he would lose all contact with reality. I reminded him of the two realities in which he still lived: that of the relational world and that of the fantasy world, the latter just as real as the former in his eyes. The threshold was crossed when the fantasy world replaced the real world; he would then lose all relational ties and find himself in a world populated only by persecutors. Francesco continued to say that he was not aware of passing from one mental state to another; this very lack of discrimination was at the root of the delusional transformation in his mind. When I reminded him that ever since he was a young child, he had built a virtual reality that he could withdraw to, he specified that, early on, he had confined himself to touching up existing reality, and only later did he end up inventing it completely.

Francesco was pessimistic about life and people: his apparent trust and friendliness towards the other could quickly change into the reverse: that is, into an experience that bordered on or paved the way for the delusion. He had taken up again one of his hobbies, painting, and went to a former close friend of his from his youth in order to buy a good deal of material. After this, he began to suspect that his friend had charged him more than he ought to have, and so he checked some prices on the internet. Having confirmed his suspicion, his trust in the world was shattered; everybody was a crook, untrustworthy and evil, and he immediately felt shrouded in the persecutory atmosphere by now familiar to him. In this case, the delusion originated in his loss of trust in his friend and in the world, and a sort of black atmosphere then invaded his whole environment.

It was clear just how difficult it was for him to understand others' intentions and behaviour. Francesco was so sure of his mental organisation that, when reality did not match his schematic expectations, he plunged into confusion and paranoia; when he misjudged people, he immediately felt disoriented and invaded by cata-strophic anxiety; at this point, he would demonise reality, and people would seem bad and hostile towards him. Similarly, he would deny suffering from ulcerative colitis, and, when his symptoms recurred, he would come to the usual conclusion that he had been poisoned. The past did not provide him with information in order to understand the present: hence, his inability to learn from experience.

In the last years of analysis, now in the twelfth year, besides working on delusional falsifications, Francesco was committed to building his identity. He dreamt he had to climb Mount Everest, which, however, seemed tamer that it actually was. A female friend of his suggested he take a helicopter. Once at the top, he found some coins left by people who had been there before him. He took lots of them, but then at a certain point, he wondered whether it was right to appropriate money belonging to others. It is clear that in the dream, alongside the symbols of grandeur, such as Mount Everest and the helicopter, there is a genuine wish to better define his personal value and give up the personality 'theft' he was so used to. We may recall that he would imitate his father when he was young, and in analysis, he had wanted to become a renowned psychologist to imitate me.

During the last period of his analysis, caring for his son had enriched Franc-esco's affective world and distanced him from new delusional productions. His days were now busy as he would get up early in the morning and help Anna take care of their child. He would often look at his child and think about how different his own childhood had been from his son's. I felt he had treasured the analytic work on his childhood experience and that he wanted to be an affectionate and present father, who could positively contribute to his child's growth and develop-ment. His son rewarded him with affection and the fact that he was growing up well. In both his family and his working life, Francesco had made steady progress: he had acquired a greater sense of responsibility and a deeper understanding of others and was no longer interested in megalomaniacal initiatives, which would certainly have ended in failure.

Francesco often drew and painted, a hobby he had pursued since childhood and which he had kept up during his analysis; he had also enrolled at art school but left without a qualification. He no longer felt special, though, believing that someday he would become a great artist, the grandeur of his ideation having significantly lessened.

A psychoanalytic therapy   125

To demonstrate how the underlying delusional structure could still reawaken, I would like to mention the following episode. Francesco had managed to have some of his paintings exhibited and to sell two of them. It was the first time this sort of thing had happened, so he ought to have been happy about it; instead, after the sale of the two paintings, the surrounding environment became threatening, and he heard a conversation that two women were having, which, in his mind, certainly alluded to a death threat. I was struck by the fact that even after many years of work, Francesco could still plunge into a delusional atmosphere. But then again, as stated previously, each time Francesco improved, persecutory threats were unleashed as if some envious demonic being were hostile towards his achievement. This time, Francesco's fear had been that of having unveiled some secret through his paintings or of having challenged someone's reputation, thereby deserving to be punished. Clearly, he felt like a little David who had challenged a gigantic Goliath. I did not understand why this dangerous dynamic of provoking a powerful rival who then persecuted him had reoccurred.

It seemed that Francesco mixed up legitimate success and megalomaniacal triumphs (which triggered the persecutory response); that is, he mistook what was permitted for what was transgressive. Once again, I realised that I needed to explore in greater depth this area of Francesco's mind; I needed to fully prepare for ploughing land that I was under the impression had been cleared but which was still rocky underneath.

I carried out this work methodically, re-examining all the most significant past delusional episodes. Francesco, while this work was carried on and the past and present compared, continued to be struck by how childishly he presented himself in the world and by his megalomaniac constructions and use of words as revelations about imaginary and delusional worlds.

Two dreams seemed further progress towards freedom from his grandiose falseself personality. In the first dream, they are interviewing him about art. While he is speaking to the journalist, he wonders whether or not he should admit that his knowledge of modern artists is limited. During the dream, he decides to be himself and admit his weak point. When commenting on the dream, Francesco added that he had always falsified who he really was in order to seem perfect in others' eyes.

In the second dream, the analyst is speaking constantly and intensely to him because the end of his analysis is approaching, as if he were trying to fill him with advice now that life would have to be faced alone.

In fact, the preparatory work for the end of the analysis lasted a further two years. (Francesco finished his therapy in the fifteenth year.) The content of sessions was now more centred on everyday life; this constant connection to real life made me think that the danger of his returning to psychosis had passed. Common topics were the relationship with his partner and his parents, inevitable conflicts with them, his son's upbringing and the need to renew friendships that had been wrecked during the many years of his psychotic state.

These last two years saw Francesco constantly thinking back over his past in search of meaningful connections between his childhood, so full of triumph and

126   *Part 3*

pathological identifications with his parents, and the development in adulthood of the delusion and persecutory megalomania. One important aspect of re-elaboration was understanding better what the psychic premises were that had determined the onset of the delusional experience. Helpful to us was his reaction of anger and hatred deriving from disappointment that his much beloved aunt had caused.

Francesco understood that his violent reaction to emotional frustration was one of the factors that pushed him towards the delusion. When this happened – after graduating and when he lost his best friend, for instance – violent anger that led him to hate the world would be unleashed; then the feeling would come over him of being totally alone against everyone, at the mercy of others, leaving him pervious to the persecutory experience.[2]

Francesco returned many times to the past to understand what had made him feel persecuted by his partner's southern relatives. It seemed that he had found it difficult to integrate their good and their frustrating parts; in other words, he had been unable to hold inside the idea that people are human beings with specific limits and not diabolic objects. Significant work that Francesco did was comparing subsequent delusions in order to identify the roots and constants of his delusional constructions.

An important acquisition was his acknowledging the psychotic operation as a two-stage process that was initially pleasant but then distressing.

Francesco was always wanting in the capacity to foresee the negative effects of psychotic transformation, which explains why the psychotic crisis, once overcome, never seemed to worry him; he was oblivious to it, neither mentioning it nor discussing it with me. As I have frequently underlined, after the psychotic experience had been overcome thanks to analytic work, it was as if it were 'forgotten' or, rather, set 'aside' somewhere in the mind, in a sort of implicit memory that made the content inaccessible and therefore unusable.

During a session in the last part of his analysis, Francesco spoke to me about a further delusional crisis. He told me that while leaving his session the previous day, he had seen a big car outside that was there for him: in fact, it left as soon as he detected it. Then he went to the swimming pool and after a while saw two women having a lively chat with one another. He was sure they were criticising him and referring to the fact that he had gone to the pool just to look at girls. A man there was wearing a T-shirt with an eye inscribed in a triangle: for Francesco, this carried disquieting but clear overtones.

I was really dispirited during that session, having had to note that once again Francesco had 'relapsed' into psychosis. I just said to him, without being too convinced, that since he had told me that those were his days off, perhaps a holiday meant an absence of thought, losing touch with himself and being taken back once more to an alien world.

The following day, Francesco took me by complete surprise with his unexpected ability to process what had happened. He said he realised that for him, having almost reached middle age and having a son, going to the swimming pool to eye up girls was absurd, but this was not the point. Going to the swimming pool meant looking for mental excitement, the swimming pool therefore representing the land of milk and honey, built, however, in opposition to the world of relations. That day, he had been invited by a group of friends to spend the afternoon with them, but he turned the invitation down, seeing the pool as an alternative and superior world of pleasure. He remembered that he had done the exact same thing during his first analytic holidays when he had been very ill; he had gone back to being delusional and then decided to ask me for two sessions. On that occasion, he had turned down a sailing holiday with some friends as he wanted to go to a tourist resort by himself to look for girls, and when there he relapsed into delusion.

He told me that in the past I had repeated to him many times over that the persecution delusion followed his maniacal excited state; on this occasion, however, he was convinced that this concept had come to his mind without me telling him. He had listened to me on those previous occasions, acknowledged what I had said, but nothing stayed with him. Only then did he realise that his creating a world of excited pleasure was to wipe out all human relations, and he understood that the result following this operation was catastrophic.

This step was very important because it meant that Francesco could finally understand the nature of psychotic excitement and its aftereffect. Not until he was able to visualise psychotic development as a two-stage event (exciting and persecutory) that was the product of one and the same mental state could he manage to contain the delusion. In fact, he had told me many times that he found it difficult to catch the initial aspects of the psychotic transformation in time to defend himself from it. After this session, Francesco's perception of the insidiously dangerous nature of that mental excitement was sharpened, and he began to control it and escape its power.

Prior to the persecution delusion, Francesco had had an individualistic vision of the world and a narcissistic-grandiose projection of the Self. Ever since he was a child, he had felt superior to others, seduced by maternal appreciation and paternal licence, and had seen his peers as rivals. The good-bad, friend-foe divide stemmed from here.

His deep conviction of rivalry that pits men against one another and can even lead to their wishing the other dead nurtured his persecution delusion. Always lacking in him was the idea of basic brotherhood that ties people together beyond conflict. In people, destructive envy prevailed, even when there were affective ties or common interests, as had been clear to him from the delusional experience that included his partner, who had borne him a son. In a continuous antagonistic confrontation, even success, such as when he sold two of his paintings at the exhibition, meant stirring up others' hatred and greed.

Simultaneously to his general improvement, in this period Francesco began to conduct what I refer to as the *deconstruction of the delusion*. Not only did he think back to his great past delusional constructions, identifying the single constituent parts, but, by being able to foresee their nature, he also managed to halt even the slightest delusional or interpretative cues. He made a distinction between *delusional component* and *delusional process*. The delusional component is a thought, a suspicion or a fantasy that appears in his mind by itself and which is not yet a delusion. If he does not capture its psychotic nature, this delusion component

128 *Part 3*

broadens and merges with other psychic constructions to produce a psychotic process proper. It is therefore important to understand the nature of the delusional component immediately in order to deprive it of its power, given the danger it poses.

At times, it was possible to understand *in vivo*, moment by moment, how the delusional transformation occurred, in that a mental transition which seemed absent or not consciously registered was rendered representable.

The following example can illustrate this.

During a session after a weekend break, Francesco told me that he and his son had been invited to a party by his son's classmate's mother. It was at a nice house with a swimming pool; Francesco chatted to the host for a while and discovered that she was a psychologist. While speaking to her, he thought she seemed a very insecure and anxious mother. His curiosity was aroused by the fact that she worked at a school, and so he asked if he could listen to some rap music that this psychologist's young students were keen on. After a while, the repetitive and relentless music began to bore and annoy him; he did not ask to stop it and passively took it in. At a certain point, he perceived that the lyrics threateningly referred to him. Here, I said to Francesco that the delusion transformation had been facilitated by his passiveness as well as his submitting to the context, which he had been unable to change. I added that on other occasions, too (and reminded him of a few), he had tolerated situations imposed by others in which he had not adopted an active mental attitude, and from there, a delusion then developed. I believe that this passive state of mind, which many psychotic individuals have, can trigger a delusion when others' wishes are felt as being dangerously invasive and persecutory. On that occasion, Francesco wiped out his emotional intuition that up until that moment had enabled him to understand this lady's personality; without this intuition his persecutory delusional ideation was nourished yet again.

Particular to this therapy was the patient's recurring delusional experiences, as constant relapses, I believe, are not the norm for all psychotic patients. Once, when I asked Francesco why he thought his being delusional recurred so frequently, he said that he felt like a river whose banks had burst, entirely flooding adjacent plains. Thanks to therapy, the riverbanks had been rebuilt, but channels that had opened up during the overflow remained, and now and again, water would spill out. Francesco also added that he had clearly been withdrawn for too long in his grandiose fantasy world during childhood and adolescence and that his overflows of thoughts ended up just being out of habit.

I think this is true and that the duration and recurrence of various psychotic forms may differ according to the expansion and duration of the infantile withdrawal; the deeper and lengthier the withdrawal, the more conditions favouring psychic modifications will be created, which in turn will facilitate reality alteration and the production of delusional experiences.

Despite Francesco's delusional tendencies not having been curbed completely, it set my mind at rest to see him grow as a free person, no longer seduced by the anxiety and megalomania of the past. His healthy part had developed progressively, and he had acquired sufficient ability to train himself to reflect on and examine what occurred in his mind. In one session during the last part of his analysis, he told me that before falling ill, he had understood nothing about others because his only purpose had been to make himself liked; he had been unable to consider others or understand what they were like. Now he felt able to do so and to learn from experience.

Notes

1 This subject matter was transposed to Kubrick's film *Eyes Wide Shut*.
2 In my book *Vulnerability to Psychosis* (p. 108), I have described the case of a psychotic patient, who, when he felt sad and isolated, would make violence and hatred against the world grow inside him. The peak of his hatred coincided with the collapse of his psychic border, resulting in the production of perceptual holes through which aggressive hallucinatory people who terrorised him came in.

10 Clinical considerations

Francesco's clinical story enables us to understand how the psychotic process develops progressively and unpredictably. Once one pathological construction was demolished, another immediately appeared, all the work done up to that point being to no avail: the new psychotic break would cancel out any insight gained as well as the patient's opportunity to learn from experience.

The fact that Francesco slowly became aware of his overpowering tendency to replace the world of reality with that of the imagination was positive; he therefore understood that he needed another mind to help him circumscribe the pathological process and develop his healthy part, which was not particularly distinct from his ill part. As I had said to him once, his mind was like a sieve, allowing thoughts of every kind to pass through it indiscriminately.

In my description of this case, I have underlined above all how Francesco deceived himself by creating an alternative reality. It is clear from my way of working that only on rare occasions did I formulate symbolic or transference interpretations as they would not have been understood and would have added to the patient's state of confusion; I worked instead to describe and analyse his psychotic mental functioning, giving a description of his mental functioning each time his 'little worm' would get the better of him. As can be inferred from my account, I worked mainly on the delusion formation.

It was clear in my mind that, in Francesco's delusions, not only had the distinction between internal and external reality been obliterated, but psychic reality had been replaced with sensory reality: he could *hear* and *see* from his mind. His delusion was characterised by confusion between external and internal and by a *concrete fact* quality, his psyche being unable to free itself of it, let alone transform it, given its sensory nature. Had Francesco been able to confine himself to *dreaming*, he would have understood that the dream represented an unconscious conflict (for example, with Anna's relatives) and could therefore have contained his fear in a processable symbolic narration. Instead, his delusion was a sensory construction (he heard and saw his persecutors), unlike the representation of the dream entirely, which can be transformed and understood.

The delusion is purely sensory and therefore has no access to representation and symbolisation; it is made up of symbolic equations (Segal 1957), and it is in this sense that Bion's inversion of the alpha function should, I believe, be understood:

in the delusion, the imagination, which in normal conditions conveys an ideative or representative content, is transformed outside awareness into beta elements: that is, into pure sensorial elements. (*'I can see through the mind's eyes'*.)

The delusion uses the psychotic mind's capacity to *make imaginative thought sensory*: the delusion cannot enter dream work to produce transformative psychic experiences such as fantasy or thought because it corresponds to a non-thought, to Bion's –K (1992). How the mind constructs the delusion must be explained repeatedly to the patient so that he becomes aware of this process.

The specific difficulty in this particular therapy was the fact that the delusion remained silent – always ready, however, to virulently reactivate; despite free intervals, the pathogenic potential of the delusion remained intact, prepared at any moment to re-explode. It was important that Francesco and I, in spite of the presence of the delusion themes, were able to reconstruct his childhood experience and see that the psychotic process had been formed in a grandiose infantile withdrawal. Francesco had grown up in a well-to-do, middle-class cultivated family, without any evident traumas. Despite this, he was not a 'normal' little boy; there were episodes in his childhood that had worried his teachers and his parents, such as when he ran away from school (sometimes with an adventure companion) to do great daring deeds or defy adults; once he had hidden for such a long time that his parents, naturally worried, called the police.

The first time we met, Francesco told me that he had wonderful parents who had never scolded or punished him. Afterwards, I understood what this meant: his parents had not been able to provide the necessary frustrations or structure his personality. Francesco had lived in a grandiose infantile withdrawal that his parents knew nothing of; on several occasions, however, they had been concerned, as they had taken him to a psychologist to whom the child said that he scolded and tried to beat his parents. The psychologist did not consider this a problem and, instead, advised Francesco's mother to see a therapist.

I was convinced that Francesco, who for a long time had lived in a fantasy world, could not bear the frustrations and hurdles of real life; while growing up, conflicts proved to be harder than his constant state of exaltation could tolerate, and, at a certain point, hatred towards frustrating objects stained his world with sombre colours.

Being outstanding and unbeatable had been his childhood and teenage *leitmotiv*. He had to beat every record: he would organise tournaments with his younger cousins, who obviously lost, or he would ask his father to explain mathematics to him to astound his teachers and classmates. Naturally, he could not tolerate being scolded by adults, and when this happened, he would react with fierce anger. We might say that he had already structured a maniacal false Self that needed to be sustained in every way possible; after university, the collapse of this defensive structure contributed to the psychotic explosion.

Fundamental in this long and complex therapy was that neither Francesco nor I lost faith in the analytic work, even when the umpteenth crisis would wipe out all our prior work. When each relapse occurred, I tried to understand what had happened, what had brought on the episode and how his mind worked. Francesco

132   *Part 3*

really was a good patient, attached to his analysis and collaborating always, thus making it possible to discuss and rebuild what had happened.

I believe that the reappearance of delusion themes is a very frequent occurrence in psychotic conditions. I once carried out the supervision of a chronic female patient in the care of a group of psychiatrists in a psychiatric ward; she had been in the care of three psychiatrists from the group for fifteen years, one after the other, and it had been observed that the delusion repeated itself with the same pattern despite the characters and contexts changing.

Francesco's delusional structure, too, presented itself each time with the same nucleus, which never changed in spite of the new characters who would come onto the scene and the increased strength the delusion would gain. My initial hope was that once the structure had been clarified, the delusion could be *deconstructed* and treated like a dream, which, once understood, can be *forgotten*. Unfortunately, as I am not tired of repeating, I was not dealing with a dream but sensory delusional reality, and I continued to ask myself how it could be transformed, given that it had a concrete and not a symbolic nature.

I noted that the psychotic episodes often appeared when there were signs of improvement. Francesco clearly felt driven towards having new experiences, but he was not quite ready to really live them. For example, when he tried to have a girlfriend, he was unable to understand the other's character and personality; he just went about things blindly, and when faced with the complexity of emotions, he would be in a state of chaos that then led him into the delusion. He did not understand emotions, nor did he place himself in others' shoes to understand their character, wishes or thoughts; for example, if he found himself facing someone who was stern and lacking empathy, he immediately felt that this person was an enemy. More often than not, he was unable to understand people who were different from him, and when he was unable to get to know someone, he would consider them bad; from here derived his suspicion, followed by the persecutory delusional construction. My job was to describe those psychic processes that he was unable to grasp the meaning of and which led to his constructing delusional realities.

The delusion did not suddenly present itself as a well-organised structure but proceeded slowly, as can be seen with respect to Anna's relatives: it stemmed from small cues that were limited to the behaviour of a few of the relatives, from some random utterance or a smile or absent greeting. Francesco felt left out by this girl, who maintained close ties with her family members; anger followed, as did their transformation into evil villains. All the little delusional interpretations stayed in his mind, no critical awareness whatsoever imparted to them, and they would then suddenly merge into one coherent whole, like tesserae in a mosaic.

From a certain point of view, it had been easier for me to work on Francesco's last delusional pattern as it regarded the world of his family affects. Here, it had been simpler to talk about the double truth of his delusional experience, given that the projection was not onto alleged distant, anonymous enemies, but his partner that he himself appreciated being close to; the delusional territory was circumscribed, which enabled a better comparison with his emotional reality. In the first part of the analysis, his delusions had a universal dimension: his enemies moved around from one country to another, from one city to the next, and on one occasion the CIA and KGB had been brought into it.

As mentioned earlier, Francesco's inability to tolerate frustration created a strong push towards the delusion: a triumphant entrance was expected into the girl's family, which did not happen. If anything, great enthusiasm was lacking, and there was perhaps even a little indifference. He then realised, however, that he had become angry because of his disappointment and had projected his worst aggressive instincts onto these people.

We understood together that frustration was unbearable, above all when he found himself in a mental state of grandeur. In the case of his partner's family, the tepid welcoming had hugely disappointed his expectations, which disintegrated like a sandcastle, leaving him disoriented and gripped by violent narcissistic resentment. Those responsible for his frustration – in this case, the girl's relatives – then became his enemies.

On this subject, I would like to recall what Freud (1915b) stated with regard to the primitive Ego:

> The ego hates, abhors and pursues with intent to destroy all objects which are a source of unpleasurable feeling for it, without taking into account whether they mean a frustration of sexual satisfaction or of the satisfaction of self-preservative needs. Indeed, it may be asserted that the true prototypes of the relation of hate are derived not from sexual life, but from the ego's struggle to preserve and maintain itself.
>
> (Freud 1915a, p. 138)

These considerations perfectly suit Francesco's grandiose mental state and describe exactly what happened in his exalted mind when he experienced frustration.

The delusion is in itself a traumatic event: like trauma, it gets dissociated and remains an unprocessed fact that cannot be *forgotten*. The following is a short fragment to illustrate how the delusion remains encysted in the mind and then suddenly re-emerges, out of apparently random associative links.

After meeting Anna, Francesco decided to buy a single bed to put next to his in order to sleep with her in his studio flat. When the shop assistant suggested a particular bed and mattress that, in his opinion, were good and reasonably priced, Francesco suddenly became distressed about this offer, was suspicious of the shop assistant and thought that he was part of a conspiracy to kill him.

What had happened? What link had made the delusion re-emerge and transform the shop assistant's friendly sales proposal into a death threat?

To an outside observer, the connection between a sales proposal for a mattress and a persecutory threat would be difficult to understand, and perhaps, even the patient himself might have had some difficulty explaining it. Having remembered the work done on his previous delusional experiences, the connection between the mattress, the shop assistant and the persecution was immediately clear: I imagined Francesco awake at night, gripped by fear, staring at the shimmering light

134   *Part 3*

coming from the mattress, his clear proof that radioactive material had been put there by his enemies. When the shop assistant said the mattress was selling at a good price, Francesco immediately thought that he was an agent, working for his enemies, who wanted to kill him with a tailor-made mattress. In this case, my associations connected to the development of Francesco's previous delusional episodes were helpful to contain a new take of the delusion.

The delusional experience was recreated from associative links: the word became a concrete fact that would unleash the delusion. Freud (1915a) wrote that, in psychosis, words enter the primary process: 'In schizophrenia words are subjected to the same process as that which makes the dream-images out of latent dream-thoughts – to what we have called the primary psychical process' (p. 198). And he added:

> These endeavours are directed towards regaining the lost object, and it may well be that to achieve this purpose they set off on a path that leads to the object via the verbal part of it, but then find themselves obliged to be content with words instead of things.

> (p. 203)

The sensory and fantasy world of the delusion, as stated earlier, presented itself in Francesco's case as *another* reality that never encountered psychic reality or the relational experience.

The two visions – that of the sensory withdrawal and that of psychic reality – although existing side by side, could not integrate to produce insight. In Francesco's words, his vision was divided in two; it was bi-ocular: with one eye he could live inside the world of the withdrawal, and with the other he could go back to seeing reality. Since the two visions did not come together, Francesco could not experience binocular vision, which would have promoted his understanding that the delusion had a falsified nature. It was as if the mind created the delusion availing itself of the same sensory channels and structures that build the perception of true and shared reality. The delusion and psychic reality, constructed within the same circuits, alternately occupied the place of the other without ever being contradictory.

In the delusion, in fact, the principle of non-contradiction fails, and therefore if a statement is true and its negative is true, too, then any statement is true; this result is defined by logicians as the *principle of explosion*. This is why the difference between true, real, improbable, probable, possible and impossible is lost in the delusional system, and an unstoppable omnipotent mechanism that knows no boundaries is implanted; the absurd, with all loss of the notion of time, place, separateness and identity, are thus possible and potentially progress endlessly.

An example that is particularly reminiscent of the dual reality in the psychotic process is reported by Mark Solms, who cites the case of a patient who suffered a stroke, causing paralysis to her left arm.[1] Solms repeatedly tried to make her understand that her left arm was paralysed, but she would firmly deny it. Even when it seemed that she had accepted reality, immediately afterwards she would go back to denying the paralysis. When Solms showed her once more the difference in mobility between her right and left arm, the patient said that she did not want to be thought of as ill and that 'with her "mind's eye" she sees her arm moving, while with her "physical eyes" she sees that her arm is not lifting as it should' (Oppenheim 2013, p. 5). It is clear in this case that the internal image of the arm moving is just as real as the image perceived by the eyes and that both can coexist without being contradictory.

Facilitating the creation of Francesco's persecutory world was his fascination with evil. A great deal of his time in childhood and adolescence had been spent reading comics and stories about villains who would get fired up in their cynical exploits; thus, his delusional persecutory world became populated by these same figures, the comic characters he had read about in his youth, who were fascinated by absolute evil. When people he met seemed indifferent to him, it meant they were bad; it was clear that Francesco had preserved a childish way of seeing the world.

In addition, he was influenced by reports he heard, by films and TV news; he seemed to know about the world not through direct experience but via the filter of his imagination; his future projects therefore could not but be unrealistic, based on alleged abilities only and an unrealistic lack of difficulty. His thought functioned by categories: good-bad, sensitive-insensitive, success-failure, without considering the complexities of the real world.

Important working through done in the last period regarded the 'reparative' aspect of the omnipotent persecutory delusion. At its base was the megalomaniac idea to reform the world and free it of all its injustice. Francesco wanted to be the new Gandhi. What he was endeavouring to do, though, was not raise humanity from inevitable, objective injustice that leads to suffering but fight against enemies who bring about evil. It was thus an individual, maniacal and omnipotent attempt at reparation, a struggle against the powerful that, should they have obtained knowledge of it, would have unleashed the persecution.

In the last period of analysis, Francesco showed growing emotional maturity: he had acquired a greater ability to understand others and had a more realistic idea of his parents; not only did he love them and feel grateful to them, but he had also begun to weigh himself up against them. Keeping his distance from his father's idealised and grandiose parts was important for Francesco's mental growth, and his maturation went hand in hand with his inner transformation.

In several dreams from his final period of analysis, it was clear that Francesco was making an effort to work out the falsified parts of his personality; as you may remember, his grandiosity was accompanied by the construction of a megalomaniac false Self (he was a great artist, psychologist, computer scientist, economist and so forth), which exposed him to disappointments and failures. His grand mythomaniacal part made me think that had Francesco had a sturdier personality structure, he could have become an imposter.

One fact that really struck me in analysis during this last period was that, when examining the first years of his life more closely, Francesco realised that he remembered nothing of his childhood. He had no memory of his childhood before

136   *Part 3*

the age of seven or eight: no recollections of his nursery school, his first years at school or his playmates, for instance. Comparing himself to his own son, whom he had continued to take care of over these past few years, this difference seemed even more profound to him. He remembered that on one occasion when he was little, he had hurt his arm and gone into hospital: he claimed that he stayed alone without his parents for a week, not even complaining about missing them. This points to a very marked detachment from emotions and a strong tendency towards passivity, as if Francesco had already built a withdrawal from the emotional world during those early years. Comparing himself to his son, his own childhood life seemed listless, almost non-existent; Francesco spent a good part of his free time with his child, who was lively and interacted with him, indirectly contributing to his emotional recovery.

The revival and development of the emotional field during the last period of analysis seemed capable also of enlightening the past. Recollecting his school days, secondary school in particular, Francesco was amazed at being able to see his classmates with depth never experienced before. Back in his school days, his classmates had seemed distant, homogeneous, undifferentiated.

I should like to make just a brief comment on the transference. During the first part of Francesco's therapy, transference was of a psychotic nature: Francesco projected distrust and persecutoriness onto me, to the extent that he considered me a potential ally of his enemies. The psychotic transference, which on one occasion visibly manifested, could have distanced him from the analysis, but the danger was averted. Only later, when basic trust had been established between us, and Francesco's psychotic part was less dominant, did the transference take on a neurotic-type quality, with an evident oedipal hue that repeated the childhood relationship with his parents, his father in particular. He even began to experience with me a relationship of admiration, mixed with competition and imitation.

This experience with Francesco made me understand that analytic therapy for a psychotic patient should not be limited to treating the symptoms only – that is, hallucinations and delusions, extremely destabilising as they may be – but it should favour the patient's affective development and his acquisition of tools in order to deal with life and develop a true personality. It is clear that Francesco had, for various reasons, preserved a very infantile and naive character: having lived for a long time in a fantasy world, it seemed he had been unable to develop strength of character via continuous experience in relation with significant others.

Much work was also done on Francesco's inability to understand reality, above all emotional experiences, in themselves rather complex and which he seemed to have no experience of. It was as if he had been used to observing the world from a certain distance without any real participation, cataloguing it using simple attributions that more often than not were moral: good-bad, empathic-nonempathic, familiar-strange etc. Luckily, though, Francesco was intelligent and versatile; he was well educated and had been selected to do highly professional work.

The following theme was central to my analytic work. I tried to create triangulation based on dialogue between two non-psychotic minds: that is, the non-psychotic parts of the patient's mind and the analyst's mind, which collaborated in order to analyse the third vertex of the triangle – the patient's psychotic part (Williams 2014). In Francesco's case, the difficulty lay in having to treat a *continuous psychotic process* that transformed perceptions, thereby pushing the healthy part into madness; it was a much more complex task than when dealing with a relatively stable *pathological construction*, which can be contrasted with the healthy part of the personality.

Lastly, we come to dreams. At the start, Francesco's dreams were of a psychotic nature. They did not convey a comprehensible narration and were fragmented and concrete; that is, they were in line with his condition of suffering and his psychic fragmentation. Later on, however, they displayed narrative continuity, and some dreams could describe to the patient his *psychotic functioning*: for example, the dream in which Mirò's flight of steps appears describes to the patient his very own construction of the delusion.

This kind of dream is quite typical during the therapy of psychosis and also in other psychotic patients who undergo analytic treatment, often appearing when there is improvement; it means that the mind is beginning to be aware of the mechanism of the delusion transformation, and it can therefore begin to describe it. In these dreams, the mad part is represented by a figure who transforms reality, such as the artist Joan Mirò, which is the way Francesco described his fascination for the delusion and the possibility of changing reality through fantasy.

As I have already mentioned and underlined, this type of dream is important because through it the delusional experience can be shown to involve the patient's psychic participation and to be a construction of his own mind, despite his experiencing it as a sudden and concrete event coming from the outside. The nature of the delusion can thus be better analysed and, with the patient's help, its uncontainable and unstoppable nature modified. As can be seen from the clinical material of this case, dreams progressively changed until they became similar to neurotic dreams, with symbolic language that enabled suitable interpretations to be made to unveil implicit emotional meaning. This means that Francesco had begun to make his unconscious operate to represent, albeit it in a disguised fashion, psychic reality and emotional states; then transference dreams were brought, which could not have appeared earlier, not only because Francesco was unable to experience me, the analyst, as a person who was emotionally tied to him, but also because the transference is formed via symbolic operations, which he had been unable to carry out prior to then.

Note

1 The transcript of the video of this interview with Mark Solms can be found in *Imagination from Fantasy to Delusion* by Lois Oppenheim (Routledge 2013).

11 Future perspectives

We are well aware that psychosis is a progressive illness that once implanted is difficult to halt. I hope I have been able to clarify the various reasons why the psychotic process is hard to transform, above all in those patients who have had more than one psychotic episode. The cases I have treated or supervised have almost all been at the first episode, when the patient is still disoriented by the catastrophe that has overwhelmed him, and he oscillates between wanting to leave this psychotic experience behind and enjoying the appeal it exerts on him. Francesco began his analysis in this mental state.

However, in patients who have had various breaks or who have been in a psychotic state over a long period of time, pathological mental structures that distance the patient from reality are already well organised and activate continually, sustained by the brain's neuroendocrine circuits.

I believe that the psychotic process can begin in childhood in those children who isolate themselves and avoid the company of other children their own age. Some have been severely traumatised, which has brought about suffering or a weakness in their personality; being unable to feel important to others and entitled to a place in the world, they take refuge in an alternative world of dissociated fantasies they themselves have created in order to flee from this intolerable reality.

Often, this kind of child is described as shy and isolated, but these are stereotypes; the apparently shy, isolated child frequently is not really so, but can be impulsive, chaotic and unable to regulate his emotions. According to Nacht and Racamier (1958), these children frequently live in a world of *artifice*: they come from very formal families and conform to their parents' expectations, in the meanwhile developing fantasying that absorbs their emotional energy. Thus, they become automatons, with a life devoid of authentic emotional relations. Given that they rely less on relations and on the world around them, they progressively lose vital aggressiveness needed for development; their tendency to passiveness is in contrast with their fantasy world, which sees them as protagonists of heroic exploits, at times violent and omnipotent. Intuitive-emotional abilities, having the possibility to develop only in the context of human relations and dependence on significant others, therefore become atrophied.

As stated repeatedly, there is a radical structural difference between neurotic and psychotic functioning which must never be overlooked. When we speak of psychotic anxieties or psychotic nuclei of the personality in analytic clinical work, we are not referring to clinically evident pathological structures but ways of *functioning*.

Transference cannot be used as the main tool with psychotic patients, based as it is on the assumption of there being symbolic capacities that process the figure of the analyst; when the psychotic patient equates the therapist with a parent, the therapist is not *like* a parent; *he is the parent*. Therefore, being unable to work with transference, we must analyse and sustain the analytic relationship; the risk here is that, being based entirely on the healthy part, the analytic relationship may disappear when the healthy part is invaded by the psychotic part.

The main therapeutic objectives when treating a psychotic patient are two: the first is to try to rid the patient of his perception problems and thought distortions (hallucinations and delusions); the second is to develop his personality, for a long time trapped within the psychotic construction. Patients of this kind have not grown emotionally, so when they improve during treatment and are free of delusions and hallucinations, they find themselves with a structureless, insubstantial personality, thereby preserving inside all the prerequisites for a new break.

As for prognosis, the relationship between the psychotic part and the healthy part needs to be assessed to understand how far the psychotic process has advanced. The most favourable condition for therapy is when the patient has not had a psychotic break and is at the clinical onset of the disease; should he have had a first episode, he will have been hospitalised and prescribed psychotropic medication.

From the start, it is possible to evaluate whether the patient experiences his psychotic part as disturbing and dangerous or whether he prefers to deny or trivialize it to then allow himself to be seduced by it. The pathogenic power of the illness depends also on past life events: if the childhood withdrawal began very early on, it is clear that the psychotic part will have acquired full right to citizenship, making its transformation more difficult.

With Francesco's case, I believe I have described the *therapy of a specific case*, each case being different and analogies among various different patients being difficult to establish; despite the specific nature of each case, I hope I have been able to highlight the various articulations of psychosis, its psychic origins and the nature of this process. Therapy is an extremely complex course, similar to guiding a river that has burst its banks back to the riverbed or herding a drove of wild horses into a pen. In a psychotic break, thoughts run in every direction, wreaking havoc. The therapist has to reset a system that began to deviate in childhood, that has turned the rules of thought upside down and has a strong tendency towards self-sensory withdrawal, which is then bound to create perceptive (hallucinations) and ideative (delusions) distortions. Although psychosis does not always involve irreversible deterioration today, the path towards recovery clearly requires considerable effort by patient and therapist alike.

It is not easy to describe the psychotic transformation: that is, what happens when spatio-temporal parameters that organise experience are abolished. Thoughts lose their meaning; they expand to invade spaces that should remain neutral. An occurrence from years past comes to the fore and is experienced as if it were in the

140   *Part 3*

present, and the mind undergoes endless transformations. In psychotic thought, things do not match up because everything happens within absolute omnipotence. Psychosis is the transgressive manifestation par excellence precisely because it wipes out the rules of thought and becomes as rampant as it sees fit, unimpeded, like that drove of wild horses. It is a condition in which the tools of knowledge are grossly distorted. And needless to say, this runaway mental state tallies with biochemical tempests, alterations to the functions of various brain regions and connections between them.

Francesco constantly produced delusions using *language in place of real facts*. By using language, he could distance himself from reality and dilate his mind omnipotently. He could play with words, match them up and obtain causal meanings that revealed existent realities through simple relations of contiguity or verbal assonance. I would like to point out that, whereas for Freud the use of words in place of things stems from both a failed attempt by the psychotic patient to recover the world of reality and the fact that he must be content with words only, I had been able to observe that, for Francesco, the use of words in place of things was a privileged path to expanding his omniscient delusional system.

As for the dynamics of the psychotic disorder, my orientation, as I hope is clear from what I have written thus far, is not in line with the theoretical and clinical contribution of the group of analysts inspired by Melanie Klein, including Bion. Naturally, their contributions are enlightening, but in my opinion, they are in need of being developed and integrated into theory and practice. I do not believe, for example, that in order to understand the origin of the psychotic process one must always refer to the death instinct or to destructiveness. I believe instead that the potential psychotic patient distances himself from reality by replacing it with an alternative world built in fantasy; more precisely, this world dissociated from reality is not really a world of fantasy, given that fantasy would correspond to a representation and, by virtue of this, would be modifiable. Fantasy that leads to psychosis is founded not on representations of objects or on aspects of reality, but on *sensory impressions* proper; and what is produced via a *sensory use of the mind* is unfortunately not easily modifiable.

In psychotic transformation, awareness of what is happening is maintained for a certain length of time; during the first stage of the delusional experience, the patient can, in fact, recover if he pays heed to the healthy part of the Self. Later, however, when self-awareness disappears, it becomes very difficult to turn back; the patient ceases to be alarmed and passively abandons himself to the psychosis while it steadily continues to advance.

The seduction that the psychotic part exercises on the healthy part is important: when the patient constructs his world of sensory fantasies, he behaves as if he were God creating the world, convinced that he is superior to other human beings, his analyst included; it is obvious that, in these conditions, the patient lacks awareness and does not understand interpretations directed at his omnipotence. So it is better to work, as I did with Francesco, to develop the healthy part and contain the invasion of the delusion. Megalomania defends from awareness of the mental catastrophe; we may understand Freud's statement, according to which the delusion would correspond to an attempt to reconstruct reality in this sense.

It must be remembered though, even when Freud's hypothesis is accepted, that the delusion invasion increasingly compromises mental functioning and, in many cases, proceeds until it leads to a state of fragmentation.

Why is the therapeutic task in psychosis so long and arduous? One of my hypotheses is that it operates in the deepest layers of the unconscious that cannot be easily understood or reached via words. The unconscious matrixes of creative thought have been studied by numerous scholars, among whom are several eminent mathematicians such as Poincaré (1908) and Hadamard (1945), who described the feeling of delight that accompanies creative intuition when the chaotic field of phenomena and perceptions organises around a figure that stands out against a background and arranges all the elements present so as to form a meaningful order. It is a moment of pleasure that accompanies scientific discovery and highlights the birth of a new idea.

Besides the unconscious laid down by Freud – that is, the foundations of psychoanalytic theory – there is a host of data on many mental functions of communication that lie outside awareness; one part of contemporary psychoanalysis and neuroscience has focused on these functions, about which we still know relatively little.

Now being investigated is the *emotional* unconscious, with its knowledge outside awareness that differs from that of the dynamic unconscious, which uses repression.

Psychoanalytic method uses the mind's natural employment of intuitive emotions connected to the capacity for self-observation of mental and emotional processes. Increasingly mentioned in psychoanalysis are structures outside awareness, implicit relations, the digestion of primitive emotions or unconscious creativity; in psychosis, these functions are distorted or weakened, and it is at this level that the illness is located.

For this reason, psychosis still largely remains an enigma. The psychotic patient does not use intuition that exercises doubt when acquiring knowledge or understanding, but proceeds by *revelations* and finds unquestionable truths that suddenly appear in his mind. Knowledge by revelation is direct knowledge obtained only by the power of the mind that creates it, unmediated by experience.

Francesco would tell me that the delusion originated in his viscera, like an intuition that flooded his body and mind. Intuitions by revelation or enlightenment cannot be transmitted to the rest of human society – something that does not perturb the psychotic patient, however, as he considers it as confirmation that he is indeed superior: the world remains in the dark while he is enlightened.

Many innovations in the contemporary psychoanalytic movement will, in my opinion, help us better understand the psychodynamics of the psychotic process; among these, as mentioned earlier, the broadening of the concept of the unconscious is surely positive.

Bion is certainly among the forerunners of this direction of research: in his theorizing, the unconscious loses its ontic meaning of place – that is, a space where the repressed is deposited – and it becomes a function of the mind. In Bionian thought, there is no longer that clear contrast between conscious and unconscious, but relationships between objects and functions, links between them intuitable but

142   *Part 3*

remaining outside awareness; the dream is not only the product of repression, but also a function that fashions and registers emotions, a daytime activity that is ever present. The unconscious is a metaboliser of psychic experiences that allows the mind to produce thoughts.

An unconscious exists that communicates and understands the meaning of experience: that is, a *function of awareness* (of external and internal reality, the emotional field, body perception, time and space) that is *outside awareness* and which becomes altered in psychosis. We still do not know what the processes are that blend individual consciousness, nor do we know how they operate, but we do know that in the psychotic process they become altered; I touched on these processes when writing on the sensory transformation of mental functions, something that can probably be equated with a primordial function of the mind that is yet to be connected to intersubjective reality.

On this subject, we must not forget that consciousness and awareness, at times considered as superimposable concepts, are different processes. A patient may be conscious but unaware, in that, as Bion stated, there are thoughts with no thinker; the psychotic patient, for instance, is conscious of the delusional experience but unaware of what it means.

In psychotic states, thoughts are without a thinker because the Ego has undergone fragmentation. Francesco did not use his mind to think, but to produce a flow of sensory images to the detriment of the thought function. We shall probably understand the mystery of psychosis when scientific thought (psychoanalytic, neuroscientific, cognitivist) has thoroughly investigated the immense territory of the mind's processes that lies outside awareness, including the construction of thought, territory that was dealt with for the first time by Sigmund Freud who, like Columbus, believed he had arrived in the Indies when what he had actually discovered was a new, endless world yet to be explored.

Another recent achievement of psychoanalysis that can help us understand psychosis in greater depth is new knowledge on child development. We have confirmed the idea that children are born with innate relating abilities and that they acquire communicative and intentional behaviour early on: important messages are communicated between parents and infants when the newborn is only a matter of days old, and they contain all the characteristics of real dialogue, except for the fact that, needless to say, newborns are not equipped with speech. Some analysts, inspired by attachment theory and findings from infant research, have proposed a conception of the mind that is structured according to unconscious organising principles that form in infancy and remain unchanged. The relational and intersubjective contribution to psychoanalysis has brought into the foreground a conception of development immersed in an intersubjective relational matrix. All these openings have seen Freud's drive model move away from the spotlight while attention has shifted onto models focused on psychological and emotional development and on the reciprocal relationship with the mother. Unfortunately, these openings have not entered clinical work with severe patients in an organised fashion and therefore have not brought about – at least, not yet – substantial enrichment to our knowledge of the psychopathology of psychosis.

A significant contribution has come from neuroscience. Mark Solms and Jack Panksepp (2012) have worked above all on the limbic emotional brain, which communicates with the prefrontal cortex where cognitive and executive functions are located. On this subject, out of the abundant data available, in Chapter 7 I have summarised interesting research on hallucinations that are produced when higher cortical functions are inhibited and no longer control the sensory brain regions. I am convinced that neuroscience will provide further knowledge that will help us understand the neuropathology of the delirious experience.

On a final note, we may say that research at a clinical psychopathological and neurobiological level on psychosis is set to continue. At an international level, we can find a number of study groups organised by psychoanalysts on psychosis, several of which are the *Association for Psychoanalytic Psychotherapy in the Public Health Sector* in England; the *Centre Evelyne et Jean Kestenberg* in the 13th Arrondissement in Paris; the *Turku Schizophrenia Project* in Scandinavia, headed by Yrjo Alanen; the *International Society for the Psychological Treatments of Schizophrenia and Other Psychoses* and the *Center for the Advanced Study of the Psychoses*, both in San Francisco; and the *International Society for Psychological and Social Approaches to Psychosis* (*ISPS*), with its headquarters in New York, which promotes psychological treatment for psychotic patients.

As stated earlier, it seems clear that following the significant development of analytic theory on psychosis, which I sought to describe in the first few chapters, no corresponding advancement has been witnessed in clinical practice. After the initial enthusiasm, it appears that the development of analytic theory on psychosis came to a halt due largely to difficulty in grasping the nature of the illness and the complexity of its process.

Psychoanalytic research on the clinical front could benefit from an organised method permitting comparisons between homogeneous clinical cases with regard to symptomatology and development; what tends to happen today is that each author reports cases that are different, are at different points along development and start from different genetic hypotheses. This is why I decided to provide an extended account of Francesco's case as it contains several aspects that are common and specific to the psychotic process. In particular, I focused on the delirious experience, on the communicative function of some psychotic dreams and on the patient's extreme identity fragility, his functioning before the crisis seemingly that of a healthy personality that was, in fact, falsified. It was important to identify the direct link between the patient's childhood and the explosion of the psychotic crisis.

I hope that I have been able to convey some core points in the study of the psychotic illness through simple and precise concepts that, despite the extreme variability of the illness, underpin this process. I sincerely believe that, in order to come to grips with psychosis, several clear core reference points are needed.

I would lastly like to express my gratitude to Francesco, from whom I have learnt so much and whose tenaciousness and determination were fundamental to the positive outcome of the therapy.

References

Abraham, K. (1924). *A Short Study of the Development of the Libido, Viewed in the Light of Mental Disorders*, Selected Papers on Psychoanalysis. London: The Hogarth Press, 1927.

Alanen, Y.O. (2009). The pioneering work of Paul Federn. In Y.O. Alanen, M. Gonzales De Chávez, A.S. Silver, & B. Martindale (Eds.), *Psychotherapeutic Approaches to Schizophrenic Psychoses*. New York: Routledge.

Arieti, S. (1955). *Interpretation of Schizophrenia*, 2nd edition. London: Crosby Lockwood Staples, 1974.

Arlow, J.A., & Brenner, C. (1969). The psychopathology of the psychoses: A proposed revision. *International Journal of Psychoanalysis*, 50: 5–14.

Aulagnier, P. (1975). *The Violence of Interpretation*. Hove: Routledge, 2001.

Aulagnier, P. (1985). Hallucinatory withdrawal: Is it the same thing as autistic withdrawal? In Lefer, J. (Ed.). *Reading French Psychoanalysis*. New York: Routledge, 2011.

Bateson, G. (Ed.) (1961). *Perceval's Narrative: A Patient's Account of His Psychosis*. Palo Alto: Stanford University Press.

Benedetti, G. (1980). *Alienazione e personazione nella psicoterapia della malattia mentale*. Turin: Einaudi.

Benedetti, G. (1997). *La psicoterapia come sfida esistenziale*. Milan: Cortina.

Bion, W.R. (1957). Differentiation of the psychotic from the non-psychotic personalities. *International Journal of Psychoanalysis*, 38: 266–275. [Also in Bion, 1967, pp. 43–64.]

Bion, W.R. (1958). On hallucination. *International Journal of Psychoanalysis*, 39: 341–349.

Bion, W.R. (1959). Attacks on linking. *International Journal of Psychoanalysis*, 40: 308–315.

Bion, W.R. (1965). *Transformations: Change from Learning to Growth*. London: Heinemann.

Bion, W.R. (1967). *Second Thoughts: Selected Papers on Psycho-Analysis*. London: Heinemann.

Bion, W.R. (1992). *Cogitations* (F. Bion, Ed.). London: Karnac Books.

Blechner, M.J. (2005). Elusive illusions: Reality judgment and reality assignment in dreams and waking life. *Neuro-Psychoanalysis*, 7: 95–101.

Bleuler, E. (1911). *Dementia Praecox or the Group of Schizophrenias*. New York: International Universities Press, 1950.

Bonifati, L.S. (2000). *La psicosi in Jacques Lacan*. Milan: Franco Angeli.

Caper, R. (1998). Psychopathology and primitive mental states. *International Journal of Psychoanalysis*, 79: 539–551.

Capozzi, P., & De Masi, F. (2001). The meaning of dreams in the psychotic state: Theoretical considerations and clinical applications. *International Journal of Psychoanalysis*, 82: 933–952.

Carrère, E. (1993). *I Am Alive and You Are Dead: A Journey into the Mind of Philip K. Dick*. New York: Metropolitan Books, Henry Holt, 2004.

References   145

David, A.S., Woodruff, P.W., Howard, R., Mellers, J.D., Brammer, M., Bullmore, E., et al. (1996). Auditory hallucinations inhibit exogenous activation of auditory association cortex. *Neuroreport*, 7: 932–936.

de Masi, F. (2000). The unconscious and psychosis: Some considerations on the psychoanalytic theory of psychosis. *International Journal of Psychoanalysis*, 81: 1–20.

de Masi, F. (2006). *Vulnerability to Psychosis: A Psychoanalytic Study of the Nature and Therapy of the Psychotic State*. London: Karnac Books, 2009.

de Masi, F., Davalli, C., Giustino, G., & Pergami, A. (2015). Hallucinations in the psychotic state: Psychoanalysis and the neurosciences compared. *International Journal of Psychoanalysis*, 96: 293–318.

Dick, P. (2011). *The Exegesis of Philip K. Dick*. New York: Houghton Mifflin Harcourt Publishing Company.

DSM-5. (2013). *Diagnostic and Statistical Manual of Mental Disorders*. Washington, DC: American Psychiatric Association.

Fairbairn, W.R.D. (1952). *Psychoanalytic Studies of the Personality*. London: Tavistock.

Federn, P. (1952). *Ego Psychology and the Psychoses*. London: Imago, 1953.

Fonagy, P., & Target, M. (1996). Playing with reality: I. Theory of mind and the normal development of psychic reality. *International Journal of Psychoanalysis*, 77: 217–233.

Freeman, T. (2001). Treating and studying schizophrenias. In P. Williams (Ed.), *A Language for Psychosis: Psychoanalysis of Psychotic States*. London: Whurr, pp. 54–69.

Freud, S. (1894). The neuro-psychoses of defence. *S.E.*, 3.

Freud, S. (1900). The interpretation of dreams. *S.E.*, 4–5.

Freud, S. (1910). Psychoanalytic notes upon an autobiographical account of a case of paranoia (dementia paranoides). *S.E.*, 12: 3–82.

Freud, S. (1915a). The unconscious in *papers on metapsychology and other works. S.E.*, 14 (1914–1916).

Freud, S. (1915b). Instinct and their vicissitudes. *S.E.*, 14.

Freud, S. (1915c). A metapsychological supplement to the theory of dreams. *S.E.*, 14.

Freud, S. (1922). Some neurotic mechanisms in jealousy, paranoia and homosexuality. *S.E.*, 18.

Freud, S. (1924a). Neurosis and psychosis. *S.E.*, 19 (1923–1925).

Freud, S. (1924b). The loss of reality in neurosis and psychosis. *S.E.*, 19.

Freud, S. (1932). New introductory lectures on psycho-analysis. *S.E.*, 22.

Freud, S. (1938a). Constructions in analysis. *International Journal of Psychoanalysis*, 19(4): 377–387.

Freud, S. (1938b). Splitting of the ego in the process of defence. *S.E.*, 23 (1937–1939).

Freud, S. (1938c). An outline of psycho-analysis. *S.E.*, 23.

Fromm-Reichmann, F. (1959). *Psychoanalysis and Psychotherapy: Selected Papers of Frieda Fromm-Reichmann*. Chicago: The University of Chicago Press.

Greenberg, J. (1964). *I Never Promised You a Rose Garden*. New York: St. Martin's Press.

Hadamard, J. (1945). *An Essay on the Psychology of Invention in the Mathematical Field*. Princeton, NJ: Princeton University Press, 1996.

Hartmann, H. (1953). Contribution to the metapsychology of schizophrenia. In *Essays on Ego Psychology*. New York: International Universities Press, 1964.

Hoffman, R.E., Anderson, A.W., Varanko, M., Gore, J.C., & Hampson, M. (2008). Time course of regional brain activation associated with onset of auditory/verbal hallucinations. *British Journal of Psychiatry*, 193: 424–425.

Hugdahl, K. (2009). Hearing voices: Hallucinations as failure of top-down control of bottom-up perceptual processes. *Scandinavian Journal of Psychology*, 50: 553–560.

Israëls, H. (1989). *Schreber: Father and Son*. Madison, CT: International Universities Press.

Jackson, M. (2001). *Weathering the Storms*. London: Karnac Books.

146　*References*

Jacobson, E. (1954). On psychotic identifications. *International Journal of Psychoanalysis*, 35: 102–108.

Katan, M. (1954). The importance of the non-psychotic part of the personality in schizophrenia. *International Journal of Psychoanalysis*, 35: 119–128.

Klein, M. (1929). Personification in the play of children. *International Journal of Psychoanalysis*, 10: 193–204.

Klein, M. (1930a). The importance of symbol-formation in the development of the ego. In *Contributions to Psycho-Analysis 1921–1945*. London: Hogarth, 1965, pp. 236–250.

Klein, M. (1930b). The psychotherapy of the psychoses. In *Contributions to Psycho-Analysis 1921–1945*. London: Hogarth, 1965, pp. 251–253.

Klein, M. (1946). Notes on some schizoid mechanisms. In *Envy and Gratitude and Other Works 1946–1963*. London: Hogarth, 1987, Chapter 1.

Kosslyn, S. (1994). *Image and Brain*. Cambridge, MA: MIT Press.

Kraepelin, E. (1883). *Compendium der Psychiatrie (Compendium of Psychiatry)*. Leipzig: Abel.

Lacan, J. (1932). *De la psychose paranoïaque dans ses rapports avec la personnalité, suivi de Premiers écrits sur la paranoïa*. Paris: Éditions du Seuil, 1975.

Lacan, J. (1981). *The Seminar of Jacques Lacan. Book III: The Psychoses, 1955–1956*. New York: W.W. Norton & Company, 1993.

Lombardi, R. (2005). On the psychoanalytic treatment of a psychotic break-down. *Psychoanalytic Quarterly*, 74: 1069–1099.

London, N.J. (1988). An essay on psychoanalytic theory: Two theories of schizophrenia. In *Essential Papers on Psychosis*. New York: New York University Press, pp. 5–48.

Lucas, R. (2009). *The Psychotic Wavelength*. London: Routledge.

Mariotti, P. (2000). Affect and psychosis (Panel report). *International Journal of Psychoanalysis*, 81: 149–152.

McGuire, P.K., Shah, G.M., & Murray, R.M. (2003). Increased blood flow in Broca's area during auditory hallucinations in schizophrenia. *Lancet*, 342: 703–706.

Meltzer, D. (1979). Un approccio psicoanalitico alla psicosi. *Quaderni di Psicoterapia infantile. Le Psicosi*, 2: 31–50, Borla, Roma.

Meltzer, D. (1982a). Interventi in allucinazione e bugia. *Quaderni di Psicoterapia Infantile*, 13: 161–175, Borla, Rome.

Meltzer, D. (1982b). Una indagine sulle bugie: loro genesi e relazione con l'allucinazione. *Quaderni di Psicoterapia Infantile*, 13: 187–191, Borla, Rome.

Meltzer, D. (1983a). Aux frontières des rêves et hallucinations. *Revue Belge de Psychanalyse*, 3: 1–12.

Meltzer, D. (1983b). The borderland between dreams and hallucinations. In *Dream-life: A Re-examination of the Psychoanalytic Theory and Technique*. London: Karnac Books, pp. 114–123.

Meltzer, D., Hoxter, S., Bremner, J., Weddell, D., & Wittenberg, I. (1975). *Explorations in Autism*. London: Karnac Books.

Miller, J.A. (2000). Jacques Lacan and the voice. *Psychoanalytic Notebooks of the London Circle*, 6, 2001: 93–104.

Nacht, S., & Racamier, P.C. (1958). La théorie psychanalytique du délire (the psychoanalytic theory of delusion). *Revue Française de Pychoanalyse*, (3), May–June, 1958. XXe Congrès des Psychoanalystes de Langues Romanes (Bruxelles, 15, 16, 17 February 1958).

Niederland, W.G. (1951). Three notes on the Schreber case. *Psychoanalytic Quarterly*, 20: 579–591.

Ogden, T. (1982). *Projective Identification and Psychotherapeutic Technique*. Northvale, NJ: Jason Aronson.

References 147

Ogden, T. (1989). *The Primitive Edge of Experience*. Lanham, MD: University of Michigan, Jason Aronson.

Oppenheim, L. (2013). *Imagination from Fantasy to Delusion*. London: Routledge.

O'Shaughnessy, E. (1992). *Psychosis: Not Thinking in a Bizarre World*. In R. Anderson (Ed.), *Clinical Lectures on Klein and Bion*. London: Tavistock, pp. 89–101.

Pally, R. (1997). Memory: Brain systems that link past, present and future. *International Journal of Psychoanalysis*, 78: 1223–1234.

Pao, P.N. (1979). *Schizophrenic Disorders*. New York: International Universities Press.

Poincaré, H. (1908). *Science et méthode*. Paris: Flammarion, 1968.

Racamier, P.C. (2000). Un espace pour délirer. *Revue Française de Psychanalyse*, 64: 823–829.

Read, J., & Ross, C.A. (2003). Psychological trauma and psychosis: Another reason why people diagnosed schizophrenic must be offered psychological therapies. *Journal of American Academy of Psychoanalysis*, 31(1): 247–268.

Read, J., van Os, J., Morrison, A.P., & Ross, C.A. (2005). Childhood trauma, psychosis and schizophrenia: A literature review with theoretical and clinical implications. *Acta Psychiatrica Scandinavica*, 112(5), November: 330–350.

Resnik, S. (1972). *Persona e Psicosi*. Turin: Einaudi, 2001.

Rey, H. (1994). *Universals of Psychoanalysis in the Treatment of Psychotic and Borderline States* (J. Magagna, Ed.). London: Free Associations Books.

Risi, N. (1968). *Diary of a Schizophrenic Girl*. IDI Cinematografica.

Romme, M., Escher, S., Dillon, J., Corstens, D., & Morris, M. (2009). *Living with Voices*. Monmouth: PCCS Books.

Rosen, J.N. (1962). *Direct Psychoanalytic Psychiatry*. New York: Grune & Stratton.

Rosenfeld, D. (1992). *The Psychotic*. London: Karnac Books.

Rosenfeld, H. (1947). Analysis of a schizophrenic state with depersonalization. *International Journal of Psychoanalysis*, 28: 130–139.

Rosenfeld, H. (1950). Notes on the psychopathology of confusional states in chronic schizophrenia. *International Journal of Psychoanalysis*, 31: 132–137.

Rosenfeld, H. (1952). Notes on the psycho-analysis of the super-ego conflict in an acute schizophrenic patient. *International Journal of Psychoanalysis*, 33: 111–131.

Rosenfeld, H. (1965). *Psychotic States: A Psycho-Analytical Approach*. London: Hogarth Press Ltd.

Rosenfeld, H. (1969). On the treatment of psychotic states by psychoanalysis: An historical approach. *International Journal of Psychoanalysis*, 50: 615–631.

Rosenfeld, H. (1971). A clinical approach to the psychoanalytic theory of the life and death instincts: An investigation into the aggressive aspects of narcissism. *International Journal of Psychoanalysis*, 52: 169–178.

Rosenfeld, H. (1978). Notes on the psychopathology and psychoanalytic treatment of some borderline patients. *International Journal of Psychoanalysis*, 59: 215–221.

Rosenfeld, H. (1987). *Comunicazione ed interpretazione*. Turin: Bollati Boringhieri, 1989.

Saks, E. (2007). *The Center Cannot Hold: My Journey Through Madness*. New York: Hyperion.

Schacter, D.L., Reiman, R., Curran, T., Yun, L.S., Bandy, D., McDermott, K.B., et al. (1996). Neuroanatomical correlates of veridical and illusory recognition memory: Evidence from positron emission tomography. *Neuron*, 17: 267–274.

Schäfer, I., & Fisher, H.L. (2011). Childhood trauma and psychosis – What is the evidence? *Dialogues in Clinical Neuroscience*, 13(3): 360–365.

Schreber, D.P. (1903). *Memoirs of My Nervous Illness*. London: Dawson, 1955.

Searles, H.F. (1959). Oedipal love in the countertransference. *International Journal of Psychoanalysis*, 40: 180–190.

148 *References*

Searles, H.F. (1961). Schizophrenia and the inevitability of death. *Psychiatric Quarterly*, 35: 361–365.

Searles, H.F. (1965). *Collected Papers on Schizophrenia and Related Subjects*. New York: International Universities Press.

Searles, H.F. (1975). The patient as therapist to his analyst. In *Tactics and Techniques in Psychoanalytic Therapy, Volume II: Countertransference*. New York: Jason Aronson.

Searles, H.F. (1979). The schizophrenic's individual experience of his world. In *Countertransference and Related Subjects: Selected Papers*. New York: International Universities Press.

Sechehaye, M. (1951). *Autobiography of a Schizophrenic Girl: The True Story of 'Renée'*. New York: Grune & Stratton.

Segal, H. (1950). Some aspects of the analysis of a schizophrenic. *International Journal of Psychoanalysis*, 31: 268–278.

Segal, H. (1956). Depression in the schizophrenic. *International Journal of Psychoanalysis*, 37: 339–343.

Segal, H. (1957). Notes on symbol formation. *International Journal of Psychoanalysis*, 38: 391–397.

Segal, H. (1974). Delusion and artistic creativity: Some reflexions on reading 'the spire' by William Golding. *International Journal of Psychoanalysis*, 1: 135–141.

Segal, H. (1991). *Dream, Phantasy, and Art*. London: Routledge.

Silver, A.L. (Ed.) (1989). *Psychoanalysis and Psychosis*. Madison, CT: International Universities Press Inc.

Solms, M., & Panksepp, J. (2012). The 'Id' knows more than the 'Ego' admits: Neuropsychoanalytic and primal consciousness perspectives on the interface between affective and cognitive neuroscience. *Brain Sciences*, 4: 147–175.

Steiner, J. (1993). *Psychic Retreats: Pathological Organisations of the Personality in Psychotic, Neurotic, and Borderline Patients*. London: Routledge.

Symington, N. (2002). *A Pattern of Madness*. London: Karnac Books.

Tarizzo, D. (2003). *Introduzione a Lacan*. Rome and Bari: Laterza.

Telfer, J. (2013). *Psychotic Processes in Everyday Life and Clinical Practice*, read at the APAS Conference in Melbourne in October 2013 (unpublished).

Tustin, F. (1986). *Autistic Barriers in Neurotic Patients*. London: Karnac Books.

Tustin, F. (1991). Revised understandings of psychogenic autism. *International Journal of Psychoanalysis*, 72: 585–591.

Van Der Kolk, B. (2014). *The Body Keeps the Score: Brain, Mind, and Body in the Healing of Trauma*. New York: Penguin Group.

Volkan, V. (1997). *The Seed of Madness: Constitution, Environment, and Fantasy in the Organization of the Psychotic Core*. London: Karnac Books.

Williams, P. (2004). Incorporation of an invasive object. *International Journal of Psychoanalysis*, 85: 1333–1349.

Williams, P. (2014). Orientations of psychotic activity in defensive pathological organizations. *International Journal of Psychoanalysis*, 95: 423–440.

Winnicott, D. (1954). Metapsychological and clinical aspects of regression within the psycho-analytic set-up. In *Collected Papers: Through Paediatrics to Psycho-Analysis*. New York: Basic Books, 1958, pp. 278–294.

Winnicott, D. (1971). Dreaming, fantasying, and living: A case-history describing a primary dissociation. In *Playing and Reality*. London: Tavistock, pp. 26–37.

Index

Abensour, L. xiin4
Abraham, K. 10, 15, 16, 93
absent-mindedness 92
aggressiveness 17, 32, 35, 39, 44, 45, 58, 59; hallucination 129n2; Super-ego and 91, 93, 94; vital 110, 117, 138
Alanen, Y.O. 143
Allen, P. 84
'Analysis of a Schizophrenic State with Depersonalisation' (Rosenfeld) 33
anamnesis 78
anxiety 3, 4, 27, 49–51, 92, 93, 102, 107, 119, 124, 139; death 20–21, 38, 100, 121; delusion and 64, 66, 76, 79, 110, 118; hallucination and 82, 84, 87; Klein on 31, 32, 33, 34, 38–39, 42, 43, 44; psychic withdrawal and 55, 57, 58, 60
appersonation 28
Arieti, S. 16, 75
Arlow, J.A. 16
arrogance 39
artifice, world of 138
Association for Psychoanalytic Psychotherapy in the Public Health Sector 143
associations 2, 3, 11, 38, 39, 64, 107–108, 115, 122, 134; of dreams 63; free 15, 25, 49; verbal 103
associative thought 13
attack on linking, concept of 38
auditory hallucination 70, 71, 74, 75, 81, 83–88
auditory memory 82
Aulagnier, P. ix, 16, 90
autism 84
autistic shapes 84
autobiographical memory 1
Autobiography of a Schizophrenic Girl (Sechehaye) 21–23

autoeroticism 54
autosuggestion 86
awareness 53, 59, 60, 75, 121, 132, 140–142; analyst's 53; dissociative state as separation from 62, 65; emotional 13; function of 142; of illness 78; loss of 3, 72; outside 44, 46, 51, 69, 88, 90, 92, 101, 107, 120, 131; of self 1, 3, 12, 14, 51, 67, 69, 89; of unconscious functioning 10

Bateson, G. 14n1
befuddlement 64, 65, 93, 94
behaviour 42, 73, 115; abnormal/ maladaptive 55–56; acceptance of patient's 17; psychotic 11
Bellevue Sanatorium 15
Benedetti, G. 5, 16; non systematic/ eclectic models 26–28
Bergman, I. xiin3
Binswanger, L. 15, 26
bi-ocular vision of reality 120, 134
Bion, W.R. vii–ix, 16, 36–40, 44–45, 140; on hallucination 83; inversion of the alpha function 130–131; on psychic withdrawal 56; on psychotic part of the personality 58–59, 69
bizarre objects 37–38, 83
Blechner, M.J. 81
Bleuler, E. 15
Bleuler, M. 26
borderline states, and psychosis 13–14
Brenner, C. 16
Brill, A. 15
Broca's area, during hallucination 85
Burghölzli Psychiatric Clinic 15, 26

Caper, R. 11, 69
Capgras syndrome 73–74

150   *Index*

care: authoritarian concept of 23–24;
    effective 9; of patients 5, 9–10, 23–24
caregiving 56
Carrère, E. 78
censorship 1, 11
*Center for the Advanced Study of the
    Psychoses* 143
Centre Cannot Hold, The (Saks) 92–93
Centre Evelyne et Jean Kestenberg 143
Chestnut Lodge Sanitarium 15
childhood 90–91, 107, 109, 113–115,
    116–118, 124–125, 131, 135–136;
    autism during 84; early development
    44, 142; origin of psychosis in 10, 14,
    17–18, 21–22, 39, 42–43, 45, 49,
    54–57, 60, 67–68, 69, 83, 138, 139;
    psychosis during 3, 4, 5, 37; severe
    illness during 30–33; sexual abuse
    during 65; trauma 13, 17, 21, 33
clinical considerations 130–137
communicative projective identification
    38–40
confusional anxiety 34
congenital aggressiveness 39
consciousness 18, 37, 83, 142; dissociation
    from 84; outside 43; reflexive 1;
    transformation of 3
constitutional component, of psychosis 39
Constructions in Analysis (Freud) 66
container defect 39
continuous/unitary hypotheses, of
    psychotic state 11
countertransference 20, 21, 51

daydreaming xi, 5, 65, 73
death anxiety 20–21, 38, 100, 121
declarative psychotic dreams 65
defence viii, x–xi, 3, 10, 11, 17, 31, 32, 54,
    66, 67, 69, 73
delusion 3, 14, 25, 27, 28, 58–61,
    65–70, 127–128; deconstruction of
    127; distinguished from dreams 73,
    86; distressing 110; exciting 110; of
    guilt 22; love 76; persecutory 76, 101;
    phases of 110; pleasure in 70–74;
    psychoanalytic therapy for 99–129;
    relapsing into 74–80; understanding 67;
    see also psychosis
delusional activity 2
delusional omnipotence 68, 77, 83, 105,
    106, 107 108
delusional process 128
delusional thinking 70, 116–118
delusional transference 45, 51–53
delusional withdrawal 56, 64

dementia praecox 9
denial 10, 31, 67
depersonalisation 32–34
depression 42
'Depression in the Schizophrenic'
    (Segal) 42
depressive position 32
destructive impulses 34
destructive phantasies 44
diabolical disposition 94
Dick, P. 31, 78–80
direct psychoanalysis 23–24
discontinuous hypotheses, of psychotic
    state 11
disintegration 56, 83
dissociated reality 45–46
dissociated world viii, ix–x, 45–46, 56,
    57, 59, 78, 138, 140
dissociation 14, 54–55, 62, 67, 78, 86, 92,
    94, 109; delusional 68, 133; experience
    of 11–12; and hallucination 83, 84;
    psychotic 32
distortion: delusion as 66, 69, 77, 78,
    90, 118, 139; hallucination as 88, 139;
    psychosis as 11, 12, 13, 14, 18, 24, 25,
    46, 59, 64, 93, 94, 140, 141; withdrawal
    as 57
dreams 5, 27, 62–65, 108–110, 112,
    114–115, 116, 122–123, 124,
    125, 134, 137; distinguished from
    delusion 73, 86, 130, 131, 132; and
    hallucination 81, 86; psychotic 12,
    25, 37, 57, 59–60, 62–80, 143
Dream Story (Schnitzler) 103
dual reality 134
Dukas, P. 46

eclectic models *see* non systematic models
ego 19, 31; boundary 25; development
    43; primitive 133; splitting 31, 58, 69;
    Super-ego 34, 35, 38, 75, 83, 93–95
Eitingon, M. 15
emotional maturity 135
emotional trauma 51, 90–91
emotional unconscious 141
emotions: awareness of 13; intense 81;
    receptiveness to 39
endogenous trauma 76
environmental component, of psychosis
    10, 22, 26, 39, 44; in hallucination 88
envy 35, 39, 58–59, 127
excessive congenital predisposition 39, 59
excitedness 52
Exegesis of Philip Dick, The (Dick) 80
Eyes Wide Shut (film) 129n1

Index 151

face-to-face therapies 50, 70
Fain, M. ix
Fairbairn, W.R.D. 16
Fantasia (film) 46
fear of death *see* death anxiety
Federn, P. 5, 16, 44, 67; non systematic/
  eclectic models 24–26
Ferenczi 10
foreclosure viii, 28–29, 84
Fornari, F. 21
fragmentation 27, 28, 31, 34–38, 43, 50,
  69, 83, 84, 94, 100, 101, 122, 133, 137,
  141, 142
Francesco (patient): clinical considerations
  for 130–137; psychoanalytic therapy of
  99–129
free associations 15, 25, 49
Freeman, T. 16
Freud, A. 21
Freud, S. vii, viii, 1, 10–11, 16, 25, 31,
  134, 140, 141; on autoeroticism 54;
  on hallucination 82–83; on primitive
  Ego 133; on psychic reality 65–67; on
  psychic withdrawal 57; on psychosis–
  neurosis distinction xiin2; on psychotic
  part of the personality 58, 60; on Super-
  ego 93; on transference 51–52
Fromm-Reichmann, F. 5, 15–19, 21,
  25, 44, 70; non systematic/eclectic
  models 17–19; on psychotic part
  of the personality 61; on Rosen's
  interpretations 24
frustration viii, ix–x, xi, 31, 32, 55, 58–59,
  105, 109, 112, 116, 126, 131, 133

grandiosity 13, 14, 17, 76, 77, 88, 103,
  104–107, 118, 125, 127, 128, 131,
  133, 135
Greenberg, J. 18–19, 70

Hadamard, J. 141
'hallucinating brain, The' (Allen and
  colleagues) 84–85
hallucination viii, x, 27, 42, 81–89, 143;
  auditory 70, 71, 74, 75, 81, 83–88;
  mind's eyes 86–89; neuroscientific
  contribution to 84–86; psychoanalytic
  contribution to 83–84; psychoanalytic
  viewpoint of 82–83; tactile 85; verbal
  85; visual 22, 70, 71, 84, 85, 87, 88
Hartmann, H. 16
hebephrenic schizophrenia 42
Hour of the Wolf (film) xiin3
Hugdahl, K. 85, 86
hyperactivation 85

idealisation, of madness 78
illness: awareness of 78; psychosomatic
  89; psychotic 20, 42, 45, 77, 89
imagination 67–68
implicit knowledge 13
implicit memory 126
I Never Promised You a Rose Garden
  (Greenberg) 18–19, 70
infantile psychosis 31–32
infantile withdrawal 54, 55, 60, 131
inner and outer world, confusion between
  42–43
intensive psychotherapy 17
*International Society for Psychological
  and Social Approaches to Psychosis*
  (ISPS) 143
*International Society for the Psychological
  Treatments of Schizophrenia and Other
  Psychoses* 143
Interpretation of Schizophrenia (Arieti) 75
interpretation 41; Benedetti 27–28; Bion
  37–38, 45; of dreams 65, 67, 70;
  Federn 25, 26; Fromm-Reichmann 17;
  intrapsychic 60; as reverse projective
  identification 43; Rosenfeld 32–36;
  Rosen 23–24; wrong 53
intersubjective transitivism 27
intrapsychic interpretations 60
invasive object 90
ISPS *see* International Society for
  Psychological and Social Approaches to
  Psychosis (ISPS)
Israëls, H. 66

Jackson, M. 16
Jacobson, E. 69
judgement dissociation 12
Jung, C.G. 15, 26

Katan, M. 16, 58
Klein, M. vii–viii, 4, 5, 16, 21, 30–32,
  66, 140; contributions of 30–46; on
  projective identification 31–33, 35–40,
  43, 44, 69; on psychotic part of the
  personality 58; on Super-ego 93; on
  transference 52
Kosslyn, S. 81
Kraepelin, E. 9
Kubrick, S. 129n1

Lacan, J. 5, 16, 43, 44, 83–84; non
  systematic/eclectic models 28–29, 30
language 36, 43; and delusion 28, 140; and
  hallucination 84, 85; symbolic 42, 59,
  76, 137

152 *Index*

libidinal impulses 34
Living with Voices (Romme, Escher, Dillon, Corstens & Morris) 83, 91
Lombardi, R. 16
loss of Self 26
love: countertransference of 20; delusion of 52, 71–72, 73, 74, 76; fantasies of 20, 29n1, 57
Lucas, R. 16

madness, idealisation of 78
maladaptive behaviour 55
Masi, F. de vii–xi, 16; Francesco patient case study 99–137
maternal figure 18, 44, 116
maternal function 43
maternal receptiveness 39
maternal violence 90
McAfee, L. 69–70
Medioli, Marina 80n1
megalomania 65, 94, 102, 104–106, 108, 109, 112–114, 116, 117, 122, 124–126, 128, 135, 140
melancholic Super-ego 93, 95
Meltzer, D. 16, 56, 57, 84
memory: auditory 82; autobiographical 1; implicit 126; procedural 13, 92; traumatic 83
mental stability 43
Miller, P. ix
mind: as organ of knowledge 88; as sensory organ x, 56, 69, 88
mind's eyes 86–89
Miró, J. 109
monotasking 121
mourning 74, 81
Müller, C. 26
multitasking 121
mutual dependence 20

Nacht, S. 138
nameless dread 39, 92–93
negative transference 24–25
neuroimaging 82, 84, 88, 92
neuroscience, contribution to hallucination 84–86
neurosis 11, 67; distinguished from psychosis vii, x, xiin2, 11–12
neurotic functioning 138–139
Niederland, W.G. 66
non-psychotic personality *vs.* psychotic personality 37–38
non systematic analysts 5

non systematic models 15–29, 43; Benedetti, G. 26–28; Federn, P. 24–26; Fromm-Reichmann, F. 17–19; Lacan, J. 28–29; Rosen, J. 23–24; Searles, H. 19–21; Sechehaye, M. 21–23
normal projective identification 38–40
Notes on Some Schizoid Mechanisms (Klein) 31
'Notes on the Psychoanalysis of the Super-Ego Conflict of an Acute Schizophrenic Patient' (Rosenfeld) 34
'Notes on the Psychopathology of Confusional States in Chronic Schizophrenia' (Rosenfeld) 34

object idealisation 31
'Oedipal Love in the Countertransference' (Searles) 20
Ogden, T. 16
omnipotence 2, 46, 59, 60, 111, 114, 140; in children 31, 43, 93; delusional 68, 77, 83, 105, 106, 107 108
O'Shaughnessy, E. 55, 69

Panksepp, J. 143
Pao, P.N. 16
paranoia viii, 28, 31
paranoid-schizoid position 32
pathological construction 137
pathological splitting 16, 17
'Patient as Therapist to His Analyst, The' (Searles) 20
Perceval, J. 9, 87–88
persecution, delusion of 31, 34, 41, 76, 88, 100, 101, 104–105, 106, 109, 111, 112, 114, 117, 121, 127, 135
personality 50, 84, 86, 89, 93, 118, 121, 124, 125, 131, 135, 136, 138–139, 143; fragmentation of 34, 94; integration of 37, 92; non-psychotic/healthy part 18, 37–38, 51, 64, 67, 77, 88, 108, 137; projection of 40; psychotic part 13, 36–39, 43; 49, 56, 54–61, 69
phobic symptomatology 57
pleasure, in delusion ix, 56, 60, 64, 70–74, 76, 77, 78, 88
Poincaré, H. 141
positive asymmetry 27
positive relation *see* positive transference
positive transference 24, 26
post-Kleinian systematic models 16
primitive Ego 133
primitive mental states 93–94

Index 153

principle of explosion 134
procedural memory 13, 92
progressive psychopathology 26–27
projective identification 31–33, 35–40, 43, 44, 46n1, 52, 58, 66, 68, 69; communicative 38–40; normal 38–40
proto-symbols 27
Psicoterapia Come Sfida Esistenziale, La (Benedetti) 26
psychic reality 3, 12, 14, 26, 31, 37, 44, 51, 54, 56, 59, 65–69, 71, 78, 86, 92, 130, 134, 137
psychic withdrawal 54–57, 87
psychoanalysis 1; contribution to hallucination 83–84; viewpoint of hallucination 82–83
'psychoanalytic approach to the treatment of psychoses, A' (Segal) 42–43
psychoanalytic theory: delusion, thinking 116–118; double reality 118–129
psychoanalytic therapy 99–129; beginning of 99–102; delusional threatening figure 113–116; grandiosity 104–107; islands of clarity 109–113; in middle period 107–109; revelations of 102–104
psychopathological constructions 69; of withdrawal 56
psychosis: borderline states and 13–14; distinguished from neurosis vii, x, xiin2, 11–12; infantile 31–32; as specific technique 10–13; theoretical discourses of vii–viii; transference 33, 51–53; as trauma 92–93; treatment for xi–xii, 12–13; use of the term 9–10; *see also individual entries*
psychosomatic illness 89
psychotic breakdown 57, 70–71, 74
psychotic episodes 40, 50, 51, 59–60, 62, 67, 72, 75–76, 78, 80, 85, 87, 92–93, 132
psychotic functioning 59, 64, 65, 71, 77, 108, 137, 138–139
psychotic illness 20, 42, 45, 77, 89
psychotic personality *vs.* non-psychotic personality 37–38
psychotic state 3, 36, 54, 61, 65, 142; analytic theory of 11; identification of 2, 4, 25, 33; long-term 35, 44, 45, 125, 138
Psychotic States (Rosenfeld) 32–33
psychotic transference 19, 34–36, 43, 44, 52, 106, 136
psychotic transformation 4, 46, 65, 126, 139–140

psychotic withdrawal 3, 54, 60
psychotropic drugs 3, 10, 77, 89

Racamier, P.C. 16, 138
Read, J. 91
regression, of patients 9–10
relapse 1, 3, 4, 10, 12, 22, 37, 49, 50, 68, 73, 74–80
repression 1, 11, 13, 25, 31, 37, 38, 51, 67, 82, 141, 142
Resnik, S. 16
revelations 141
Rey, H. 16
Risi, N. 21
Rosen, J. 5, 16; non systematic/eclectic models 23–24
Rosenfeld, H. 13, 16, 32–36, 45; on psychic withdrawal 56; on psychotic part of the personality 58; on splitting of the Ego 58, 69
Russo, R. 80n6

Saks, E. 92–93
Saussure, R. de 21
schizophrenia 9, 16, 19, 21, 29, 31, 32–33, 75
Schreber, D.P. 12, 57, 66–67, 82
Schwing, G. 24
Searles, H.F. 5, 15–17, 27, 29n1, 44, 75; non systematic/eclectic models 19–21
Sechehaye, M. (Madame Sechehaye) 5, 16, 26, 44; non systematic/eclectic models 21–23
Second Thoughts (Bion) 36
Segal, H. 16, 40–45, 68
self-awareness 69
self-idealisation 103
Self, loss of 26
sense organs, use of 37, 45–46, 83, 84
sensorial self-stimulation ix
sensory organ, mind as x, 56, 69, 88
sensory reality 35, 69, 86, 88, 130
sensory withdrawal 55, 88, 134, 139
setting, establishing formal 49–51
sexual abuse 91–92; childhood 65, 83
Sheppard and Enoch Pratt Hospital 15
Solms, M. 134–135, 137n1, 143
'Some aspects of the analysis of a schizophrenic' (Segal) 40–41
'Sorcerer's Apprentice, The' (Goethe) 46
Spitz, R. 21
splitting 10, 33, 35–37, 42; ego 31, 58, 69; pathological 16, 17

154 *Index*

Steiner, J. 55
Sullivan, H.S. 15–16
Super-ego 34, 35, 38, 75, 83; and psychosis 90–95; psychotic 93–95
symbiosis 19
symbolic equation 43, 68
symbolic realisation method 21–23
Symington, N. 16

Telfer, J. 73
theoretical-systematic models 16, 43
therapeutic phantasmatisation 27
therapeutic symbiosis 19
threshold functioning 123
transference 10; countertransference 20, 21, 51; delusional 45, 51–53; negative 24–25; positive 24, 26; psychosis 33, 51–53; psychotic 19–20, 34–36, 43, 44, 52, 106, 136, 139
trauma 5, 18, 22, 28, 33, 45, 73–76, 90–93, 131, 133; childhood 13, 17; infantile 91, 92; and psychosis 90–95; violent 90–91; emotional 3, 21, 51, 90–91

traumatic memory 83
treatment/case study, of Francesco 99–129
Turku Schizophrenia Project 143
Tustin, F. ix, 84

unitary hypotheses, of psychotic state 11

Van der Kolk, B. 92
verbal hallucination 85
violence 90–91
visual hallucination 22, 70, 71, 84, 85, 87, 88
Volkan, V. 16
Vulnerability to Psychosis (de Masi) 2, 80n5, 129n2

Williams, P. 16, 90
Winnicott, D.W. viii, 14n2, 16, 21
withdrawal: delusional 56, 64; infantile 54, 55, 60, 131; psychic 54–57, 87; psychopathological constructions of 56; psychotic 3, 54, 60; sensory 55, 88, 134, 139
Working with Difficult Patients 80n1